MEN AND MARRIAGE

George Gilder

Men and Marriage

PELICAN PUBLISHING COMPANY
GRETNA 1987

First printing, August 1986
Second printing, February 1987

This book is a revised and expanded edition of *Sexual Suicide* © 1973,
published by Quandrangle/The New York Times Book Company

Library of Congress Cataloging-in-Publication Data
Gilder, George F., 1939–
 Men and marriage.

 Rev. ed. of: Sexual suicide. 1973.
 1. Sex customs—United States. 2. Family—United States. 3. Love.
4. Sex role—United States.
I. Gilder, George F., 1939-   . Sexual suicide.
II. Title.
HQ18.U5G55   1986   306.8′5′0973   86-9340
ISBN 0-88289-444-7

Manufactured in the United States of America
Published by Pelican Publishing Company, Inc.
1101 Monroe Street, Gretna, Louisiana 70053

Contents

To my Mother and Gilly

Preface
to the Revised Edition

Men and Marriage is a revised edition of *Sexual Suicide,* my book on the drive to deny and repress the differences between the sexes. It is also about the redemptive joys and crucial functions of marriage and family, the roots of human civilization.

In a sense the project began some thirteen years ago in the July 1973 issue of *Harper's* magazine, when I was first plunged into the maelstrom of emotions and ideologies surrounding sex. In a cover story entitled "The Suicide of the Sexes," adroitly excerpted by editor Nelson Aldrich, I declared that "the differences between the sexes are the single most important fact of human society." I asserted that "the drive to deny them—in the name of women's liberation, marital openness, sexual equality, erotic consumption, or homosexual romanticism—must be one of the most quixotic crusades in the history of the species." The response reverberated indignantly in hundreds of letters to the magazine and scores of reviews of the book.

I later wrote other books that drew on the themes of *Sexual Suicide.* First was *Naked Nomads,* an extended essay on unmarried men. Then followed *Visible Man,* a nonfiction novel about demoralization and violence in the welfare culture, and *Wealth and Pov-*

erty, a worldwide best seller on capitalism and supply-side economics that also continued my family theme in several chapters. After *Wealth and Poverty* brought publishers galore to my door, offering me large sums for new works, I thought it would be opportune to republish *Sexual Suicide,* the book where it had all begun. Indeed, several prominent publishers did offer to reissue the book. But in every case they called back later to tell me—or imply strongly—that protests from feminist editors had balked them. Finally Milburn Calhoun of Pelican Publishing Company of New Orleans asked to publish an updated version. A brave man, he rushed in where all the New York publishers feared to tread. He also assigned me a trenchant and punctilious editor, Frumie Selchen, who helped shape the project to the end.

As I sat down to the editing job, though, I realized that it was too late to republish the book without substantial revision. The radical feminist movement, once a dominant force in the nation's affairs, had suffered serious setbacks. The more obviously extreme figures, much assailed in *Sexual Suicide,* no longer command serious attention. While Kate Millett's *Sexual Politics* gained an almost unprecedented two-part rave from Christopher Lehmann-Haupt in the daily *New York Times,* her subsequent celebrations of lesbianism were largely dismissed. Germaine Greer rode the best-seller list for months with *The Female Eunuch,* but *Sex and Destiny,* her pronatalist near-recantation, was little noticed. Defeat of the Equal Rights Amendment broke the movement into several warring factions. Indeed, *The New York Times Magazine,* in a long and agonized report, embalmed feminism on the campuses, the unreal world in which it always flourished best. Even Betty Friedan, who had launched the movement as an intellectual force with her book *The Feminine Mystique,* declared herself in favor of the nuclear family— previously denounced in the pages of the *Times* as "a cradle of evil."

As a critique of the feminist movement and its politics, *Sexual Suicide* now seems less telling. But the central themes of the book remain vitally important. Though rejecting feminist politics and lesbian posturing, American culture has absorbed the underlying ideology like a sponge. The principal tenets of sexual liberation or sexual liberalism—the obsolescence of masculinity and femininity, of sex roles, and of heterosexual monogamy as the moral norm—have diffused through the system and become part of America's conventional wisdom. Taught in most of the nation's schools and colleges and proclaimed insistently in the media, sexual liberalism prevails even where feminism—at least in its antimale rhetoric—seems increasingly irrelevant.

Rather than expressing hostility to men and masculinity, sexual liberals simply ignore or deny male nature. Encouraged by male feminists writing books about the male mystique and the "myth of masculinity," American intellectuals and social scientists reduce manhood to androgynous mush. With men seen longing for the "right to cry" or to stay home and nurture children, virility becomes a mere derivative of femininity. As Steven Goldberg has remarked, masculinity is treated like sex in Victorian England: a fact of life that the society largely condemns and tries to suppress and that its intellectuals deny. And as in Victorian England, when suppression of sex led to an efflorescence of lurid flowers in the secret gardens of society, so the denial of male nature in modern life warps and perverts the natural play of male aggression, leading to violence and pornography, to fear and exploitation of women, to the quest for potency through drugs and alcohol, to punch-drunk music, and to fighting at sports events. Millions of men feed on the masculinity of a few heroes—boxers, football players, rock stars, entrepreneurs, macho film and TV avengers.

The result is a society that at once denies the existence of natural male aggressiveness and is utterly preoccupied with it. While academic intellectuals and media sociologists ruminate on the feminized "new man," male aggression and violence, muscles and madness, guns and technologies animate our movies, TV shows, magazines, newspapers, politics, music. From Patton to Bond to Rocky to Rambo to Conan the Barbarian and scores of imitators—from Mick Jagger to Bruce Springsteen—the popular culture reeks and reverberates with male aggression. From hijacker threats to guerrilla terror, our public life revolves around male violence. Our city streets quail before it. Our city schools are paralyzed by fear of it. "Liberated" women are obsessed by it, laboring through hours of karate, declaring a national crisis of battered wives, palavering endlessly through rap sessions on rape. All the while, most academic theorists maintain that men could be mild and maternal if somehow "the culture" would socialize them like women.

The imperious power and meaning of male sexuality remains a paramount fact of life and the chief challenge to civilized society and democratic politics. Failing to come to terms with masculinity, a society risks tearing its very ligaments, the marriage and family ties that bind men to the social order. For it is only their masculinity, their sexual nature, that draws men into marriages and family responsibilities. When our social institutions deny or disrespect the basic terms of male nature, masculinity makes men enemies of family and society.

Although some observers believe that feminism and sexual liberalism no longer threaten family values, little in fact has changed. Contemporary sexual liberals are merely less honest than earlier feminists in facing the inevitable antifamily consequences of their beliefs. They continue to maintain that the differences between men and women, such as men's greater drive to produce in the workplace, are somehow artificial and dispensable. They still insist that men and women can generally share and reverse roles without jeopardizing marriage. They still encourage a young woman to sacrifice her twenties in intense rivalry with men, leaving her to clutch desperately for marriage as her youthfulness and fertility pass. Although they declare themselves supporters of the family, they are scarcely willing to define it. They often maintain that the traditional family is dead because at any one time only some 10 percent of all households may contain a working man, a housewife, and children (though some 80 percent take this form for some period of time). In seeking a broader definition of the family, they seek to overthrow the normative pattern of a male with the chief provider role and a woman who focuses on child care while her offspring are young.

Sexual liberals often declare that their true end is sexual freedom for both men and women. But nothing is finally free, least of all sex, which is bound to our deepest sources of energy, identity, emotion, and aesthetic sense. Sex can be cheapened, as we know, but then, inevitably, it becomes extremely costly to the society as a whole.

In the most elemental sense, the sex drive is the survival instinct: the primal tie to the future. When people lose the power of sexual polarity, they also lose their procreative energy and faith in themselves and their prospects. They seize on the bomb as a reason for a life of child-free futility. They promote abortions and distribute contraceptives "nonjudgmentally" to teenagers without telling their parents (i.e., "squealing"). They delay marriage and family. They exert moral pressure and impose financial penalties on families with more than one or two children. They promote a program of zero population growth that leaves the nation unable to support its increasing array of programs for the elderly, who themselves are increasingly cast beyond the care of family. They foster a politics strangely hostile to our own genetic perpetuation as a nation and an economics based on the foolish notion that population growth hurts economic progress.

It is an ideology of personal hedonism based on fear of the future, the old sophomoric canard of "eat drink and be merry, for tomorrow we die." The advocates of this view may indulge a lot in what they call sex. But it is a kind of aimless copulation having little to do with the deeper currents of sexuality and love that carry a community into the future.

So in spite of all the protests and denunciations thirteen years ago, I am happy to return to the themes of *Sexual Suicide*. I do not want my son to be told that he does not have to be masculine to succeed as a man—that he can be happily supported by a mothering wife and never really grow up. I do not want to see my daughters grow up to be like the feminist leaders now reportedly longing to have children as they approach their fifties. I do not want my wife to feel she is unequal to me if she earns less money than I do, or unequal to the careerist women I meet in my work. I understand that sexual liberalism chiefly liberates men from their families, and I love my family more than I long to relive a bachelor freedom or marry a coed. I understand the terrible losses inflicted by sexual liberalism on the men and women I know who try to live by its remorseless egalitarian code, who attempt to twist their lives and bodies into the unisex mold, who tangle in loveless sterility on the procrustean beds of emancipation.

Perhaps these more personal reasons for opposing the ideology of sexual liberalism are the most important, because such personal intuitions explain its continuing failure to prevail in America despite its dominance in the media and the academy. Most men and women know at heart that masculinity is no myth, that marriage largely depends upon it, and that civilization depends on marriage. This book attempts to explain these facts of life.

The new edition, however, also springs from the increasingly grim and nearly conclusive vindication of my previous arguments. With the illegitimacy rate approaching 80 percent in Central Harlem and over 40 percent in Sweden, it is no longer tenable to defend the welfare state as an answer to social problems. With recent studies of census data indicating that single women who wait until their mid-thirties have less than a 5 percent chance of finding a husband, my attacks on the feminist argument for delayed marriage seem pathetically understated. With women still earning less than 17 percent of family income in intact families, my argument that wives would never make income their prime goal stands entirely unshaken by 15 years of so-called "social change." With the outbreak of AIDS and a slew of other medically baffling venereal diseases, my case against liberated lifestyles seems unconscionably timid. With birth rates 40 percent below replacement level all over Europe, my prophecy that sexual liberalism leads to social suicide is no longer very controversial. The fact is that *Sexual Suicide*, declared an outrage in all centers of established opinion, has proved to be true beyond my worst fears and boldest predictions in 1973.

The process of revision owed much to the the help of many friends and associates and the encouragement of scores of unprompted letter writers who have been urging me for years to publish an updated edition of the book. *Sexual Suicide* was originally published by Times Books under the bold leadership of Sidney Gruson and Herbert Nagourney. Midge Decter contributed to the development of many of these themes and her husband Norman Podhoretz published sections from part two in *Commentary*. Natalie Gittelson, then of *The New York Times Magazine,* commissioned and bravely defended the article from which chapter 12 has been adapted. William F. Buckley, Jr. and *National Review* have offered continual guidance and encouragement in my steady move toward conservatism, and published parts of chapters 5, 10, and 13. Crucial in reducing a large manuscript to a coherent book and giving it a title was *National Review*'s superb article editor Richard Vigilante, who—with his wife Susan—gave indispensable aid, both editorial and inspirational. Josh Gilder was always willing to turn from his vital work at the White House to give advice and encouragement, and Bruce Chapman—then director of the Census Bureau—helped continually with statistics and themes. My wife Nini has proven to me that all my early celebrations of marriage underestimated its joys.

PROLOGUE:
The Princess
and the Barbarian

Once upon a time in a distant mountainous land there was a young and beautiful princess who loved to wander in the woods. The forest was deep below the snowcapped peaks and the valleys were quiet and safe. She could go freely without care or fear. She could saunter along the trails that took local merchants and messengers toward the passes to neighboring lands and brought them back laden with news and commerce. She could watch for birds radiant among the leaves and sometimes glimpse a deer dancing through the brush. In summer she could swim in the brooks that hurtled down the mountains and gathered in pools in the crevices. She was carefree and gay, at ease with nature and the world.

Then one year trouble struck this halcyon land. A barbarian moved into a cave somewhere in the woods and began to prey on the merchants and messengers making their way through the mountain passes. Although groups of young men formed posses to pursue him, he was so strong and swift and so resourceful in the ways of the woods and canyons that no one could catch him. Commerce slowed and the kingdom grew steadily poorer. Merchants could travel only in large groups protected by warriors. The king and queen bade the princess to halt her wanderings and stay in the castle night and day. Someday, they said, she would be queen, but until then she would have to learn the ways of the palace. She pined for her dark and secret places among the trees, but she did not disobey.

One night, however, her sleep was beset with dreams of serpents. She woke in fear as shadowy shapes lurched on her walls and sinister sounds whirred outside her window. She went to the sill, parted the curtains, and gasped at the wild beauty beyond. Through the trees, waving their arms in the night winds and glistening in the moonlight, she could see deep into the forest that she longed to explore. She yearned to run along the sylvan paths and feel the pine needles under her bare feet and the breezes against her face and in her hair. She longed to spy on the creatures of the night. Surely, no one would notice or care if she should steal down the stone stairs and step out on the moonlit path.

As it happened, that same evening the barbarian, also restless in the night season, set forth into the lunar darkness down the path that led toward the castle. He walked quietly, like a cat slinking through the woods, until, startled by the sound of steps, he slid behind a huge oak. At first he thought he had heard some animal and raised his club. Then he sensed a human rhythm in the paces and steeled himself for a robbery. When the princess finally came into view, he gasped at the sight of her—a beautiful girl garbed only in a silken gown—gliding barefoot along the trail.

Never before had a vision moved him so powerfully. The luminous night and the woman alone, the shape and the shadows, reached in beyond his bearded face and bristling chest and touched his sinuous heart. He stepped forward and asked her if he might walk with her a while. She screamed and fled. He pursued her, caught her, and pulled her to the ground, ripping her gown. Then he seized her flailing arms and shook her to silence.

Soon, however, he sensed that he wanted less to overpower than to please her. Entranced by the wonders of her strong young body, he pleaded with her to stop struggling—he meant her no harm. She told him to go ahead and kill her if he wanted her, but to do it quickly and mercifully. He insisted he had no desire to have her dead. He wanted her alive; he wished to hold her body against his in the night. She said she would die first.

He then changed his approach and asked her again if she would walk with him for a while in the woods. She consented; it was a way to gain release from his grasp. But as they strolled along, his gruff voice softened. With quiet authority he described his life in the woods among the fierce animals that threatened his survival and that he sometimes had to kill to escape. She listened and marveled as he told her fantastic tales of the barbarian life. She had never before heard of the struggle for life in the wilds beyond the castle walls. They walked together until the glow of dawn shocked her to her senses and she said she had to run back to the castle. The great barbarian slumped in helpless anguish. She assured him she would be back the next week to learn more. But to the barbarian, a week seemed an eternity.

The next week she once more sneaked away from her bed after midnight and walked in the woods with the barbarian. When the sun rose he lunged for her, and she delicately slipped aside, saying she would be back again in another seven days. The next week they once again walked and talked for hours in the night. Finally he asked her to come back to see the etchings on the walls of his cave.

She said no, she would never go back to his lair until he halted his attacks upon the merchants and messengers of the realm. He said robbery was his way of life; all men robbed in one way or another; the king's entire territory had been stolen from the barbarian's forebears, the natives of the land. She told him severely that he had better find another way of living if he expected her ever to visit him in his cave. He should make a clearing, build a cabin, and grow a garden in the woods. He could collect nuts and berries and hunt small game. With all his knowledge of the wilderness he could live well, and she would come weekly to hear his tales of the night wood.

The barbarian was heartbroken. The idea of a different life frightened and repelled him. He was a nomadic predator, born to run in the forest and prey on the weak. But finally he saw that he had no choice. To avoid losing the princess, he recognized at last that he would have to give up the barbarian life and get to work. And so he did. By the time he met her seven days hence, he had cleared a large space among the trees. Within six months he had planted a garden and built a cabin.

During that time no robberies were reported on the road. Commerce with neighboring kingdoms expanded rapidly as travel grew safer and merchants could go through the mountain passes without an expensive guard of young warriors. With the country growing richer, the barbarian did well selling wood and nuts to the people. At last one day, after showing her his trove of produce, his cabin enlarged with an octagonal wing, and his large gardens and herds of goats, he asked the princess to marry him. Joyfully she said yes and brought him back to the castle to meet her father and mother, the king and queen.

At first the king declared that the barbarian's background made him entirely unsuitable to be the mate of his precious daughter. But the queen replied with a smile that he too had been something of a barbarian in his day and he had to confess that this was true. The barbarian was certainly a refreshing change from the unctuous courtiers who had previously pursued the princess. The king and queen soon welcomed the youth as a strong and resourceful husband for their daughter and an asset to the realm.

The wedding brought a huge celebration throughout the kingdom. After a nostalgic honeymoon in the cabin in the woods, the couple moved into the castle. Freed from the ravages of the barbarian, the land continued to prosper. After the princess's parents died, the barbarian himself became king and expanded his domains deep into the mountains and the forest. In the course of time the new queen bore a daughter and the daughter too grew into a beautiful young princess, who, like her mother, hearkened to the call of the wild.

As the realm grew ever richer, the king and queen invited famous wise men from a neighboring kingdom to entertain at court. These men told of seductive new ideas. They chilled the king and queen with tales of the death of God and the eclipse of law, and excited them with accounts of the joys of libertine sex. They brought books and art celebrating the new freedoms that followed the breakdown of traditional morality and religion. They told of a city called New York where everything indeed was new and free.

The young princess listened avidly. Poring over the books, she learned of the powers that princesses held in other nations. She learned to disdain the stodgy, hardworking life of her parents' kingdom and to long for a land where happiness was the only goal. As time passed these ideas gnawed at her nocturnal thoughts. Like her mother she found her sleep disturbed by serpentine dreams, and she would walk in the woods to quell the disquieting desires that flooded her young body.

Then a crisis struck the country. Another barbarian—as young and strong, ruthless and resourceful as his predecessor—moved into the forest and began preying on the commerce between the kingdom and the neighboring realm. Once again the land became poor, and this princess too was forbidden to walk in the woods. The princess, however, rebelled against her parents and continued her excursions.

One night she found herself suddenly confronted by the young barbarian. She was even more beautiful than her mother, and the barbarian surged with admiration and desire. He asked her if she minded if he walked with her for a while. Deeply bored by her life in the castle, she agreed. They sauntered along the path discussing the flaws of the king and the oppressive rules within the walls. Shortly he put his arm around her shoulders and she pulled away and said please, not yet. He asked her if she would return with him to see the etchings in his cave. She suggested they first walk longer and get to know one another better. But eventually they visited his cave together. When she left at dawn, she promised to return the next week. "Wow," she exclaimed, "you're good!"

For the next several months she visited with the barbarian every week and they reveled in the cave. Then one day, a king arrived from the progressive country of the wise men to visit with the father of the princess. This foreign king was the most charming and cosmopolitan man the princess had ever seen. He told her of the great riches and romantic forests of his land, of the advanced universities and museums, of the flourishing commerce and art. And after everyone went to bed, there was a knock on the door of the princess's chamber.

The princess opened the door and saw the foreign king outside, garbed in a robe of purple velour. He asked to come in. He stayed until dawn, and as the morning light suffused the room, along with the royal aroma of his Paco Rabanne, he asked her to return with him to his kingdom. He would divorce his queen and marry her. They had "drifted apart," he said, and his marriage "was no longer a growthful experience." His wife needed "more space," and in his progressive views and liberated lifestyle, he discovered he had far more in common with youth than with his own generation. The princess agreed joyfully. Banishing the barbarian in the woods from her thoughts, she returned the next day with the king to her new land.

Each week the barbarian waited in the forest for his princess. But she never came. After a while he gave up waiting and angrily escalated his attacks on the commerce between the two nations. As time passed, the mood of license fostered by the wise men induced many young men to join the barbarian in the woods. The nation fell into ruin and the forest became a jungle, ruled by barbarians, where no princess ever dared to tread.

MEN AND MARRIAGE

PART ONE

THE FACTS OF LIFE

CHAPTER 1

The Necessities of Love

Love is a desire for generation and birth in beauty.

PLATO

The crucial process of civilization is the subordination of male sexual impulses and biology to the long-term horizons of female sexuality. The overall sexual behavior of women in the modern world differs relatively little from the sexual life of women in primitive societies. It is male behavior that must be changed to create a civilized order.

Men lust, but they know not what for; they wander, and lose track of the goal; they fight and compete, but they forget the prize; they spread seed, but spurn the seasons of growth; they chase power and glory, but miss the meaning of life.

In creating civilization, women transform male lust into love; channel male wanderlust into jobs, homes, and families; link men to specific children; rear children into citizens; change hunters into fathers; divert male will to power into a drive to create. Women conceive the future that men tend to flee; they feed the children that men ignore.

The prime fact of life is the sexual superiority of women. Sexual love, intercourse, marriage, conception of a child, childbearing—even breast-feeding—are all critical experiences psychologically. They are times when our emotions are most intense, our lives are most deeply changed, and society is perpetuated in our own image. And they all entail sexual roles that demonstrate the primacy of women.

The central roles are mother and father, husband and wife. They form neat and apparently balanced pairs. But appearances are deceptive. In sexual terms, there is little balance at all. In most of these key sexual events, the male role is trivial, even easily dispensable. Although the man is needed in intercourse, artificial insemination has already been used in hundreds of thousands of cases. Otherwise, the man is altogether unnecessary. It is the woman who conceives, bears, and suckles the child. Those activities that are most deeply sexual are mostly female; they comprise the mother's role, a role that is defined biologically.

The nominally equivalent role of father is in fact a product of marriage and other cultural contrivances. There is no biological need for the father to be anywhere around when the baby is born and nurtured. In many societies the father has no special responsibility to support the specific children he sires. In some societies, paternity is not even acknowledged. The father is neither inherently equal to the mother within the family, nor necessarily inclined to remain with it.[1] In one way or another, the man must be *made* equal by society.

In discussing the erotic aspects of our lives—even when we are focusing on men—we must concern ourselves chiefly with women. Males are the sexual outsiders and inferiors. A far smaller portion of their bodies is directly erogenous. A far smaller portion of their lives is devoted to sexual activity. Their rudimentary sexual drive leads only toward copulation. The male body offers no sexual fulfillment comparable to a woman's passage through months of pregnancy to the tumult of childbirth and on into the suckling of her baby.

In primitive societies men have the compensation of physical strength. They can control women by force and are needed to protect them from other men. But this equalizer is relatively unimportant in a civilized society, where the use of force is largely restricted by law and custom. In successful civilized societies, man counterbalances female sexual superiority by playing a crucial role as provider and achiever. Money replaces muscle.

If society devalues this male role by pressing women to provide for themselves, prove their "independence," and compete with men for money and status, there is only one way equality between the sexes can be maintained: Women must be reduced to sexual parity. They must relinquish their sexual superiority, psychologically disconnect their wombs, and adopt the short-circuited copulatory sexuality of males. Women must renounce all the larger procreative dimensions of their sexual impulse.

This is precisely what sexual liberals advocate. They assiduously deny that women have a maternal instinct and assert women's "right" to adopt male sexual attitudes and ape male sexual drives. At the very same time they argue that men can find sexual fulfillment in "nurturant" activities like child-rearing.

Whether "instinctive" or not, however, the maternal role originates in the fact that only the woman is necessarily present at birth. Only the woman has a dependable and easily identifiable connection to the child—a tie on which society can rely. No matter how "equally" the functions of child-rearing are distributed, the man will always know that the woman's role with the children was more important, more organically indispensable. There is no way the man can share in the euphoria that many women feel—along with the pains—when pregnant, for it is a sensation of warm separateness and independent fulfillment. There is no way that men can share in the "mothering hormone" that many authorities believe the woman secretes in childbirth. There is no way the man with the bottle will experience the sense of sexual affirmation and sensual fulfillment felt by the woman with a child at her breast.

The man's dependence on women begins in his earliest years. A male child is born, grows, and finds his being in relation to his own body and to the bodies of his parents, chiefly his mother's. His later happiness is found in part on a physiological memory. Originating perhaps in the womb itself, it extends through all his infant groping into the world at large, which begins, of course, in his mother's arms. In trusting her he learned to trust himself, and trusting himself he learns to bear the slow dissolution of the primary tie. He moves away into a new world, into a sometimes frightening psychic space between his parents; and he must then attach his evolving identity to a man, his father. Almost from the start, the boy's sexual identity is dependent on acts of exploration and initiative.

Throughout the lives of men we find echoes of this image, of a boy stranded in transition from his first tie to a woman—whom he discovers to be different, and perhaps even subtly dangerous to him—toward identification with a man, who will always deny him the closeness his mother once provided. At an early age he is, in a sense, set at large. Before he can return to a woman, he must assert his manhood in action. The Zulu warrior had to kill a man, the Mandan youth had to endure torture, the Irish peasant had to build a house, the American man must find a job. This is the classic myth and the mundane reality of masculinity.

Female histories are different. As Margaret Mead observed: "The worry that boys will not grow up to be men is much more widespread than the worry that the girls will not grow up to be women, and in none of these South Sea societies [that she studied] does the latter fear appear at all."[2] A girl's sexuality normally unfolds in an unbroken line, from a stage of utter dependency and identification with her mother through stages of gradual autonomy. Always, the focus of female identification is clear and stable.

Anthropologist Ashley Montagu has reported evidence that women treat girls and boys differently from the time of birth, fondling and caressing the girls more and making them feel more a part of their initial environment.[3] The mothers may unconsciously recognize that girls can enjoy a continuous evolution of identity with their mothers, while boys relatively soon must break this primary tie.

This analysis is essentially confirmed by the studies of Karen Horney and Erik Erikson.[4] Moreover, the pattern these earliest events might be expected to create—of a more stable and secure femininity and a more insecure and questing masculinity—is later enforced by the radically contrasting ways in which men and women emerge into their sexuality.

Male sexual consciousness comes as an unprogrammed drive. Nothing about the male body dictates any specific pattern beyond a repetitive release of sexual tension. Men must define and defend the larger dimensions of their sexuality by external activity.

As a physical reality, the male sexual repertory is very limited. Men have only one sex organ and one sex act: erection and ejaculation. Everything else is guided by culture and imagination. Other male roles, other styles of masculine identity, must be learned or created. The most important and productive roles—husband and father in a durable marriage—are a cultural invention, necessary to civilized life but ultimately fragile.

A woman is not so exclusively dependent on copulation for sexual identity. For her, intercourse is only one of many sex acts or experiences. Her breasts and her womb symbolize a sex role that extends, at least as a potentiality, through pregnancy, childbirth, lactation, suckling, and long-term nurture. Rather than a brief performance, female sexuality is a long, unfolding process. Even if a woman does not in fact bear a child, she is continually reminded that she can, that she is capable of performing the crucial act in the perpetuation of the species. She can perform the only act that gives sex an unquestionable meaning, an incarnate result.

Thus, regardless of any anxieties she may have in relation to her sexual role and how to perform it, she at least knows that she has a role of unquestionable importance to herself and the community. Whatever else she may do or be, she can be sure of her essential female nature.

On this point the sexes do not understand each other. Women take their sexual identity for granted. They assume that except for some cultural peculiarity, men might also enjoy such sexual assurance. Women are puzzled by male unease, by men's continual attempts to prove their manhood or ritualistically affirm it. Judith Hole and Ellen Levine, in the *Rebirth of Feminism,* show typical female complacency when they call sexual identity "an almost immutable fact," like "the location of one's head."[5] Seymour Fisher's elaborate research of female sexuality for the National Institute of Health confirms this greater security of women: "It was my conclusion, after reviewing all available studies," Fisher writes, "that the average woman is more 'at ease' with her own body than is the average man. . . . Her body 'makes sense' to her as one of the prime means to become what she wants to become."[6] This assurance about sexual identity leads to a certain impatience with men.

Throughout the literature of feminism there runs a puzzled complaint: "Why can't men *be* men and just relax?" The reason is that, unlike femininity, relaxed masculinity is at bottom empty, a limp nullity. While the female body is full of internal potentiality, the male is internally barren (from the Old French *bar,* meaning man).

Manhood at the most basic level can be validated and expressed only in action. A man's body is full only of undefined energies—and all these energies need the guidance of culture. He is therefore deeply dependent on the structure of the society to define his role. In all its specific expressions, manhood is made, not born.

Nancy Chodorow ends her otherwise fine essay on "Being and Doing" by envisioning a world in which "male identity does not depend on men's proving themselves by doing."[7] Like so many other feminists, she wonders whether men can be "humanized." Chodorow laments that in our society men's "doing" is "a reaction to insecurity" rather than "a creative exercise of their humanity."

She is essentially right. The male sexual predicament, like the female, is not the sort of arrangement that might have been invented by social engineers. It has a tragic quality that is difficult to adapt to egalitarian formulas. Men must perform. There is no shortcut to human fulfillment for men—just the short circuit of impotence. Men can be creatively human only when they are confidently male and overcome their sexual insecurity by action. Nothing comes to them by waiting or "being."

This inferior sexuality, this relatively greater sexual insecurity, is the reason intercourse plays a role in the lives of males different from its role in the lives of females. Lacking the innate insecurity of males and possessing an unimpeachable sexual identity, women are not usually so reliant on intercourse. As Alfred Kinsey's colleague, Mary Jane Sherfey, observes in her liberationist book on female sexuality[8]—and as the Masters and Johnson experiments showed—women can both enjoy sexual relations more profoundly and durably and forgo them more easily than can men. In those ways they are superior. Whatever other problems a woman may have, her identity *as a woman* is not so much at stake in intercourse. She has other specifically female experiences and does not have to perform intercourse in the same sense as her partner; she can relax and usually please her man.

The man, on the other hand, has just one sex act and he is exposed to conspicuous failure in it. His erection is a mysterious endowment that he can never fully understand or control. If it goes, he often will not know exactly why, and there will be little he or his partner can do to retrieve it. Even if he succeeds in erection he still can fail to evoke orgasm—and he can lose out to other men who can. Unlike the woman's physique, the man's physical endowment—his phallic size and endurance—is crucial to the success of intercourse. And if he is impotent, it will subvert all the other aspects of his relationship and will undermine his entire personality. As Robert Musil has written, "the man's most masculine part is also the most easily intimidated."[9]

In general, therefore, the man is less secure sexually than the woman because his sexuality is dependent on action, and he can act sexually only through a precarious process difficult to control. Fear of impotence and inadequacy is a paramount fact of male sexuality. For men the desire for sex is not simply a quest for pleasure. It is an indispensable test of identity. And in itself it is always ultimately temporary and inadequate. Unless his maleness is confirmed by his culture, he must enact it repeatedly, and perhaps destructively for himself or his society. Particularly in a society where clear and affirmative masculine activities are scarce, men may feel a compulsive desire to perform their one unquestionable male role. It is only when men are engaged in a relentless round of masculine activities in the company of males—Marine Corps training is one example—that their sense of manhood allows them to avoid sex without great strain.

Under most conditions, young men are subject to nearly unremitting sexual drives, involving their very identities as males. Unless they have an enduring relationship with a woman—a relationship that affords them sexual confidence—men will accept almost any convenient sexual offer. This drive arises early in their lives, and if it is not appeased by women it is slaked by masturbation and pornography. The existence of a semi-illegal, multibillion-dollar pornography market, almost entirely male-oriented, bespeaks the difference in sexual character between men and women. One can be sure that if women passionately wanted porn, it would be provided. Though sexual liberals have denied it so often as to thoroughly confuse each sex about the feelings of the other, the fact is that women lack the kind of importunate, undifferentiated lust that infects almost all men.[10]

This view is strongly confirmed by a cross-cultural study of 190 different societies made by Clellan S. Ford and Frank A. Beach.[11]

Males almost everywhere show greater sexual aggressiveness, com-pulsiveness, and lack of selectivity. Over the whole range of human societies, men are overwhelmingly more prone to masturbation, homosexuality, voyeurism, gratuitous sexual aggression, and other shallow and indiscriminate erotic activity. Male sexuality is a physi-cal drive and a psychological compulsion. This voracious need can rise to a pitch at the slightest provocation; it demands nothing but an available body; at its height it aspires less to a special love than to an orgiastic rut.

In virtually every known society, sex is regarded either as a grant by the woman to the man or as an object of male seizure. In most societies, the man has to pay for it with a gift or service. Although women are physiologically capable of greater orgasmic pleasure than men—and thus may avidly seek intercourse—they are also much better able to abstain from sex without psychological strain. In the United States the much greater mental health of single women than single men may be explained in part by this female strength. But greater sexual control and discretion—more informed and deliberate sexual powers—are displayed by women in all socie-ties known to anthropology. Indeed, this intelligent and controlled female sexuality is what makes human communities possible.

This difference between the sexes gives the woman the superior position in most sexual encounters. The man may push and pos-ture, but the woman must decide. He is driven; she must set the terms and conditions, goals and destinations of the journey. Her faculty of greater natural restraint and selectivity makes the woman the sexual judge and executive, finally appraising the offerings of men, favor-ing one and rejecting another, and telling them what they must do to be saved or chosen. Managing the sexual nature of a healthy society, women impose the disciplines, make the choices, and summon the male efforts that support it.

Modern society relies on predictable, regular, long-term human activities, corresponding to the sexual faculties of women. The male pattern is the enemy of social stability. This is the ultimate source of female sexual control and the crucial reason for it. Women domesti-cate and civilize male nature. They can jeopardize male discipline and identity, and civilization as well, merely by giving up the role.

The female responsibility for civilization cannot be granted or assigned to men. Unlike a woman, a man has no civilized role or agenda inscribed in his body. Although his relationship to specific children can give him a sense of futurity resembling the woman's, it always must come through her body and her choices. The child can never be *his* unless a woman allows him to claim it with her or unless he so controls her and so restricts her sexual activity that he can be sure that he is the father. He cannot merely come back nine months later with grand claims. He must make a durable commitment.

Even then he is dependent on the woman to love and nurture his child. Even in the context of the family, he is sexually inferior. If he leaves, the family may survive without him. If she leaves, it goes with her. He is readily replaceable; she is not. He can have a child only if she acknowledges his paternity; her child is inexorably hers. His position must be maintained by continuous performance, sexual and worldly, with the woman the judge. The woman's position, on the other hand, requires essentially a receptive sexuality and is naturally validated by the child that cannot ordinarily be taken away. The man's role in the family is thus reversible; the woman's is unimpeachable and continues even if the man departs.

The man's participation in the chain of nature, his access to social immortality, the very meaning of his potency, of his life energy, are all inexorably contingent on a woman's durable love and on her sexual discipline. Only she can free the man of his exile from the chain of nature; only she can give significance to his most powerful drives.

The essential pattern is clear. Women manipulate male sexual desire in order to teach men the long-term cycles of female sexuality and biology on which civilization is based. When a man learns, his view of the woman as an object of his own sexuality succumbs to an image of her as the bearer of a richer and more extended eroticism and as the keeper of the portals of social immortality. She becomes a way to lend continuity and meaning to his limited erotic compulsions.

This intuition of mysterious new realms of sexual and social experience, evoked by the body and spirit of woman, is the source of male love and ultimately of marriage. In evoking marriages love renders the woman in a way transparent: the man sees through her, in a vision freighted with sexual desire, to the child they might have together. This vision imposes severe social conditions, however. For it is a child that *he* might have only if he performs a role: only if he can offer, in exchange for the intense inner sexual meanings she imparts, an external realm of meaning, sustenance, and protection in which the child could be safely born.

In the man's desire, conscious or unconscious, to identify and keep his progeny is the beginning of love. In a civilized society, he will not normally be able to claim his children if they are born to several mothers. He must choose a particular woman and submit to her sexual rhythms and social demands if he is to have offspring of his own. His love defines his choice. His need to choose evokes his love. His sexual drive lends energy to his love and his love gives shape, meaning, and continuity to his sexuality. When he selects a specific woman, he in essence defines himself both to himself and society. Every sex act thereafter celebrates that definition and social engagement.

Without a durable relationship with a woman, a man's sexual life is a series of brief and temporary exchanges, impelled by a desire to affirm his most rudimentary masculinity. But with love sex becomes refined by selectivity, and other dimensions of personality are engaged and developed. The man himself is refined, and his sexuality becomes not a mere impulse but a commitment in society, possibly to be fulfilled in the birth of specific children legally and recognizably his. His sex life then can be conceived and experienced as having specific long-term importance like a woman's.

Obviously the most enduring way to make this commitment is through marriage. Yet because sexual liberals deny the differences between the sexes, their explanations of why there are marriages and why marriage is needed and desired ignore the central truth of marriage: that it is built on sex roles. Pressed to explain the institution, they respond vaguely that human beings want "structure" or desire "intimacy." But however desirable in marriage, these values are not essential causes or explanations of it.

In many cultures, the wife and husband share very few one-to-one intimacies. Ties with others of the same sex—or even the opposite sex—often offer deeper companionship. The most intimate connections are between mothers and their children. In all societies, male groups provide men with some of their most emotionally gratifying associations. Indeed, intimacy can deter or undermine wedlock. In the kibbutz, for example, where unrelated boys and girls are brought up together and achieve a profound degree of companionate feeling, they never marry members of the same child-rearing group.[12] In the many cultures where marriages are arranged, the desire for intimacy is subversive of marriage.

Similarly, man's "innate need for structure" can be satisfied in hundreds of forms of organization. The need for structure may explain all of them or none of them, but it does not tell us why, of all possible arrangements, marriage is the one most prevalent. It does not tell us why, in most societies, marriage alone is consecrated in a religious ceremony and entails a permanent commitment.

As most anthropologists see it, however, the reason is simple. The very essence of marriage, Bronislaw Malinowski wrote, is not structure and intimacy; it is "parenthood and above all maternity."[13] The male role in marriage, as Margaret Mead maintained, "in every known human society, is to provide for women and children."[14] In order to marry, in fact, Malinowski says that almost every human society first requires the man "to prove his capacity to maintain the woman."[15]

Marriage is not simply a ratification of an existing love. It is the conversion of that love into a biological and social continuity. The very essence of such continuity is children—now fewer than before, but retained far longer within the family bounds. Regardless of what reasons particular couples may give for getting married, the deeper evolutionary and sexual propensities explain the persistence of the institution. All sorts of superficial variations—from homosexual marriage to companionate partnership—may be played on the primal themes of human life. But the themes remain. The natural fulfillment of love is a child; the fantasies and projects of the childless couple may well be considered as surrogate children.

A man without a woman has a deep inner sense of dispensability, perhaps evolved during the millennia of service in the front lines of tribal defense. He is sexually optional. Several dominant males could impregnate all the women and perpetuate the tribe. It is this sense of dispensability that makes young men good fighters, good crusaders, good martyrs. But it also weakens the male ability to care deeply and long and stunts young men's sense of the preciousness of human beings. Because the woman has always been directly responsible for infants and almost always exclusively responsible, she is dubious about the dying and killing that have surrounded male activities.

Once the man marries he can change. He has to change, for his wife will not long have him if he remains in spirit a single man. He must settle his life, and commit it to the needs of raising a family. He must exchange the moral and spiritual rhythms of the hunt for a higher, more extended mode of sexual life. He must submit, ethically and sexually, to the values of maternal morality and futurity.

When the man submits to female sexuality, therefore, he not only adopts an ethic of long-term responsibility for the life and death matters of his own children's upbringing but he also adopts a new perspective on life and death itself. His life is no longer so optional, because his wife and children depend on him. Thus individual life assumes a higher value within the monogamous marriage than it does in a male group.

As a social institution, marriage transcends all individuals. The health of a society, its collective vitality, ultimately resides in its concern for the future, its sense of a connection with generations to come. There is perhaps no more important index of the social condition. It is the very temperature of a community. A community preoccupied with the present, obsessed with an immediate threat or pleasure, is enfevered. A social body, like a human body, can run a very high fever for short periods in order to repel a specific threat or to meet an emergency, a war or domestic crisis. But if it finds itself perpetually enfevered, it begins to run down and can no longer provide for the future. Its social programs can fail to work, its businesses can fail to produce, its laws can become unenforceable. The will and morale and community of its people can founder. A society, apparently working well, can stand impotent before its most important domestic and external threats and opportunities.

The sense of social vitality and balance does not "just happen." In civilized conditions it is love, marriage, and the nurture of children that project a society into the future and make it responsible for posterity. There does not seem to be any other dependable way to do it, throughout an entire population over time. Militarism, chauvinism, religious fanaticism, even the leadership of a charismatic psychopath can serve briefly—and at a major cost to individual freedom. But in general it is only through love for specific children that a society evokes long-term commitments from its members.

That is why the social temperature of single men is so high—why they end up so often being sent to war or jail or other institutions, and why they burn out so young. A society does not run into real trouble, however, until its culture begins to adopt the unmarried male pattern, until the long-term commitments on which any enduring community is based are undermined by an opportunistic public philosophy. The public philosophy of the unmarried male focuses on immediate gratification: "What did posterity ever do for me?" A society that widely adopts this attitude is in trouble.

The power of a woman springs from her role in overcoming these socially and personally self-defeating ways of men. She can grant to the man a sexual affirmation that he needs more than she does; she can offer him progeny otherwise permanently denied him; and she can give him a way of living happily and productively in a civilized society that is otherwise oppressive to male nature. In exchange modern man gives his external achievement and his reluctant faithfulness. It is on these terms that marriage—and male socialization—are based.

The ideology of the sexual liberationists sees society as a male-dominated construct that exploits women for the convenience of men. In evidence, they cite men's greater earning power, as if economic productivity were a measure of social control rather than of social service. But it is female power, organic and constitutional, that is real—holding sway over the deepest levels of consciousness, sources of happiness, and processes of social survival. Male dominance in the marketplace, on the other hand, is a social artifice maintained not for the dubious benefits it confers on men but for the indispensable benefits it offers the society: inducing men to support rather than disrupt it. Conventional male power, in fact, might be considered more the ideological myth. It is designed to induce the majority of men to accept a bondage to the machine and the market-place, to a large extent in the service of women and in the interests of civilization.

Any consideration of equality focusing on employment and income, therefore, will miss the real sources of equilibrium between the sexes. These deeper female strengths and male weaknesses are more important than any superficial male dominance because they control the ultimate motives and rewards of our existence. In child-bearing, every woman is capable of a feat of creativity and durable accomplishment—permanently and uniquely changing the face of the earth—that only the most extraordinary man can even pretend to duplicate in external activity.

Women control not the economy of the marketplace but the economy of eros: the life force in our society and our lives. What happens in the inner realm of women finally shapes what happens on our social surfaces, determining the level of happiness, energy, creativity, morality, and solidarity in the nation.

These values are primary in any society. When they deteriorate, all the king's horses and all the king's men cannot put them back together again.

CHAPTER 2

The Biological Difference

In recent years, a new professional has emerged in America: the sexologist. Usually a woman, conservative in dress and temperament, confident, with formidable credentials, she comes forth to utter the final word on contemporary sexual behavior. In this oracular role, though, she does not speak for herself. She represents an institution or an academy—some large and august first-personage plural—the learning of which looms up behind the speaker like a convocation of eminent ghosts, for which she is only a modest medium.

This would not matter necessarily. Her views are more significant if widely and prestigiously held. But what has this Delphic corporation learned about sex? Ask it any question and the answer is the same: "We don't know this"; "We have no evidence for that"; "Our experiments are inconclusive"; "Our knowledge is limited"; "We just don't know." In fact, if one presented in one place all the expressed opinions of these collective experts, one might suppose they were discussing some great mystery—the nature of God, perhaps—and one would have to conclude that all the "available data" from the "most knowledgeable sources" and most learned authorities, commanding all the "best experimental evidence," had as yet failed to substantiate widely heard rumors and superstitions concerning the existence of "sex." To be sure, *something* is going on out there, but as to what it is exactly . . . well, "we have very conflicting data on that point. We need more research."

19

The issue about which "we" are most assuredly and doggedly agnostic is the existence of two biologically different sexes. Dr. Babette Blackington, for example, a few years ago alerted a presumably perplexed television audience to the hitherto unknown possibilities of male breasts. "Men's breasts, you know, can be induced to lactate," she said, "and the woman's clitoris can be made to ejaculate." Thus she expressed in vivid terms the ultimate vision of the sexual liberationist: the two sexes are essentially identical, inessentially and arbitrarily divided.

To most people over the centuries this view would have seemed preposterous. And so it is today. For after all these years, scientists are finally affirming what nonexperts have always known: that there are profound and persistent biological differences between the sexes, with which every society must come to terms.

Some of the most formidable evidence comes from the studies of Dr. John Money and his colleagues at Johns Hopkins University in Baltimore, who for decades have been treating hermaphroditism and other sex anomalies.[1] Other persuasive material comes from the University of Wisconsin laboratories of the Harlows, who have long been examining the habits of Rhesus monkeys.[2] Further evidence comes from the studies of baboons, chimpanzees, and other primate cousins, both in captivity and in the wild. Then there are hundreds of interesting experiments with the hormonal systems of rats. Finally, there are scores of experiments and observations among humans from infancy to adulthood, in virtually every kind of society from the most primitive to the most advanced.[3] The evidence in fact is so hugely voluminous that our sexperts could be excused for their confusion—if all the material, without important exception, did not point in the same direction: that from conception to maturity, men and women are subjected to different hormonal influences that shape their bodies, brains, and temperaments in different ways.

The man is rendered more aggressive, exploratory, volatile, competitive and dominant, more visual, abstract, and impulsive, more muscular, appetitive, and tall. He is less nurturant, moral, domestic, stable, and peaceful, less auditory, verbal, and sympathetic, less durable, healthy, and dependable, less balanced, and less close to the ground. He is more compulsive sexually and less secure. Within his own sex, he is more inclined to affiliate upwards—toward authority—and less inclined to affiliate downward—toward children and toward the weak and needy.

Of course these tendencies are shaped by environment and culture, and are modified in crucial ways by the relations between men, women, and children in any society. But most of these propensities are substantiated by a large amount of cross-cultural material, combined with a growing body of physiological—particularly neuro-endocrinological—data.

Among the many interesting cross-cultural comparisons is a study by B. Whiting of six separate cultures—one each in India, Okinawa, the Philippines, Mexico, Kenya, and New England. In all, the boys are more aggressive and violent than the girls and, in all, the girls are more nurturant and responsible with younger children.[4]

Steven Goldberg, in preparing his fine study, *The Inevitability of Patriarchy*,[5] examined most of the anthropological and sociological literature on the subject of political leadership and authority. In particular he scrutinized every report of an alleged matriarchy, where women were said to hold political power. He found no evidence that a matriarchy had ever existed or is in any way emerging today. He found no society in which authority was associated chiefly with women in male-female relations. In a review, Margaret Mead agreed with these findings and described his presentation of the data as "faultless."[6] The degree to which women take power seems to depend on the extent to which the men are absent.[7] George Murdock compared some 500 cultures and found that, in all of them, fighting and leadership were associated with the men.[8]

Now there are two essential ways to deal with a pattern so universal. One can go to the thousands of human societies and find ingenious explanations for each incidence of masculinity and femininity. The men provide most of the food, so they dominate. Or they don't provide most of the food, but the women, feeling secure, allow them to dominate. The men are free from child-care responsibilities and can spend time competing for power. Or the men really have as much responsibility for the children as the women do, so the men create a pattern of dominance from generation to generation.

One can offer a similar catalogue of particular explanations for the other general patterns. One can find as many partial or apparent exceptions as possible. One can show how the general tendencies can be overcome by conditioning under some circumstances—as when a male Rhesus monkey grooms and fosters an infant put in its cage. One can write a lot about gibbons, beavers, marmosets, golden hamsters, and the few other animals that are less dimorphic than man, and in which the female is the same size as the male or larger.[9] One can assemble the various tests that fail to register differences between the sexes in humans. One can design and give new ones. Then if one wishes, one can say, "We just don't know." "The data on these points is very confusing." "We need more research."

It is simpler, however, to consult the existing research and arrive at a biological or physical explanation. The evidence is ample.

The sexes become significantly different, even in the very organization of their brains, during the time in the womb. There the presence or absence of a Y sex chromosome determines whether the embryo will be a boy or a girl. The fetus with a Y chromosome will develop testicles rather than ovaries. When the fetus develops male gonads, they will secrete small amounts of androgenic (from *andro*—male, and *genic*—creating) hormones, chiefly testosterone. The testosterone eventually acts on the brain, giving it a male form. So far, neuroendocrinologists have shown that the hypothalamus is measurably dimorphic, with different cell structure and weight for each sex. The hypothalamus is the part of the brain that governs such impulses as hunger, anger, and sex drive. In the man, it also ultimately controls the secretion of the androgens, chiefly testosterone, which themselves have a deep relationship to aggression and sexuality.

The female hypothalamus administers a more complex hormonal system, involving two major sex hormones, estrogen and progesterone, rather than essentially one, as in the male. It also ultimately governs the hormones involved in breast-feeding, both in causing lactation (prolactin) and in creating a desire to nurse and stimulating the flow of the milk (oxytocin). Oxytocin is also a tranquilizing hormone that encourages nurturant behavior.

The male neuroendocrinological system—chiefly the hypothalamus and the gonads—is thus less various and flexible than the woman's. The chief male hormone, testosterone, is very powerful, and small amounts of it given to a woman greatly stimulate her sex drive (her natural libidinal hormone is an androgen produced in the adrenal glands). But testosterone is almost the man's whole repertory, the only way he can respond hormonally to a sexual stimulus.

In a sense, sexual inequality begins in the fetus. The basic human form (template) is female. Even a male fetus will become a healthy *female* if, for some reason, the gonads do not secrete sufficient testosterone in the womb. The fetus becomes male only when it both has a Y chromosome and is acted upon by androgenic hormones. On the other hand, androgenic hormones cannot make a healthy male out of a female fetus, a fetus with X chromosomes. But the androgens can cause dramatic virilizing effects. By studying such accidents, one can learn much about the influence of the different hormonal and hypothalamic forms of males and females.

A hormonal accident or malfunction in the womb may cause a later sex confusion, or even a hermaphrodite, with the organs of both sexes. If one has a child of ambiguous sex, one may take it to the clinic conducted in Baltimore by Dr. Money and his colleagues. They have been treating and examining such patients for several decades and have become the world's leading authorities on the subject.

Many of their findings are presented in *Man and Woman, Boy and Girl* by Dr. Money and Anke Ehrhardt.[10] Described by the *New York Times* on publication in 1972 as the most important study published in the social sciences since the Kinsey reports, it is a fascinating exploration of the causes of sexual dimorphism or of its failure to occur.

In order to judge the impact of fetal masculinization on men, it is useful to appraise its effect on the female. Thus one can distinguish to some extent the impact of fetal testosterone on the brain from the continuing influence of testosterone secretions after birth.

Money and Ehrhardt compared a group of girls accidentally exposed as fetuses to an androgen with a group of girls suffering from a genetic disorder known as Turner's syndrome, in which they are born without sex hormones. Both groups—the androgenized girls and the girls without sex hormones—were raised as females and identified themselves as such. The results of the comparison are summarized succinctly by Corinne Hutt, an experimental psychologist at Oxford, in *Males and Females,* perhaps the most readable study of the biology of sex differences:

> Whereas none of the patients with Turner's syndrome showed "intense outdoor physical and athletic interest," all but one of the androgenized females did so; whereas none of the Turner cases regarded themselves or were considered by others to be a tomboy, most of the [androgenized] cases did, and were also regarded so by others. The majority of the androgenized girls preferred boys' toys to girls' toys, some of them playing *only* with boys' toys, while all the Turner girls preferred girls' toys to boys'. The same was true of clothes . . .[11]

Perhaps the most remarkable result, however, was the apparent influence of fetal experience on career and marriage priorities.

> No androgenized girls put marriage before a career, some put a career before marriage and many wanted both; of the girls with Turner's syndrome, some put marriage before career, more wanted both, but only one put a career before marriage and she wanted to be a nun.[12]

The point is that these genetic girls, exposed to a male hormone as fetuses, can develop a fully masculine childhood pattern as a result. They consider themselves girls, but they consistently reject most of the attempts of the culture to feminize them. One might plausibly conclude, therefore, that the similar biases in boys, massively reinforced at puberty, are not cultural fictions. In other words, boys are more aggressive, career-oriented, and physically exploratory chiefly because of the way they are born, not the way they are raised. Their brains are fetally masculinized. The major impact is on the hypothalamus as the center of appetites and emotion and the thalamus, which controls the erection, but some experts believe that the cortex is affected as well.

Many studies of small children indicate that the chief effect of masculinization is more roughhousing, aggressiveness, and competition, together with a tendency to affiliate upward, toward male leaders. The Harlows have demonstrated that, in monkeys, these effects are slightly diminished rather than heightened by maternal influence. Male monkeys raised in cages and fed artificially by simulated cloth "mothers" are more aggressive with their peers than normal monkeys (while females show just as much feminine "grooming" activity as normal monkeys and vastly more than the males).[13]

It is at puberty that the major hormonal crisis occurs in the lives of boys. Although they are not at that time significantly larger than girls, their bodies begin secreting testosterone in enormous quantities, ten to twenty times the amount of androgens received by girls. This has several effects beyond the obvious changes in external sexual characteristics. Testosterone promotes protein synthesis and thus greatly increases physical strength. By fifteen, the boys have shot ahead of the girls in all indices of athletic ability involving muscular strength, height, speed, and cardiorespiratory capacity. Testosterone vastly boosts sexual drive, to the extent that boys reach a peak at age sixteen or seventeen; such "peaking" does not happen to women. And, finally, testosterone fosters aggression and competition. Although the precise way testosterone works remains open to question, tests both on humans and monkeys have linked levels of testosterone secretion with levels of aggressive or dominant behavior. Scientists have succeeded in changing the dominance order in groups of monkeys by injecting testosterone in the lower-ranking males.[14]

Although older men learn to "hold their hormones" to some degree, the young man is full of both aggression and sexual appetite. He wants to join with older boys and participate in highly charged group activity. He wants to define and fulfill his male sex drive. He is swept from day to day by waves of glandular emotion. The feminists who suppose that "the cortex has liberated men from hormonal influence" could not have much observed the behavior of young men.

It is not the exalted cortex that impels their passion for acceptance by the group, their eagerness to compete for a place, their obsessiveness in practicing for the test. It is not cool passages of reason that govern the adolescent's sexual fears and compulsions—his pornographic curiosities, his masturbatory sieges, his ambivalent pursuit of girls. The boy is encountering in acute form the predicament of male sexual identity: a powerful group of drives that lack a specific shape or clear, ultimate resolution in modern society.

The adolescent girl, meanwhile, is often lethargic. Her hormonal surge may depress her. Her body is changing rapidly in ways that are initially uncomfortable. She is entering "the awkward age." But as her body fills out and she becomes a woman, a clear and important sexual role unfolds. Her breasts, her womb, her temperament—together with the increasing interest of boys—remind her of her possible future as wife and mother.

It is an identity of obvious importance to the society. It offers a variety of sensual rewards, from orgasmic sexual fulfillment to childbirth and on into the deep affirmations of breast-feeding and nurture. It is a sexual role that gives a nearly irrevocable value: one's own child. Needless to say, there are also conflicts and complications. Moreover, sexual identity in itself does not resolve all identity problems. But it is an indispensable beginning—a beginning directly related in women to specific and intelligible changes in their bodies and their lives.

It is hard to exaggerate how different is the adolescent boy's experience. His body is not evolving; it is launching an insurrection. It demands to be satisfied now, by external activity. Even in women and in male homosexuals, the injection of testosterone creates a desire for immediate but undefined sexual action.

The most obvious relief, masturbation, is a flight from sexual identity rather than an affirmation of it. Relations with girls, moreover, are ambiguous and complicated at this stage. Rejection of the overwrought male by the underripe female is frequent and deepens the boy's anxieties.

A sexual identity has to involve a role. In the past, there was a direct tie between the boy's growing strength and aggressiveness and his entry into adult male groups. In fact, he might be stronger and faster, a better hunter, than his elders. Like a woman's sexuality, his purpose in life was defined and fulfilled through the changes in his mind and body. But this is no longer true.

The relationship between virility and adult acceptance may even be negative in today's society. Not only do strength and aggression fail to provide a future, they are also likely to jeopardize one's present. Voluminous testing data indicate that "feminized" boys do best in school, while the strongest and most aggressive drop out.[15]

Despite all the blather to the contrary, it is obvious that virile men remain attractive to women. They can gain some sense of identity through sex and sports. The chief social problems are created by men of insecure sexual identity who cannot either find girls or excel them in "feminized" school and career competitions. Tests among prisoners indicate that it is the ones with the greatest sexual role anxieties who commit violent and predatory crimes.[16]

A man who cannot attain his manhood through an affirmative role resorts to the lowest terms of masculinity. What can he do that is exclusively male? He consults his body. He has a cock. But he is a failure and no woman wants it. He has greater physical strength and aggressiveness. He uses it.

This social and hormonal dilemma of young men was illuminated by a series of experiments with Rhesus monkeys in Atlanta.[17] The researchers found that when male monkeys compete, their testosterone levels rise. But when the contest is over, only the winner's remains high. He feels confident, dominant, and ready to pursue females. The loser, on the other hand, is dejected, and his hormone level plummets.

In modern society, sexual relations with women are becoming the chief way many men assert their sexual identity. But in most of the world's societies, sexual relations follow achievement of manhood, or accompany it. Male affirmation may lead to high testosterone levels, and to feelings of worth, that in turn lead to sexual fulfillment. In this society, it is very hard for many youths to qualify for the company of men on the job or elsewhere. They must validate themselves in sexual terms alone. Yet they may lack the confidence and spirit to approach and win a woman.

Ford and Beach's study of nearly two hundred societies concluded that in virtually all of them sex is regarded as something the woman does for the man.[18] He needs it more urgently than she does. He has no alternative or extended sexual role.

Therefore in every human society the man has to bring something to the woman. He has to perform a service or give a gift. At the very least, he must offer more than his own urgency or he will not even be able to gratify the woman sexually.

Even when he cannot be the provider much of the time, he offers his success as a man, validated in a world of men inaccessible to her. Now, however, the man all too often comes to the woman seeking the very affirmation that he needs to have already if he is to win her. Nothing has occurred in the biology of love that significantly relieves him of this dilemma. The man still has to perform—still has to offer something beyond himself, and beyond her reach—if she is to receive him. To find the further sources of this male imperative, one must explore the realm of anthropology—the primal history of human societies.

CHAPTER 3

After the Hunt

Perhaps the clearest lesson of anthropology is that a tribe's sex roles—its births, matings, kinship ties—largely shape its nature and durability. In the modern world, the links between sex and civilization may seem more obscure, but our civilization also largely derives its forms and possibilities from sexual arrangements. A job, a custom, a ritual, an institution not only plays an immediate role in production or consumption. It also plays a role in the sexual constitution of society: the intricately woven armature of eros that generates our will, vitality, and creative force.

One of the key concerns of every society is how to respond to the unprogrammed power of male sexual energy. Mead goes to the heart of the matter: "The central problem of every society is to define appropriate roles for the men."[1] The uses and abuses of the male sex drive constitute the vital variable in civilization.

Many communities have been able to solve this problem rather easily. The men have simply performed those tasks of hunting and defense which through the long millennia have allowed women time and space to procreate the species or gather and prepare food. Hunting and defense fortunately are activities that accord with the brief but intense rhythms and compulsions of male sexuality. A hunt proceeds to a violent climax when the game is found and killed. A battle erupts suddenly, requires frenzied activity, and soon ends. The men can rise to the occasion and then subside; tension grows and is released. Gratifications are immediate and transitory. The men travel in gangs. They may copulate with the women but otherwise often have little to do with them. If in the state of nature as Hobbes described it, human existence is "solitary, poor, nasty, brutish and short," this, excluding solitude, is the masculine pattern.

Whether or not this hunting and gathering life is the earliest human arrangement, it has certain attractions today. In primitive hunting communities the males are not "sexually insecure." In Nancy Chodorow's terms, perhaps they act with the "full expression of their humanity." They are not threatened by female intrusion on their realms of activity. Women often take part in the hunt in various capacities, provided the hunting party itself is not jeopardized. Lionel Tiger, in his pathbreaking book *Men in Groups,* assumes that in most instances the hunting party would be endangered by female participation, and he concludes, plausibly enough, that segregated groups won natural selection.[2] Critics of Tiger point out that among the Australian Bushmen, the Eskimos, and the other few observable hunting societies, women sometimes participate in various ways.[3] The segregation is not legal and complete.

But surely this scholarly conflict is spurious. In hunting and gathering societies within a hostile environment, the position of males is so spontaneous, so secure, so indispensable, that no *de jure* exclusions are needed. Male roles and male sexuality coincide and affirm each other in an authentic unity. In addition, because the men in hunting and fighting parties would be most likely to succeed if they acted together, a cooperative inclination or male bonding instinct evolved. Of course, the inclination to exclude females from the hunt also reflects the intense distraction created by sexually eligible women in any gathering of men, particularly over a long period. Natural competitive instincts are exacerbated and trust and unity undermined.

In any case, the role pattern of these hunting societies is clear. The men hunt and, when necessary, defend. The women gather and prepare food, as well as bear, nurture, and raise children. The family unit thus effectively consists of the mother and child, with the man an occasional visitor seeking sexual release and sometimes displaying little interest in young children. In the pure case, where there is no agricultural activity and food is scarce, the tribe is likely to be nomadic, marching to the beat of the hunt and the battle.

Agricultural societies are in important ways superior to hunting societies. For in general, civilization evolved through the subordination of male sexual patterns—the short-term cycles of tension and release—to the long-term female patterns. Anthropologists often credit women with the initiation of agriculture. Just as the movements, crises, performances, and recoveries of nomadic hunting embodied the rhythm of male sexuality, so the seasonal phases of the farm community accorded with the extended cycles of the woman's life.

But this advance for mankind came at some psychological cost for men. The problem called by Mead the central issue of every human society arose: what to do with the males. Unlike hunting groups, immobile agricultural communities had to stress diligence, regularity, and control; they left little room for male initiatives and aggressions. A mistake would ruin a whole season of crops. In farming a bold initiative offers more danger of disaster than promise of gain. Under those circumstances male sexual insecurity arises as a social problem.

Different societies—and different kinds of men—react in different ways, but virtually every community has to respond to the new anxieties of the male when deprived of his central hunting and warrior roles. In some tribes men continue to hunt compulsively, even though game is no longer really needed. The Kalahari Bushmen devote most of their time to hunting giraffes, rather ineffectually; the women provide most of the food.

In other tribes, well described by Mead and by Spencer and Gillen, the men conduct elaborate rites that attempt to claim for the males some credit for the life-bringing miracles of procreation,[4] obviously in practical terms the most important activity of the group. Hundreds of societies perform the ritual of *couvade*, in which men enact a public display of all the pains and throes of labor in childbirth, while the actual mother quietly bears the infant in a hut to the side. Almost nowhere in the anthropological records is found evidence of Freudian penis envy (except among other men), but womb envy is ubiquitous. It confirms female sexual superiority as a basic

reality of human life, universally apparent but feverishly denied—
and aggressively countervailed in action—by posturing men in all
societies.

Margaret Mead describes a characteristic rite of male passage to
adulthood:

> . . . The basic theme of the initiatory cult . . . is that women, by
> virtue of their ability to make children, hold the secrets of life. Men's
> role is uncertain, undefined, and perhaps unnecessary. By a great effort
> man has hit upon a method of compensating himself for his basic
> inferiority. Equipped with various mysterious noise-making instru-
> ments, whose potency rests upon their actual form's being unknown to
> those who hear the sounds—that is, the women and children must
> never know that they are really bamboo flutes, or hollow logs, or bits of
> elliptoid wood whirled on strings—they can get the male children
> away from the women, brand them as incomplete, and themselves turn
> boys into men. . . . Men owe their manhood to a theft and a theatrical
> mime, which would fall to the ground in a moment as mere dust and
> ashes if its true constituents were known. A shaky structure, protected
> by endless taboos and precautions, . . . it survives only as long as
> everyone keeps the rules . . . To the Occidental, bred in a society that
> has exalted the achievements of men and depreciated the role of
> women, all this seems far-fetched, perhaps the more far-fetched when
> he realizes that the men who depend for their sense of manhood on a
> fantasy structure of bamboo flutes, played within leaf hedges imitating
> man-made wombs, are not peaceful shepherds, but bold and fierce
> head-hunters, men often six feet tall, well set-up, and capable of mag-
> nificent anger . . .[5]

Such rites gained their magical authority chiefly from the exclusion of women. In fact, these rites usually represented a rather
absurd effort by the males to simulate the awesome female achievement of childbearing and to compensate for their own organic
fecklessness. When missionaries moved in with the attitudes of
modernity and displayed the pipes and other devices to the women,
the whole system collapsed. Some of the men wandered off to be
eaten by a neighboring tribe. Others sulked. But the rituals ended.

Sex-role segregation derives as much from the sexual anxieties
that inspire such rites of passage as from the aptitudes of the sexes in
performing particular functions. In fact, the question of which sex
or which individuals can best do a particular job has little to do with
who does the work in many societies. The women sometimes do the
heaviest labor in the fields, while the men lounge in hammocks or

perform relatively untaxing tasks. The role segregation is less a function of economic utility than of the sexual constitution of the community.

Under most conditions, the males insist on some conventionally masculine activity, whether hunting or tribal warfare or elaborately mysterious religious rites. As male sexual rhythms succumb to female ones, however, the hunting in many of the agricultural communities is transformed into the management of domestic animals, either for consumption or for fieldwork. In most instances, strict role segregation is maintained, with all the large animals and all the plowing done by men. Since women can handle many domestic animals, once again it seems the segregation is established less for the benefits afforded to the animals than for the creation of a role for males.

Studies by Yale anthropologist David Pilbeam have confirmed, in fact, that male insistence on sex segregation of roles actually increases as it becomes less necessary, and thus more open to challenge. He compares groups of hunting Bushmen in Africa with groups who have moved onto farms. "Among Bushmen who are still hunters," he writes,

> sex roles are far from rigid, and in childhood the two sexes have a very similar upbringing. However, among those Bushmen who have adopted a sedentary life devoted to herding or agriculture, sex roles are much more rigid. Men devote their energies to one set of tasks and women to another, mutually exclusive set. Little boys learn only "male" tasks and little girls exclusively "female" ones.[6]

This pattern, found among the Bushmen, a most pacific and cooperative hunting society, is repeated worldwide in the annals of anthropology. Lionel Tiger contends that the tendency of men to bond with one another in purposeful and often aggressive groups precedes even the male-female tie itself.[7] The closest tie in virtually all societies, primate and human, is between women and children. But the next most common and strong connection may well be the all-male bond. The translation of the rudimentary impulse of love into intense ties between specific men and women appears to have been emphasized and sanctified later, in the course of creating civilized societies.

The male bands tend to be strongly hierarchical. There are always chiefs—what Robert Ardrey calls Alpha males—who lend the group coherence and character. Most men, particularly when young, have a strong desire to follow and emulate such leaders. It arises early and continues long. It is the kind of passion that suggests an instinctive source. And, indeed, it seems to be part of the pattern that produces the group itself: leadership, loyalty, and excitement.

The group is formed and sustained by rites of competition. One wins admission by passing tests, meeting standards, and excelling in contests that embody the values or purposes of the unit. Whether in a hunting party, a military company, a juvenile gang, a football team, or a rock group, membership has value because it is earned. Leadership is revered because it epitomizes the same values. Thus bonding, hierarchy, excellence, and excitement are all assured in the process by which boys and young men gain entry. In fact, it is the process by which they become men as well.

The desire of young men to compete is as profound and insistent as all the other motives and impulses given shape by the bond. All the bonding processes are enjoyed in themselves. It is the contest, the chase, the adventure, the speculation, the risk that enthralls, more than the purpose or the goal. The men are gratified to compete and to belong, to lead and to follow—to meet one another and the challenge. Much of the time, they couldn't care less what the ultimate purpose is, as long as the society says it is important. That is why any organization or enterprise that offers group fulfillment to young men will release great energies, whether it is a team, a political club, an entrepreneurial company, a military venture, a motorcycle gang, a criminal conspiracy, a religious movement, or a revolution. Wise societies provide ample means for young men to affirm themselves without afflicting others.

Single men could thrive in cultures that emphasized male groups of this kind. Often they died, for aggression and combat are perilous. But in most places, through most of human history, life has been short for everyone and the male band has enjoyed some of its more coveted joys: gratifications as primordial and intense in some ways as those afforded by the other crucial human connection, the one between mother and child.

In less thoroughly civilized societies in the past, sexual relations between men and women were a more episodic and casual affair. The real business of life was among the men, and among the mothers and children. This pattern prevailed through the Middle Ages in much of Europe. While millions of young men were engaged in a succession of wars and crusades, banditry and pillage, women entered one of the multifarious religious orders of the day, joined one of the many all-female guilds, or served the most powerful men and women. The women did much of the community's most essential work. But the men, as defenders and protectors, could feel important and manly. And because young men were often strongest and most daring, most committed to the group, most entranced by leadership and high rhetoric, they could at least hope to become heroes. But life was grim and short. Women died in labor, men died in battle, millions died in plagues. One prayed for better in the world to come. Few expected better on earth.

With the industrial revolution, however, a better world did in fact arrive on earth. Perhaps the most cataclysmic event in history, it changed every aspect of human society. Until it occurred, most communities faced a vicious cycle: gains in agricultural production caused rises in population that negated the agricultural advance. For example, increases in availability of food or of arable soil would lead to earlier marriages and larger families, making the entire society more vulnerable to agricultural disaster or plague. By emancipating the creativity of individual men and male groups—of capitalists, inventors, and engineers—the industrial revolution overcame this Malthusian dilemma. Increases in population could then spur economic growth at some geometric rate, more rapid than the growth in human fertility. Small enterprises could capture the imaginations and mobilize the energies of young men.

Industrialization has now become the professed goal of almost all the world's societies, from underdeveloped nations to economically backward parts of advanced countries. Exhaustive studies have been made of its causes and processes. As in most social studies—from anthropology to economics—no single model will suffice to explain the vastly diverse and turbulent flow of such a historic phenomenon. Nonetheless the evidence mounts that economic growth and capitalism depend in crucial degree on familial and sexual organization: how the sexual constitution induces men to subordinate their sexual rhythms to extended female perspectives.

"Pre-industrial men," as British demographer E. A. Wrigley puts it, "lived their lives in a moving present; short-term prospects occupied much of their attention."[8] Wrigley believes that it was the presence of relatively isolated conjugal or nuclear families that made possible the emergence of the highly motivated industrial bourgeoisie and labor force. Maintaining that "the act of marriage is necessarily one which stands centrally in the whole complex of social behavior," Wrigley points to intriguing differences between marital customs in areas that produced an early industrial revolution and those in areas that remained economically stagnant.[9]

In the seventeenth and eighteenth centuries, throughout industrially retarded Eastern Europe and Asia, marriages took place at an early age within the bounds of an extended family; the couple was not expected to support itself at the beginning.[10] By contrast, in England, where the revolution began, and in precocious parts of Western Europe, a couple generally could not get married unless it was economically independent, with a separate household.[11] Thus sexual energies were directly tied to economic growth, and since strong sanctions were imposed on premarital sex, population growth was directly connected to economic productivity. The result was that in Elizabethan England marriages tended to occur three or four years later than in England today. As Wrigley writes, "The conjugal family, consisting of father, mother, and children only, so often held to be the result of industrialization and urban living, was normal in much of Western Europe for several centuries before the industrial revolution."[12]

The virtues of this arrangement, which also prevailed in colonial America, go beyond the effective harnessing of male sexual and economic energies to the creation of family units. By concentrating rewards and penalties, the conjugal household set a pattern of incentives that applied for a lifetime. Benefits of special effort or initiative were not diffused among a large number of relatives, as in the extended family, and the effects of sloth or failure would not be mitigated by the success of the larger unit. In general, the man stood alone as provider for his wife and children. He was fully responsible for the rest of his life. Such responsibility eventually transformed large numbers of pre-industrial men, living in a "moving present," into relatively long-term planners, preparing for an extended future.[13]

In another sense, men diminished their economic ties to relatives in their own and previous generations and oriented themselves toward their children and the future. Thousands risked everything and died as failures; many struggled through lives of unremitting drudgery. But largely because their motives were tied to the future that we now enjoy, the world at last escaped its Malthusian predicament.

In terms of the relations between men and women, the industrial revolution, for all its violence and technological impetus, was probably dependent upon a draconian imposition on males of the long-term rhythms and perspectives of female sexuality. Men were made to feel that their identities as males were dependent not chiefly on religious rituals, or gang depredations, or hunting parties, or warfare, but on work, initiative, love, and responsibility for a wife and children. The new structure of motivation, which arose in agrarian England and Western Europe, created the bourgeoisie that launched the industrial revolution. It produced the Jeffersonian yeomen, the independent farmers, and the small shopkeepers of the American Revolution. And it prompted the ideas of individual responsibility, dignity, and equality that are the pride of capitalism.[14]

The human race met the challenge of transition from hunting to agriculture and from agriculture to industry in part by shifting the male pursuit from game to women. Through the wombs of women men could partake in the future of the race. But the hunter in man did not expire; his hunting energies were applied to higher and more extended endeavors: from the seasons of crops to the life-spans of domestic animals to the prolonged phases of invention and manufacture. In the process, society became strongly dependent on the institutions by which the hunter is domesticated—chiefly now the institution of marriage. In general, across the range of modern life, marriage became indispensable to socializing the mass of males.

The desire of men to claim their children thus emerged as the crucial impulse of civilized life. It is chiefly in the nuclear household that the man's connection to his children becomes central. He is the key provider. His fatherhood is direct and unimpeachable, and he identifies, loves, and provides for his offspring. His role as provider then becomes almost as crucial for the maintenance of the family as the mother's role. He thus can feel equal to the mother within the family and he can join it without damage to his sense of himself as a man.

This system of male socialization is the central enactment of our sexual constitution. If we wish to maintain an advanced civilization, technologically inventive, economically productive, and democratically organized, we must either support this complex of familial roles or provide fully adequate replacements.

In the matter of replacements the burden of proof must rest fully and heavily on the innovators: both on those who believe the nuclear family can survive the compromise of the male provider and on those who say humane values of individuality and love can survive the collapse of the nuclear family. A few partial experiments under special conditions—an agricultural commune here, embattled kibbutzim there, utopian speculations everywhere—offer a pathetically inadequate basis for the programs of sexual revolution.

CHAPTER 4

Taming the Barbarians

A fugitive and a vagabond shalt thou be in the earth . . .
YAHWEH to CAIN

Biology, anthropology, and history all tell the same essential story. Every society, each generation, faces an invasion by barbarians.[1] They storm into the streets and schools, businesses and households of the land, and, unless they are brought to heel, they rape and pillage, debauch and despoil the settlements of society.

These barbarians are young men and boys, in their teens and early twenties. If the truth be known, all too many of them are entirely unsuited for civilized life. Every society must figure out ways to bring them into the disciplines and duties of citizenship.

A young man enters the decisive phase of his life when he resolves on marriage and career. Typically, at the time, he is rebelling against his parents, his teachers, and his church. Joining with his peers, he pursues rites of virility, group tests of male identity, often defying physical danger and the law. His earnings capacity, meanwhile, is at its nadir and his sex drive is a governing passion.

At this point, economic incentives and bureaucratic rules alone are impotent to make him a useful citizen. He becomes law-abiding and productive, in essence, because he discovers it is the only way he can get sex from the women he wants, or marriage from the one he loves. It is the sexual constitution, not the legal one, that is decisive in subduing the aggressions of young men.

The outcome is set by work and women. If he finds work that affirms his manhood and a girl who demands that his sexuality succumb to hers, he is likely to become a valuable and constructive citizen. If, on the other hand, he sees long-term employment and marriage as a woman's world, he will tend to exploit both jobs and women as short-term ways to money and pleasure.

In these terms, the sexual role of most jobs is more important than their economic function. In its extraordinary complexity, modern civilization is extremely vulnerable to the outlaw—whether the alcoholic driver or the hijacker, the heroin pusher or the bearer of AIDS, the guerrilla or the computer criminal, the mugger or the assassin. The real contribution made by individual men in their work, particularly at this stage in their lives, rarely exceeds the real damage they can do if their masculinity is not socialized or subjected to female patterns.

The society thus has a much larger stake in employing young men than in employing young women. The unemployed man can contribute little to the community and will often disrupt it, but the woman may even do more good without a job than with one. Her joblessness may spur new efforts to induce a man to work, supporting her own crucial role as a mother.

In general, men are happiest working with other men in challenging and virile activity. At its best, the job can be an important mode of initiation to manhood. The male group at work can counteract the influence of the peer group on the street. The job can transmit important values to the young man coming up.

The prevailing ideal of the unisex workplace, however, can be demoralizing to young men. Where single men and women work at the same jobs, the women are socially superior. They know it and the men know it. The young secretary can marry her boss, can bear his children. She can go out with the young executive. Her social and sexual value, though influenced by class, is relatively little affected by her earnings and occupational status.

By contrast, a man with a low-income job has little chance of taking out—and only one chance in ten of marrying—a woman who earns as much or more than he does.[2] Economic failure or unemployment will tend to cripple him both socially and sexually, restricting him to brief and inconsequential relationships. Unlike men, who nearly always marry down economically, women nearly never do. A woman is understandably uninterested in wedding a man with less earnings capacity than her own, a man who will not be able to support her while she raises a child.

Although money enhances the sexual appeal and marriageability of men, and gives them both the confidence and the wherewithal for long-term sexual initiatives, a woman's financial superiority may reduce the likelihood of marriage—or diminish its duration.[3] Even when her income is necessary to support the children, as in the welfare culture, it will tend to demoralize and estrange the men around her. Not only is she less likely to want to marry, but the man realizes that if he marries her his role in the family would be inherently precarious. Enduring procreative love becomes difficult, because it places the man in an impossibly inferior position. Amid squalling infants, even his residual role of providing sexual services at once becomes more difficult to perform and declines in importance. Increasingly he wants to get out and return to the man's world of his peers on the street.

The woman's financial superiority thus leads to a society of sexually and economically predatory males. The sexual power of women, if combined with economic power, leaves many young men with no civilized way to achieve sexual identity. If they cannot be providers, they resort to the primal male assets, wielding muscle and phallus for masculine identity and attacking the fabric of society.

One popular answer to the problem is to change society. Vivian Gornick calls for "an effort in a single generation" to transform "the emotional habits of thousands of years."[4] Many idealists, particularly living in nations with a lot of material goods, demand that we move beyond materialism, beyond masculinity. They urge that men escape the "masculinity trap" of the provider role and release the more nurturant and caring side of their personalities.

Implicit in this argument is the idea that the male provider role and the woman's role as chief nurturer are mere cultural conventions. The argument is a familiar one and it ultimately rests on familiar distortions of anthropology. Many sexual liberals—for instance, the late George O'Neill and Nena O'Neill, whose best seller *Open Marriage* was reissued in 1984[5]—have claimed that the best anthropology supports their thesis of the huge elasticity of sexual roles and the optionality of masculinity. Most frequently cited is the work of Margaret Mead, perhaps the paramount genius in her field.

Among the Mead research most enthusiastically embraced by the liberationists is her study of three primitive New Guinea tribes: the

Arapesh, the Mundugumor, and the Tchambuli.[6] These three tribes do display an extraordinary sexual diversity of sex roles and temperaments. They represent extreme cases of female aggressiveness,[7] male nurturance, and other seemingly anomalous behavior.[8]

Still, each of these tribes may be said to exhibit some of the characteristics and the problems of the liberal conception. This, one could contend, is one of the reasons these groups were such pathetic failures in dealing with their environment that they were all approaching extinction when Mead studied them.

The Arapesh are the saddest because they seem the most humane. Both the males and females are deeply concerned with child-rearing. Although the chief responsibility is the woman's, the Arapesh believe that the man contributes vital nourishment to the unborn child every time he copulates with the pregnant mother. Therefore the males can claim more credit for the children than in most societies. But it is not enough, and the man not only needs an extra young wife but also spends much of his time preparing male virility rites from which the women are excluded. He is insufficiently aggressive to offer much sexual gratification, protection, or food to his family, and the tribe has been driven away from all the most productive land. He is desperately afraid of the more powerful women from neighboring areas, imagining them as witches who will come to steal his semen.

The chief positive trait of the Arapesh males seems to be their great generosity and cooperativeness, characteristic of tribes in which the males greatly value childbirth. It is in a sense a liberated marriage. The men are often in the home, doing work closely associated with women in most societies. The results in this case are an obsessive virility anxiety, alleviated in male rites, and "incompetence" in what Mead calls "all the assertive, creative, productive aspects of life on which the superstructure of a civilization depends."[9] The Arapesh created a society in which the greatest value is children but in which the children die for lack of food.

But perhaps the Mundugumor are more relevant because they do not display what the O'Neills would call the Arapesh "inflation and glorification of motherhood."[10] According to Mead, the Mundugumor regard children as a great inconvenience and treat them brusquely. The lack of concern for the mother-child tie, moreover, is reflected in a general lack of cooperation or compassion in the tribe. The women are powerful, ruthless, and aggressive, and gather most of the food. The men are even more vicious and strong, and spend most of their time headhunting among neighboring tribes. In a sense, the relationship partakes of liberationist principles because the women are extraordinarily aggressive and productive. But the males feel compelled to exceed them. The result is a society that was in dire straits because its cannibalism turned against itself, involving even small children. The group was disintegrating when Mead left it.

The Tchambuli, combining some of the female aggressiveness of the Mundugumor with the male passivity of the Arapesh, are as catastrophic a failure as either of the other tribes. The males, whom the women abuse from birth, spend their lives in a futile pursuit of their masculinity. Although they no longer have the gumption for headhunting, they purchase victims from other tribes to kill sacrificially as part of their elaborate male initiation rites. They were down to 500 people when Mead left them. Perhaps they had the most liberated marriages of all—and the most fearful and ineffectual males, who devoted themselves obsessively to various masculine displays.

None of the conclusions that can be appropriately drawn from the experience of these three tribes is at all helpful to the liberationist thesis. What Mead concluded from all her other studies as well, the New Guinea experience affirms: Males always require a special arena of glorified achievement from which women are excluded. Their concern with sexual differentiation is obsessive. Men can be passive without grave psychological damage only if the women are passive also. Aggressive and competitive women, unconcerned with motherhood, produce more ruthless men—and a society so competitive that it disintegrates. Men, on the other hand, when passively preoccupied with child-rearing, become incapable of effective sexual behavior and paranoid about aggressive women. A society with a great emphasis on child-rearing will, however, be exceedingly generous and cooperative. In none of the tribes Mead studied is there the slightest evidence that roles, however created, through culture or biology, can be switched back and forth or that the aggressiveness and volatility of males can be ignored by any society.

These realities emerge just as commandingly in the modern world as in any primitive tribe. As the massive survey of male and female attitudes by Anne Steinmann and David Fox has shown, women want "a man even more active, self-oriented, and aggressive than the men were or wanted to be."[11] This finding was heavily confirmed by *American Couples*, a more recent work, financed by the National Science Foundation[12] and rated by the *New York Times* the "largest and most comprehensive study ever undertaken" on the subject. The *Times* summed up its conclusions: "Most men are not happy when their wives earn more than they do. When roles are reversed, with men doing the housework and women providing the income, 'couples become dreadfully unhappy.' Women were found to be happier and relationships were more stable when the male partners were ambitious and successful, but the husbands surveyed often resented ambitious wives."[13]

In general, the successful woman demands that her man be even more successful than she is. In fact, the more successful a woman is in her job the larger tends to be the gap between her earnings and the earnings of her still more accomplished husband. The increasing difficulty of finding such extraordinary husbands means that career women are marrying later and divorcing more (the most successful of all lead the league in divorce.)[14] Thus the demands placed on men, insidiously tacit but inescapable, are greater than ever.

Many men today, as always, deny that such pressures bother them. To declare enthusiasm for feminist ideals is almost a new mode of macho, a way to flaunt an invulnerable virility. Many will dismiss feminism as merely a matter of domestic logistics. The man will more often hold the baby (and, on occasion, heroically change its diapers) or baby-sit while the woman attends a political meeting. The man will more often take out the garbage, wash the dishes, and do other chores around the house. It seems no large issue.

These young men do not feel threatened at work. Their jobs are fairly secure, and it is exciting to have that pretty blond lawyer on the staff. (Who is she sleeping with now, anyway?) Although they endorse equal pay for women, they almost always make more than their own wives, or are engaged in training or business that promises a superior career. Mention procreation, and they talk about the population explosion. They believe it is just as well that many women indicate disinterest in having children. And they profess delight (somewhat uneasily) with the new female sexual freedom.

The personal experience and expectations of these men, the "yuppies" of the mid-1980s, are real. But they are living in a dream world. As long as everything goes reasonably right in their lives, the sexual revolution will affect them little. But for many men, things go wrong. They lose their jobs or their wives (often both together) and find themselves suddenly in an insecure and hostile situation. Then their sexual security vanishes. The aggressiveness of a girl in bed becomes menacing. The competition of women for high-level employment is alarming. For a man in this situation, it becomes difficult to find reassurance from the women he meets on the mediocre job he finally accepts. These women seem serious about their work and know too much about his. If his finances are low, it becomes difficult to take new women out; and somehow when he accepts, more than once or twice, the old friend's offer to pay, her attitude changes.

At this point, his own view of women undergoes a shift. He wants to use them for sexual validation. Intercourse, the only male sex act, looms greater among his priorities. Long-term relationships, though desirable, diminish in attraction. He doesn't pay bills. He drinks a great deal with the boys, watches football on TV, and enjoys crude jokes about females. When someone challenges him, he wants to fight. He finds himself gravitating toward women he wouldn't have considered before—submissive and intellectually inferior. He turns to his parents for support and is grateful if it is there.

When an upper-middle-class world collapses, it can often be restored. In most cases, a good job will do the trick. When disaster strikes precariously risen middle-class men, however, the damage is more difficult to repair. Many men find themselves outside the social order altogether, following the impulsive and predatory patterns of fallen masculinity. When too many men are subverted, the society itself is jeopardized.

The role of the male is the Achilles' heel of civilized society. Sexual liberals are correct that it is a cultural contrivance and that it can be destroyed. But they are wrong to suppose that men, shorn of their current schemes of socialization, would mildly accept the role of the "new man." New roles can work only if they come to terms with the sexual inferiority and compensatory aggressiveness of the male, only if they afford a distinctive male identity that accords with the special predicament of male sexuality in civilized society.

In the long run, women will always insist on the man's continued exertions to remain chief provider, protector, and lover. The modern woman merely offers more readily her own competition and more grudgingly her respect for a special male place and virtue. Even those few women who do permit the man to stint on his material responsibilities require a psychological and sexual confidence on his part that is difficult to achieve without victories of one kind or another in those status competitions so disdained by feminists. Only a small proportion of American women even *say* they would respect a man for choosing to stay home and care for children.

Women are not wrong or culpable for demanding performance from men. They do not have to inflict the system on men, because it is already *in* men. Men already know that if they are to win a high-status woman for more than a brief sexual fling, they had better gain high status themselves. There are few facts of life that men know so well.

The need to perform is not only a deep social imperative for men. It begins in the act of love itself. The man must be potent and commanding if intercourse is to succeed. In women's literature, as in men's, there is a lot of talk about whether women are "good in bed." But the very concept is mostly a projection of male anxieties. When a man says that a woman is "good in bed" he usually means "responsive," i.e., appreciative of *his* performance. It is the men who succeed or fail in sexual relations. A woman may be more or less beautiful, more or less loving. But she cannot really fail like a man who is impotent or suffers from premature ejaculation. The man is the one who is tested—tested again and again—as much in bed as at work.

The essence of the passage to manhood, in fact, is a series of trials. Young men now may pass or fail the sexual test at an early age. They continue to bear the provider burden. And their manhood among men is also a matter of performance. This pattern obtains in our society and in every other. It is not really optional. The diffuse energies and compulsions of the teenaged boy must be shaped into the constructive activities of manhood. The barbarians must be tamed.

In modern society, the provider role is performed with money. But unlike the warrior's emblems and hunter's game, money lacks gender. Women can get it as well as men. The provider role, therefore, is losing its immediate sexual correlation. It is sustained by the greater desire of men to perform it and by their greater aptitude for competition. Together with the maternal concerns of most women, these male tendencies mean that married men, in general, earn much more money than married women. Money thus acquires a kind of concealed sex in the context of marriage.

The ulterior gender of money tends to break down among single people. The greater psychological need for single men to perform may not be joined with a significantly greater ability to earn money. The bent of men to provide for women may not be joined by a visible need of single women to be supported. In the end the young man's opportunity to qualify for a family—to validate in society his love and sex through becoming a husband and provider—may be jeopardized. Unable to love he becomes unable to make the long-term commitments to work and community that the society depends on love to evoke.

In a world where women do not say no, the man is never forced to settle down and make serious choices. His sex drive—the most powerful compulsion in his life—is never used to make him part of civilization as the supporter of a family. If a woman does not force him to make a long-term commitment—to marry—in general, he doesn't. It is maternity that requires commitment. His sex drive only demands conquest, driving him from body to body in an unsettling hunt for variety and excitement in which much of the thrill is in the chase itself.

The man still needs to be tamed. His problem is that many young women think they have better things to do than socialize single men. But in the illusory liberation of the sexual princess, the woman may have problems of her own.

PART TWO
THE BREAKDOWN
OF MONOGAMY

CHAPTER 5

The Princess's Problem

I know lots of girls who don't want to get married or have children. And very vocal they are about it. Well, they are trying to cheat on their biology . . .

DORIS LESSING

Let us dream a dream of liberation, a dream of young women. . . . Susan does, as she leans back into the softness of her chair in her nineteenth-floor office at Rancour House and lets her eyes rest on her small but privileged view of the East River.

The river flows out toward the Statue of Liberty. What does Liberty ask in 1986? Bring me your associate editors yearning to breathe free, your girl executives weary of the office air, your young lady lawyers with brisk smiles and medicated wombs, your tired and hungry heiresses with advanced degrees—all your single women moving upward behind the glowing unopenable glass windows, who gaze at the brown river and ponder the passage of time, the promise of freedom.

Susan, however, is now thinking more concretely. She is waiting for Simon, the editor in chief at Rancour House, who will soon be by to discuss a manuscript. A forty-seven-year-old married man, he often manages to discuss manuscripts with her at five. And for the last four years their discussions have continued at a quiet bar down the street, and later, for greater comfort and privacy, at his *pied-à-terre* in the city. Susan feels her breath quicken as she thinks of Simon's approach. But she has learned that there is more to liberation than comfort and privacy with the most compelling and important man in the company.

Why are there no *single* men? Susan wonders. Or why are the ones she knows—even Arnold, her former lover—ultimately so tiresome?

51

Arnold is the author of a novel that has been sitting in manuscript on Simon's desk for over two months. Occasionally Susan reminds Simon that he should read it. Two weeks ago he said he would get to it by the end of the week.

Arnold always makes Susan feel guilty. He wants to marry her, but she knows it is impossible. He is so unsettled, always struggling: for literary recognition, love from her, money from anywhere. He seems to need constant affirmation of his manhood, and even sex itself seems a test for him rather than an expression of virility and desire. Doesn't he know that she needs his manliness to feel sexual herself?

Simon, on the other hand, is already a man, tested and assured. A father, a husband, he evokes her deepest femininity. Arnold now merely evokes her affectionate concern and vague resentment. How can she want to marry Arnold when Arnold is struggling to be like Simon and she can have Simon himself? How can she make a bet on an unpublished author when she can have the editor in chief?

The rest of the single men around seem even more out of the question than Arnold. Full of sexual urgency and ego-sensitivity, vain postures and tall stories, they always try too hard. And the more they try, the more she tends to prefer, as single men go, the homosexuals who predominate in the lower echelons of Rancour House.

So Susan's dream of liberation has come to focus on Simon. She wants him to divorce his wife Jane. The hometown girl he wed when he was a young reporter in the Midwest, Jane has failed to keep up with his new cosmopolitan interests and advanced social views. Simon has told Susan that his marriage is a charade, continued only for the sake of the children. But the children are now all in college. Simon has no further obligations. He could leave his wife and marry her. Yes, Susan decides, only marriage to Simon will relieve her of the unresolved guilts and anxieties she still has as she enters her thirties as a single woman.

Simon, too, is dreaming of liberation. Earlier, he had dreamed of "men's liberation": that Susan would be willing to sleep with him more often and without such solemnity. Why was she never available in the afternoon for what a friend of his calls "matinees"? Why couldn't she be more understanding of his need to be home in the evening? But soon his feelings for her deepened. He saw that, finally, she could demand her own terms.

This meant he would need a divorce, and he wished divorces could be managed more smoothly and sensibly. Jane would not understand; and the truth was that in a way he still loved her; their life together was in general happy. And his children would certainly not understand. But however easily he had once been able to accept the routine passages of a middle-aged marriage, he had found his predicament almost unbearable since Susan first let her slip fall to the floor before him, magically dissolving his burden of years.

Simon and Susan would insist, however, that it isn't merely a matter of sex between them; together they attain a kind of human fulfillment they lack apart. They share the life of books. Ever since leaving college, Susan has lived for publishing and worshiped Simon. She understands his brilliant leadership that has made Rancour House an arena for all the most arresting and original new thinking and creativity. Simon, on the other hand, respects Susan's deft skills as an editor, her tact with sensitive authors, her sense of the coming fashion in ideas. Although Simon's wife appreciates his success, she is unwilling to plunge herself into the social whirl of New York publishing. Her heart remains in their Scarsdale home; Susan virtually lives in the office down the hall.

How can anyone deny Simon and Susan their modest but redemptive dream? A society that values freedom, sexuality, and human happiness can hardly balk at this inspiring fulfillment of its ideal. The only ones likely to object are Simon's wife (though the social politics of divorce no longer favor a woman who wants to hang on) and Arnold, who has almost no leverage to deny them anything.

The statistics of divorce and remarriage indicate that Susan and Simon, and hundreds of thousands like them, are now gaining their dream. With the problems of children, separate housing, alimony, and divorce lawyers, the dream turns out to be more conflicted than they ever imagined in those exalted moments in Simon's New York apartment. Nevertheless, growing numbers of older men are leaving their wives and children to marry young women like Susan, and these young women are increasingly able to choose men regardless of their marital status. With single men seeming such a dreary lot compared to the married ones, the limitless frontiers of married men open before ambitious young women as a liberation indeed seductive.

These are the winners of the "sexual revolution." As has long been clear to the political philosopher but strangely obscure to the sexual liberal, freedom at some point becomes the enemy of equality and the ally of power. In sex, the most powerful people are young women. The next most powerful people are successful older men. They come together with a social and sexual electricity that jolts the conventions of monogamy to their foundations.

The power of young women stems partly from the male sex drive. For millions of years of human evolution, male eroticism has focused on fertile women. Even when children are not a prime purpose of the marriage, a man is still most compellingly attracted to young women who can bear them. Moreover, while most men remain fertile into old age, women can bear children only with increasing peril and difficulty as they move into their forties. Thus by excluding from their sexual ken the millions of older women, all men put themselves at the sexual mercy of the relatively small group of unmarried women in their twenties and thirties. These women can command the sexual tribute of men aged from their twenties into their sixties.

In a society where monogamy rules—in which successful older men cannot easily leave their wives to marry again—young women exercise their power chiefly to tame the barbarians, to induce young single men to support them and their children in marriage. Under these conditions, young women have to take a chance that the single men they choose will be able to give them the lives they want. They have to bet on the Arnolds of the world; and by choosing them and loving them and bearing their children, the young women greatly enhance the likelihood that struggling young single men will in fact become successful men like Simon.

With sexual liberation, however, a young woman can conceive an escape from the predicament of choosing a man "for better or for worse, for richer or for poorer." She can pursue a man who is already well off. The demographic data show that she will have a large number of men from whom to choose.

Between the ages of twenty and forty, there are some 1.5 million more single men than single women.[1] But the available group only begins with these relatively young men. Also entering the fray to pursue young women are nearly three million divorced and separated men between forty and fifty-five. The vast majority will remarry, choosing women with a median age in the low thirties.[2] If many of the still-married men are also open to the appeals of a young princess—and they are—her possibilities rise by millions more.

Liberation enthrones young women as a sexual aristocracy. For a span of some fifteen to twenty magical years, many of them are sexual princesses who can dictate terms to the world. And yet there is something going wrong in their lives. Susan and many of her peers do not feel like princesses; they feel a little anxious and used. They even claim to be oppressed, like blacks and other minorities, and have sustained with other women a passionate national movement of feminism to press their charges. Why do young women with so much choice often feel afflicted? Why do so many of these young women with an apparent prodigality of options end up not marrying at all? What is the princess's problem?

If Susan is as smart as her reputation, she can find her clue in the river. As she looks out her exalted window, she knows that the river flows through her own life as well and erodes her throne. Simon may marry her, but he may be less of a prize than he seems, particularly since the expenses of the divorce may greatly reduce his net worth and possibly even arouse in him resentment toward Susan. He will also have demonstrated his willingness to leave a marriage. After the first, each subsequent divorce becomes statistically more likely than the one before. If he has enough money, as Susan grows older or becomes too demanding, he might decide to cash in a third time.

On the other hand, as a sexual princess Susan has lived a life of luxurious sensuality, with men competing for her favor with ardent gymnastics. Her expectations are high. But a man's sexual aptitude and enthusiasm tend to decline as he grows older. Susan may feel cheated by Simon's declining fervor and allow her own eye to wander. He will sense her restlessness and feel threatened. As he proceeds through his sixties laden with wealth, he may even fear that she would prefer him dead. He may marry his young nurse. The marriage won by our princess may be no picnic on the beach.

Nonetheless, if Susan succeeds in marrying Simon, there is no point denying they may well live happily ever after, beginning a new family of children in a setting of love and prosperity. Not everyone loses in the sexual revolution. The princess may become a queen. But it is also eminently possible—particularly as he explores in detail the painful complexities of divorce—that Simon will eventually refuse to marry her. After giving up her twenties to an obsessive drive for career advancement at Rancour House, Susan will also have given up four or five of her most marriageable years to Simon's pleasure. She will be well into her thirties without a husband.

Suddenly she will discover that the sexual power she wielded so confidently before is rapidly vanishing. She will have to marry whoever happens to be available as her thirties pass by. If she waits too long, she may well find that even Arnold is no longer interested, particularly if he has at last reached success in his career. He may reject her with regret. But reject her he finally will, in favor of a woman in her twenties. A recent study by Yale and Harvard sociologists, based on census data, shows that a woman who waits until after age 35 has only a 5 percent likelihood of marrying.[3]

Susan's search for another man will be hampered by the very code of liberation that made it possible for her to pursue Simon. She does not comprehend that men and women have radically differing sexual drives and situations. Thus she thinks that there is a close correlation between the men she can seduce and the men she might marry. But a young princess can seduce the vast majority of men. Unless very securely married, virtually any man will sleep with any attractive young woman. In Washington the liberated princess can sleep with senators. In Hollywood, with directors and movie stars. Everywhere she can sleep with her boss. Often she will be able to sleep with rising superstars and juvenile celebrities who will profess love but never contemplate marrying her. She comes to believe that she can marry such men. All too often she merely gives up her remaining marriageable years to them.

As Marilyn Monroe's career suggests, the sexual princess can even become a sex goddess without escaping the essential female predicament. Until marriage she can long exercise her sexual power only by withholding her sexual favors. The promiscuous princess quickly becomes a pawn.

As a result, the aging princess becomes bitter and cynical about men. Disdaining the ones who might love her, she gives herself to men who ultimately disdain her. Then all too often she gives herself to drugs and the bottle. Finally, she may even realize that she is a victim of a new generation of princesses like herself.

She will join many other victims. The most obvious evidence of a painful social breakdown is the ever-growing number of older divorcees. The number of divorced women nearly tripled during the 1970s and early 1980s.[4] Between the ages of thirty-five and sixty-five, there are some two million, or 50 percent, more divorced or separated women than divorced or separated men.[5] Although the number of divorced men was also rising, they were remarrying at three times the rate of the divorced women.

The differing span of fertility of the two sexes means that unlike divorced men, most of whom find new wives within three years, women over forty only rarely remarry. The median age of these divorced women was approximately forty, while the median age of the women whom the men took as their second wives was about thirty.[6] A woman divorced after forty—after her childbearing years—is likely to spend the rest of her life unmarried. After 50, only 11.5 percent of divorcees remarry.[7]

Sexual liberals have long suggested that the older divorced women wed the younger men who are prevented from marrying by the older men with new young wives. But evolutionary biology and human psychology prevail against sexual convenience. Films and women's magazines may entertain their readers with stories of love between the two available generations of old and young. But except in show business, where the men often function more as paid escorts than as husbands and fathers, such marriages are rare. Simon's ex-wife Jane will not marry Arnold.

The only undeniable winners in the sexual revolution are powerful men. Under a regime of sexual liberation, some men can fulfill the paramount dream of most men everywhere: they can have the nubile years of more than one young woman. Whether a man takes these young women at one time, staying married and having mistresses—or whether he marries two or more young women in succession, or whether he merely lives with young women without marriage—makes little difference to the social consequences. The man is no less effectively a polygamist—or more specifically a polygynist—than if he had maintained a harem. The obvious victims of this breakdown of monogamy are the women who must grow old alone when their husbands leave. But they are only the first of the victims.

The removal of restrictions on sexual activity does not bring equality and community. It brings ever more vicious sexual competition. The women become "easier" for the powerful to get—but harder for others to keep. Divorces become "easier"—except on divorced older women. Marriages become more "open"—open not only for the partners to get out, but also for the powerful to get in.

Monogamy is central to any democratic social contract, designed to prevent a breakdown of society into "war of every man against every other man." In order to preserve order, a man may relinquish liberty, property, and power to the state. But if he has to give up his wife to his boss—or hers—he is unmanned. A society of open sexual competition, in which the rich and powerful—or the sexually attractive—can command large numbers of women, is a society with the most intolerable hierarchy of all.

Monogamy is egalitarianism in the realm of love. It is a mode of rationing. It means—to put it crudely—one to a customer. Competition is intense enough even so, because of the sexual inequality of human beings. But under a regime of monogamy there are limits. One may covet one's neighbor's wife or husband, one may harbor fantasies of teenyboppers, but one generally does not act on one's lusts. One does not abandon one's own wife when she grows older, to take a woman who would otherwise go to a younger man. One does not raid the marriages of others. Thus a balance is maintained and each generation gets its only true sexual rights: the right to a wife or husband and the possibility of participating in the future of the race through children.

It is not a ruthlessly strict system. Philandering erodes love and family values, but it does not necessarily destroy them. Many divorces, particularly the 50 percent occurring among young couples without children, may be relatively harmless. But the essential rules are necessary to a just and democratic society. A breakdown in the sexual order will bring social ills and injustices far more grievous than the usual inequalities of money and power.

A society is essentially an organism. We cannot simply exclude a few million women from the fabric of families, remarry their husbands to younger women, and quietly return to our businesses as if nothing has happened. What has happened is a major rupture in the social system, felt everywhere.

Less obvious, perhaps, among the victims are the young men. They seem fortunate to some because they are left to pursue young women without being caught in the coils of female sexuality. Untamed, they can indulge their short-term and promiscuous male sexuality—and many do. They may enjoy the barbarian's dream of compliant princesses—and a few will. But as Arnold's predicament suggests, the liberation of princesses is in fact a very mixed blessing for single men.

CHAPTER 6

The Barbarians' Revenge

The single man. An image of freedom and power. A man on horseback, riding into the sunset with his gun. The town and its women would never forget, never be the same. But the man would never change, just move on. To other women, other towns. As he rides away, the sunset gilds his silhouette.

The single man. The naked nomad in the bedrooms of the land. The celebrity at the party, combed by eyes of envy and desire. The hero of the film and television drama: cool, violent, sensuous, fugitive, free.

The American dream, the Superstar. If one were only rich, young, famous, one would revel as a single man. One would be Steven Spielberg or Bruce Springsteen or Joe Montana or Mick Jagger or Sean Penn. Or whatever young man currently leads in arousing fantasies of multifarious wealth and women.

But the fact is—as every society hostess learns as she seeks "eligible" escorts for single women at her parties—if one is young, rich, and famous, one is most likely a married man. Of the men above only Jagger, at last report, was even nominally single, and he was living with the mother of his two youngest children in a near-marital setting.

If one were actually a single man, unattached—free in the spirit of our dream, our memory of youth that improves with age, our love 'em and leave 'em Lancelot, our easy-riding ranger—one would be . . . ? Well, we know from the statistics: In general, compared to others in the population, the single man is poor and neurotic. He is disposed to criminality, drugs, and violence. He is irresponsible about his debts, alcoholic, accident-prone, and susceptible to disease. Unless he can marry, he is often destined to a troubled and abbreviated life.

Of course, there are many exceptions. Millions of single men have managed to become disciplined and valuable citizens, and millions of divorced men have survived to a happy and productive old age. Bachelors are a fluid group, with every man single, at least for a while; millions are merely temporary bachelors looking for a wife, and most will eventually find one.

Nevertheless, the bachelor pattern is overwhelmingly marked by lack of sustained commitment and lack of orientation toward the future. The single man tends to move from one sexual partner to another, from job to job, city to city, rotating his life without growth or progress. And when a man gets divorced or widowed, he tends to revert in many respects to the temperament of the never-married single man.

In this syndrome of the single man lie some of the key reasons for the moral life: the need for monogamy and sexual restraint. In the single man's predicament can be found important clues to some otherwise baffling social phenomena, from homosexuality to ghetto unemployment. Singles may be peripheral in a sense; but their experience is central to the enigmas of modern life. And their numbers have been growing. Between 1970 and 1982, the ranks of single people jumped 78 percent, to 19.4 million.[1]

One striking result of the bachelor pattern is low income. With the same age and qualifications, single men have long earned about the same as single women. As early as 1966, a Labor Department study found both earned about the same hourly wages.[2] Single college graduates over age twenty-five earned about the same amount in 1969, whether male or female.[3] Single men currently have median incomes less than 10 percent higher than those of single women,[4] who are alleged to be hobbled by discrimination, even though single men work longer hours and in general tend to use their earnings capacity more.[5] Yet they are 30 percent more likely to be unemployed.[6]

Married men, however, earn some 70 percent more than singles of either sex.[7] Single college graduates earn about the same as married high-school graduates. In addition, the married high-school graduate has a nearly four times better chance than a comparable single of eventually earning over $30,000.[8] It could well be more important for an ambitious young man to get married than to go to college. Married men are the only ones in the population who in general tend to reach the high echelons of earners.

Although single men do not make more money than women, who are said to be gravely victimized by bias, discrimination is not the bachelor's problem. His chief problem is his own psychological and physical condition. In general, men have more psychological problems than women, and single men have the most problems of all.

According to famous data assembled by Jessie Bernard, single men are far more prone to mental disorders than any other large group of Americans, with the possible exception of the divorced.[9] Single men between twenty-five and sixty-five are over 30 percent more likely than married men or single women to be depressed; 30 percent more likely to show "phobic tendencies" and "passivity"; and almost twice as likely to show "severe neurotic symptoms." They are almost three times as prone to nervous breakdowns. They can't sleep (three times more insomnia), and if they do sleep, they are three times more likely to have nightmares.[10]

Perhaps the most striking data come from a study by Leo Srole and Associates, "Mental Health in the Metropolis: The Midtown Manhattan Study." Srole's report found that married men and women do not greatly differ in their mental health: about one-fifth of both are impaired. In this survey, unlike some others, single women are slightly better off. But like all other available data, the report shows single men to be in the worst condition and deteriorating most rapidly with age. Between the ages of fifty and fifty-nine, an astonishing total of 46.1 percent of all single men in the Manhattan survey suffered "mental health impairment."[11]

Even in the realm of sex single men do less well than married men. Though single men are far more promiscuous, they also have less total sexual experience than monogamous men (and women). In the younger age groups single men have only about one-fifth as much sexual activity as married men of the same age, and less than half as much sexual activity as single females. Single men also fail five times more often than married men in evoking orgasm.[12]

In addition, there is considerable evidence of a sexual crisis among young men, marked by sexual fragility and retreat. Greater female availability and aggressiveness often seem to decrease male confidence and initiative. A large survey of college students indicated that while virginity among girls was rapidly diminishing, virginity among boys was actually increasing, and at an equal rate.[13] Impotence has for some time been the leading complaint at most college psychiatric clinics. Citing evidence from "my patients, both male and female, articles in medical journals, and conversations with my colleagues," one psychiatrist called it "the least publicized epidemic" of the 1970s.[14]

Needless to say, all such anecdotes and surveys are fallible. Studies based on interviews or on vague criteria of mental health and happiness lack any final authority. But the conclusions of these studies are heavily supported by data from institutions showing that bachelors are twenty-two times more likely than married men to be committed for mental disease (and, incidentally, ten times more likely to be put in hospitals for chronic diseases).[15]

As far as society is concerned, however, the main problem of single men is not mental or physical illness, or related afflictions like alcoholism, loneliness, and sexual inadequacy. It is not discrimination or poverty. It is not that thriving old specialty of single men and their intimates: venereal disease. Single men have another way of getting the rest of society, however reluctantly and unconsciously, to take part in their problems. That way is crime.

It is by now well known that about half of all violent crime is committed by and against blacks. But the central facts about crime are not racial; they are sexual. Groups of sociologists venturing into urban streets after their seminars on violence in America do not rush to their taxis fearing attack by marauding bands of feminists, covens of single women, or angry packs of welfare mothers. Despite all the movies of avenging women with machine guns and the exploits of Kathy Boudin and her Weather Underground friends or Charles Manson's gang, one need have little fear of any group that so much as contains women—or, if the truth be known, of any group that contains men who are married to women.

Crime, like poverty, correlates far better with sex and singleness than it does with race. Although single men number some 13 percent of the population over age fourteen, they comprise 40 percent of the criminals and commit nearly 90 percent of major and violent crimes.[16] Even as adults, single men are some five times more likely to commit violent crimes than married men.[17] Single men are convicted of the ultimate sexual violation—rape—five times more often, proportionately, than married men. The reported incidence of this crime rose 28.6 percent between 1974 and 1983, more than any other major offense.[18]

Violence and crime join with mental illness, mild neurosis, depression, addiction, AIDS, institutionalization, poverty, unemployment, and nightmares to comprise the specialized culture of single men in America. Not surprisingly, the climax of the grim story is death. Of all groups, single males have the highest mortality rate—and suicide is increasingly the way they die.

Between 1960 and 1977, the suicide rate for young men between 15 and 19 rose 154 percent.[19] Suicide is not restricted to young single men, however. In fact, after the perilous early twenties, the older a man gets without marrying, the more likely he is to kill himself. Of course there are many forms of suicide that go by other names, and single men excel at all of them.

Single men have almost double the mortality rate of married men and three times the mortality rate of single women from all causes: from automobile accidents and other mishaps, as well as from the whole range of conventional diseases.[20] Most of the illnesses do not become evident until after age forty-five.

In analyzing the high death rates of single men, sociologists normally focus on the bachelors' lack of the kind of "personal maintenance" married men enjoy from their wives. Sexual liberals talk of the failure of sexist society to teach male children how to cook and take care of themselves. But the maintenance theories are inadequate to explain the all-encompassing reach of single male afflictions. Altogether the pattern of mortality among single men is so various and inexorable that it suggests an organic source: a failure of the will to live, a disconnection from the life force itself as it arises in society. Discussing the high suicide rates of single men throughout Europe in the nineteenth century, Emile Durkheim wrote: "The bond attaching the [single] man to life relaxes because that attaching him to society is itself slack."[21]

Perhaps the most dramatic evidence of the literally vital importance of the marriage tie to men is the impact of its rupture by divorce or widowhood. Contrary to the usual images of the helpless and abandoned wife, the statistics show far greater evidence of helpless and traumatized husbands. The woman tends to suffer most during the separation when the man diverts himself with dreams of bachelor freedom, and if she is over forty she has a much smaller chance of remarriage. But in terms of mental and physical disease and life expectancy, divorce damages the man far more than the woman.

Thus, divorced men are more likely to seek psychiatric help than divorced and separated women,[22] and they can be found in disproportionate numbers in mental hospitals.[23] They are also more prone to profess unhappiness than divorced women. But it is in statistics of disease and mortality that the plight of these men emerges most strikingly. According to figures from the National Bureau of Health Statistics, divorced men of every age group between thirty-five and sixty-four have a mortality rate three and a third times as high as divorced women.[24]

They die of all causes, but like single men, divorced men specialize in accidents and suicides. Divorced men are three and a half times as likely as divorced women to commit suicide, and four times more likely to die in an accidental fire or explosion. Murder claims three divorced men for every divorced woman, as does cirrhosis of the liver. And, in the realm of more conventional mortality, divorced men are six times as likely as divorced women to die of heart disease.[25]

In short, when a man, accepting an honor at the company banquet—or prefacing a book—gives much of the credit to his wife, he is not merely following a ritual. He is stating a practical fact. In all likelihood he would not have succeeded—and possibly not even survived—if he had been single or divorced.

Nonetheless, statistics are treacherous. Perhaps all these weaknesses of the single and divorced are the cause rather than the consequence of their marital failures. The man with a criminal bent or a proneness to mental illness is admittedly a poor prospect for marriage and a good one for divorce. Perhaps the man who falls off cliffs, or crashes his automobile, or drinks to excess, or takes addictive drugs, or fools around with guns, or inclines to suicide, or becomes depressed and unhappy and neurotic—even late in life— perhaps these men also, in one way or another, have opted out of successful marriage.

It is possible to explain by the process of marital selection all associations of divorced and single men with mortality, insanity, and criminality—and the associations of married men with longevity, success, and equanimity. It is possible to contend that these statistical relationships have little to do with the comparative healthiness of single and married life or the deep psychological need of men for women. But these arguments create more problems than they solve. The idea that most singles are inherently unmarriageable and the divorced unstable fails to explain the same pattern of afflictions among widowers. It fails to explain the absence of comparable patterns among single and divorced women. And the marital selection theory fails to reveal the mechanism whereby many of the symptoms that supposedly prevent marriage do not appear until after many years of singleness. In addition, the impact of marriage on character is not merely a statistical conclusion. One does not have to look far to find examples of buccaneer singles transformed by marriage or to find examples of once-stable men plunged into depression and drink by widowhood or divorce.

In the elaborate studies by John Bowlby on attachment and loss in small children in all human societies,[26] in increasing evidence that lack of "social involvement" is a key to mental illness,[27] and in the endless annals of the literature of isolation, everywhere we discover that the finding and losing of love are central to human experience. It should not be surprising that divorce is a destructive event for men or that the failure to find a wife is deeply unsettling. Men are usually the most active partners in the finding of love; they are most likely to lose everything, even the children, when love is lost; and their more limited sexuality means that they suffer a more complete sexual rejection when their overtures are refused.

Released from the cages of sexual repression, the rising numbers of single men are the male victims of the breakdown of monogamy. They are the peripheral men who cannot win a durable relationship with a woman and whose existing ties are always in jeopardy. As in a baboon troop, the powerful get the women most of the time, and the powerful father most of the children.

It is then that the peripheral men feel sexually expendable. But unlike the peripheral baboons, who are physically controlled by the dominant ones, the peripheral men are not powerless. They can buy knives and guns, drugs and alcohol, and thus achieve a brief and predatory dominance or an illusory potency. The rapist, the addict impotent, and the playboy can attain, however spuriously, a masculine "high." Most of all, the peripheral men can achieve, beyond all the dreams of other men, an orgiastic fulfillment of male sexuality.

CHAPTER 7

Cruising

In the hothouse cruises of many male homosexuals—short-term, intense, violent, abandoned to the rule and worship of the most worthy phallus; moving from body to body to hungry body with scarcely a glint of human recognition beyond the beckoning flesh; repeatedly coupling and climaxing, all beneath a clinging, heating, and lubricating blanket of anonymous steam; pulsing to the rhythm of the hunt and the chase, with no fear of procreation or entanglement and usually no expense—these men can enact for free the ultimate male fantasies of hedonistic and ecstatic sex.

This circus of the senses repels most men, particularly the ones well socialized by women, and even offends many homosexuals who lead discreet and civilized lives. The leading writers and experts on the subject assume that only a fixated homosexual could adopt such behavior. They treat the problem as an anomaly on the fringes of society, posing no threat to anyone and unrelated to other social developments. Because psychologists cannot explain homosexuality, they discuss it in terms of sickness or mystery. But homosexuality is merely the most vivid and dramatic manifestation of the breakdown of monogamy—an extreme expression of the sexuality of single men.

In denying the danger of gay liberation and its possible threat to social order, experts assume that an aroused young man is a reasonable being. They deny the possibility of a death wish lurking amidst the gardens of lust. They ignore the dark and demonic inversions

69

hiding within the sunny pursuits of sensuality. But sexual decisions all too often slide down slippery slopes of accident and compulsion rather than step rationally toward pleasure. Sexual hungers spring not from the rational heights of the brain but from its glandular depths, not from the lofty cortex but from the unruly domain of the hypothalamus. A major goal of every civilization must be to bring these compulsions under control by the force of aspiration, worship, and reason. It is not easy.

For example, society has never succeeded in controlling the related male circus of heterosexual prostitution, which is far more expensive and scarcely less repellent. The dank and dingy massage parlors, the fetid half-hour hotel rooms, the menacing mince of the streetwalker, the glower of her pimp in the shadows all defy the illusion that men are remotely reasonable about sex.

The sex business flourishes because men pursuing sex are often beyond sense or self-control. If you put up a sign offering flesh for sale and bathe it in purple light, they come like moths. You can get men to spend their last fifty dollars to sit naked on a couch in a cold room and talk to a dull girl without clothes. You can get men to risk disease, robbery, and self-loathing sleeping with a streetwalker. You can get men to sit in the darkness and watch other people copulate with animals on a screen. Men with hardly the money to pay the rent and to eat splurge on glossy magazines with bizarre pictures or squander their entire paychecks for a few minutes with a whore. In many ways the underworld of heterosexuality seems no more rational than the free-for-all of homosexual life. Yet otherwise sane and responsible men around the world lunge and flounder for the most sordid heterosexual offerings.

Similarly the homosexual arena thrives less because men want it than because they cannot help themselves. Politicians risk their lives and careers to wallow in degradation; priests and pastors tear asunder the very sinews of their characters and stain the core of their reputations to perform acts that would befoul a word processor to describe; and the *American Journal of Public Health* reports that in late 1983, in the face of the rising AIDS epidemic, more than half of all gays were still performing their usual gymnastics.[1] Robert Bauman, a leading conservative congressman, married and with children, who had repeatedly denounced gay liberation, later confessed to desperate binges in homosexual bars which finally led to his arrest for pederasty and the end of his career. The press leapt to charge him with hypocrisy, implying that he actually believed in this behavior. But his condemnation of gay rights was likely made with all sincere passion. He swerved off the tracks of civilized sexuality—yes, again and again—only in the deepest pain and regret. Lord lead us not into temptation.

Scores of theories have been presented to explain the incidence of homosexuality. Although research continues to fail us on this matter, it seems likely that some homosexuals, like alcoholics and other addicts, suffer from a profound predisposition, possibly physiological in origin. But an enormous number of homosexuals have clearly been recruited from the ranks of the physically normal. In the course of initiation they have undergone a passionate experience of discovery and conversion. This experience is entirely possible for ordinary men with fully remediable sexual problems.

There are millions of males who under the wrong conditions are open to homosexuality. A frequent catalyst is self-abasement. Failure in love or work may so deject a man that he feels incapable of rising to a relationship with a woman. He may find he lacks the confidence for the rudimentary acts of self-assertion—even the rudimentary selfhood—needed for any heterosexual exchange. He becomes fixated on his own physical limitations and begins worshiping the male members of others.

Intercourse remorselessly sets the bounds of androgyny: to have a woman, a male must to some extent feel himself a man. A man who does not feel like a man may seek to have a man. Men who feel abased may enjoy the idea of a specific enactment and affirmation of their abasement. Men incapable of deep sexuality may be relieved to offer a deep throat—to pursue sexual activity without the burden of initiative or personality or human ties. Homosexual activity does not require confidence or male identity or a face-to-face self-exposure. It does not require money and may often be a source of money. It can even be managed without an erection. It is an inviting escape for the fallen male.

Homosexuality may begin as merely a particularly elaborate form of masturbation. Among adolescents in particular it may arise as a mere exchange of reciprocal services, scarcely beyond the campfire "circle jerk." But like masturbation and its associated pornography, the more limited exchanges tend to pall, and demand ever more extreme measures to achieve the original effect. The mechanics of mutual massage give way to the passion and turbulence, fear and frenzy of sexual hierarchy and obsession.

Most men recover from sexual setbacks without an episode of homosexuality. This is the usual course of events. Even fully fledged homosexuals often return to the pursuit of women. Eighty out of Kinsey's 450 homosexual histories ended with such a recovery.[2] Psychiatrists report change to heterosexuality in as many as one-third of all motivated homosexual patients.[3] But the return is difficult and treacherous for addicted men. It is tragic, therefore, if the cultural ambience provides too easily for perversion.

In many parts of urban America this tragedy is a way of life. The precarious male is surrounded by homosexual stimuli. If he goes to a pornography shop—a frequent resort of despair—he will find homosexual literature and devices increasingly prominent and will discover that even heterosexual porn focuses more and more on male organs. In some sections of town he will meet homosexuals on every street corner, genitals pressed like vultures against their jeans. In fashionable literature he will frequently encounter the argument that homosexuality is not an addiction or a disease but merely an alternative form of sexual expression toward which all civilized men should be tolerant.

Once a homosexual culture is established it can attract others by seduction and by its inherent appeal to insecure males. When they give themselves up to a homosexual environment, their passage spurred by drugs, alcohol, and failures with women, normal young men can suddenly realize an almost physiological change and feel as if they were born gay. Like any compulsive or addictive pursuit, homosexuality gains a momentum of its own. It overmasters conscious resistance, impelling its victim into a fugue of behavior that he somehow feels he watches more than wills, that seems beyond his conscious control. With promiscuous male partners far cheaper and easier to find than females, young single men lost in the city, disdained by young women at work and dismissed at the singles bar, driven by the amorphous lusts of youth but with jobs below the demands of available women, can slip abruptly into the homosexual life.

The most powerful tool of the homosexual culture is the myth that homosexuality is a fixed and immutable condition, like the color of one's skin. Widely taught in sex-education programs in secondary schools and in college psychology and social-science courses and endlessly repeated in all the media, the message is drummed in: "You—you impressionable teenager with a crush on the football captain and anxiety about your own masculinity—you just *might* be a born homosexual. But don't worry. It's only an alternative life-style and perfectly acceptable."

This appallingly widespread message leads many perfectly normal but sexually confused or insecure young men to imagine that their random lusts and social failures signify a permanent homosexual fixation rather than a passing obsession with the phallus. In actuality, any man can be homosexual, but no man has to be. The belief in innate homosexuality, at best a half-truth propagated fervently by many homosexuals who do not want to believe they had a choice, is a key force in the growth of the movement.

The facts of male homosexuality are also endlessly misrepresented and confused by the homosexual women who often speak for gay liberation. Female homosexuality has nothing whatever to do with male homosexuality. Just as male homosexuals, with their compulsive lust and promiscuous impulses, offer a kind of caricature of typical single male sexuality, lesbians closely resemble other women in their desire for intimate and monogamous coupling. They most often explain their practice by denouncing the "meat market" of heterosexual single life and by proclaiming their own need for feminine tenderness and trust.

In a survey of homosexuals in San Francisco, 28 percent of males reported having had more than a thousand partners, and 75 percent said they had had more than a hundred partners. Not one lesbian reported having had a thousand partners and only 2 percent said they had had more than a hundred.[4] Fifty percent of lesbians have had only one partner.[5] In fact, the surveys suggest that lesbians have substantially fewer partners than heterosexual women. Unlike male homosexuals, who often become fixated as teenagers, female homosexuals tend to begin their activity later and very rarely indulge at all if they are married.[6]

The two sexes differ greatly in their ability to experiment with their sexuality. Although older lesbians, like all older women, may have trouble finding marriage partners, lesbians easily can and do return to heterosexual activity when they wish. Except that it induces some women to withdraw from conventional society until too late for marriage with children, lesbianism is a relatively trivial aberration. It gains reflected import chiefly from its mistaken association with male homosexuality and from its ascribed political content as an act of feminist protest.

For women sex is not normally the vital drama of sexual identity and momentous challenge of performance it is for young men. Nor are women so fixated by visual cues, so obsessed with physical rivalry. Rather than the fulcrum of sexual identity, sex for women is an act of pleasure or procreation that takes its part in the whole fabric of the woman's emotional life.

By contrast, the male burden of sexual initiation and performance, the avid male receptivity to charged visual images, and the compulsive short-term nature of male lust mean that for men homosexual relations, however casually entered, are far less likely to be casually abandoned. The gay life becomes a traumatic and life-changing obsession. For men, homosexual behavior is anything but a trivial event; it feeds on a powerful undertow of masculine sexual propensities that can solidify into an enduring mind-set.

Indeed, in some ways, homosexuality is more in accord with masculine nature than is heterosexual courtship. The sex drive of the young male is not only promiscuous; it also tends to merge with the male impulse to affiliate upward to worship power. Since male sexual power is embodied in physical endowment and prowess, young men with sexual confusions and anxieties, fears of inadequacy primed by rejections from women, can react passionately—and in a homosexual environment addictively—to the naked bodies of aroused and powerful men. Homosexuality can therefore feel more natural to many men than their comparatively laborious, expensive, and frustrating pursuits of young women.

Once a young man experiences the gay world—often joining it as others join a cult or a movement—the addiction may be very hard to break. The homosexual will seek to affirm his choice by finding others to join him in it. Because homosexuals are essentially like other single men, with a sexuality at least in part oriented toward the feminine, they create an important place for effeminate men. Or, unwilling to wait for the ripening, they create a marketplace for thousands of adolescents who most resemble women. As families dissolve in divorces and separations and as illegitimacy spreads, boys in increasing numbers escape parental control and slip into the ambit of the so-called chicken hawks of the gay underworld. The result is the expansion of the homosexual life to further generations and the spread of AIDS and other diseases of drugs and promiscuity.

While there are many people who accept the romantic propaganda about male homosexual existence, the life of tricks and trades is in fact agonizing for most of its followers. Lasting relationships are few and even men who live as couples tend to cruise separately.[7] The usual circuits of gay bars, returning servicemen, forlorn personal advertisements, and street pickups afford gratifications so brief and squalid that no society can morally affirm them. The social pressures for heterosexuality should not be relaxed in any way.

This emphatically does not mean harassing or imprisoning homosexuals. Perhaps the worst perversion occasioned by homosexuality is the police practice of entrapment. But at the same time it is crucial to affirm precarious males in their heterosexuality. Compassion for men who are already homosexual—and our recognition that some have adjusted happily—should not lead us to praise or affirm the homosexual alternative or to acquiesce in its propaganda.

Many homosexuals, like most heterosexuals, have sufficient discipline and self-control to avoid the slipperiest slopes, the most sordid pits. Many live decorous and civilized existences. Many others have now been shaken sufficiently by the threat of AIDS to reject or abandon the wild side of the gay scene. These men are not helped in their arduous disciplines by a gay liberation movement that attempts to move the bathhouse into the midst of society, to make the homosexual circuit more open and accessible. They are not helped by AIDS hysteria and gay protests and parades, campus dances and demonstrations. They do not benefit from demands for rights and quotas that seem designed to flush them out of the closet and onto the street where they can be exploited by the gay-rights brigade. They want to live their lives quietly and productively and safely, and most of them are knowledgeable and sensible enough not to want to inflict their problem on others.

The liberal journalists, compassionate churchmen, tolerant sociologists, pliable psychologists, pandering politicians, and valuefree sex educationists who condoned the most extreme homosexual behavior as an acceptable life-style are the true sources of the AIDS epidemic. That gay liberationists were killing themselves in a mad gadarene rut was evident to many doctors long before the new plague struck. By the early 1980s gays comprised 41 percent of all cases of syphilis and 21 percent of cases of gonorrhea. According to various surveys, they showed a rate of infectious hepatitis eight to twenty-five times higher than heterosexual males. Some 78 percent had contracted at least one venereal disease, and at any one time perhaps a fifth suffered from some stage of gonorrhea.[8] Over the last decade of liberation in San Francisco, infectious hepatitis A more than doubled, infectious hepatitis B quadrupled, amoebic colon infection rose 25 times.[9] Yet gays turning to churches and other institutions for help all too often were told not to worry. Seeking redemption for their sins they were treated as sinless. Denied repentance they could not attain expiation.

Depending chiefly on the degree that the wanton male sex drive succumbs to maternal goals and rhythms, any society is capable of a variety of sexual states. Civilized and productive societies reflect the long-term disciplines of female nature, upheld by religious and marital codes. But civilized society is not more natural than more degenerate social states. It represents a heroic transcendence of the most powerful drives of men. It is a triumph of aspiration and worship, salvation and conscience, over the compulsions of the flesh.

Because homosexuals do not control society, they are more victims than agents of its decay. The most crucial cause of the rise in homosexuality in America in recent decades is sexual liberation: the emancipation of men from monogamy. Once again when men leave their aging wives to marry young women or maintain young mistresses, they create, in effect, a system of polygyny. The annals of anthropology offer few examples of a correlation so complete as that between human societies that tolerate polygyny and societies with conspicuous practice of homosexuality. George P. Murdock's world ethnographic sample of some 580 societies examined by anthropologists indicates a nearly exact correspondence between the two forms of behavior.[10]

Best known is the legendary pattern of the Arab world: sheiks with harems and homosexuality pervasive. By allowing a man to have up to four legal wives—and concubines as well—Islam made it impossible for many young men to find nubile women. Although Islam, like other religions, condemns sodomy and pederasty—and some Moslem states have imposed the death penalty for such behavior—polygyny assures that homosexuality will be rampant in many Moslem areas.[11] Wherever monogamy breaks down, however, from Western Australian tribes studied by Edward Westermarck[12] to idyllic Tahiti, from the Mohave Indians examined by George Devereux[13] to sexually liberated Western Europe, polygyny produces homosexuality. For all the complexities of particular cases, a homosexual culture, whether in prisons, at sea, or in polygamous societies, originates with a lack of available young women.

Yet this explanation of homosexual *culture* seems inadequate to explain many *individual* homosexuals—from Rock Hudson to Robert Bauman—who have been attractive and powerful men. Indeed, many homosexual actors and models are among the men regarded as most attractive to women. When they become rich and prominent, they find women easily available. Some get married. But in most cases their traumatic experience of homosexuality—their fixation and acculturation—came much earlier, near the peak of their sex drive as young men. In the absence of a homosexual environment, the homosexual possibility, latent in most men, would rarely become an addiction. But with the existence of a gay world of orgiastic freedoms, many men succumb who otherwise would have pursued a conventional heterosexual life, and even some married men, like Congressman Bauman, are captured.

Homosexuality remains chiefly a facet of polygyny. Polygyny reflects the natural desire of men of all ages for young women, the natural human tendency toward hierarchy, and the tendency of the powerful to use their power to take the nubile years of many young women, in a succession of wives and mistresses. Like female-headed families, homosexuality reflects the state of breakdown that occurs when the constraints of civilization succumb to the demands of male power. As the longer horizons of female sexuality give way to the short-term compulsions of masculinity, civilized societies break down into polygynous and homosexual formations, with related outbreaks of feminism and pornography.

This process of moral decline is a liberation chiefly for established men who can take a series of young wives and for young women who can raid existing marriages. Homosexuals are just one of the groups who suffer from this trend of social decay and sexual revolution— and accommodate it.

The sexual revolutionary, with his talk of love and sharing and universal kinship, sounds like a rather conventional utopian: sentimental but harmless, and with his heart in the right place. In fact, however, the sexual revolutionary is more dangerous than most, because his program is at once less realistic and more feasible. Unlike the economic or political utopia, the sexual revolution can be practiced in one's own home. But unlike the economic or political utopian, who at least gestures at realities of scarcity and interdependence, the sexual revolutionary rarely transcends the closed world of his own imagination. In theory, his program is utterly misconceived, and in practice it is evil.

Monogamy is designed to minimize the effect of sexual inequalities—to prevent the powerful of either sex from disrupting the familial order. In practice, however, through history the chief offenders have been older men. Young women, supremely powerful sexually for a relatively short time, ideally exercise their powers less to gain large numbers of partners than to win permanent mates. They use their position as the rulers of the sexual realm to break men from the short-term compulsions of singleness. In general, women succumb to the male pattern only when coerced by pimps or heavily paid by powerful men.

Any sexual revolution, therefore, will tend to liberate more men than women. Larger numbers of men than women will command two or more exclusive partners. Thus a sexual revolution will exclude many more young men than young women.

What happens when sex is liberated is not equality, but a vast intensification of sexual competition, from which there is no sure haven except impotence and defeat; competition in which marriage is just another arena, or the home base from which the strong deploy; competition in which the only sure result is an ever larger band of vindictive losers, of fatherless children and childless fathers. In a world without family disciplines, many of them can be found in the ghetto.

CHAPTER 8

Ghetto "Liberation"

Nowhere in America is the breakdown of monogamy so dire and drastic as in the ghetto. Detailed statistics are not available for the inner city itself, but overall black totals are heavily influenced by ghetto conditions. The black illegitimacy rate is 56.5 percent, more than five times higher than the white rate.[1] Only 41 percent of black children under eighteen are living with two parents, a level 39 points below the white figure of 80 percent.[2] Because the ghetto often cannot enforce monogamy or perpetuate marriage, most older ghetto women lack husbands and young ghetto men lack the stabilizing influence of legal links to wives and children. Marriages are under siege. Even some 22 percent of nominally wedded black couples actually live apart.[3] With nearly 60 percent of black men single (compared to 38 percent of white men), the temper of the community is shaped by unmarried males.[4]

The results are predictable. Some half of our violent crimes—murders, robberies, rapes, and other felonies—are perpetrated by and against ghetto residents. In proportion to their numbers young ghetto males commit seven times more homicides and 30 percent more suicides than young white males.[5] Perhaps half of our addict population—and a similar proportion of our prisoners—comes from the ghetto. Although such statistics are not fully reliable, it is not prejudice or paranoia that defines the inner city, in the words of Daniel Patrick Moynihan, as "a tangle of pathology," or as the epitome of our domestic problems.

79

The cause is not racial. A similar syndrome of familial collapse and social disorder is spreading in Scandinavian welfare states, in the U.S. suburbs, and in the street slums of white dropouts and runaways. Charles Murray has uncovered evidence that in poverty areas the white illegitimacy rate was over 60 percent in 1970.[6] The majority of black families are no more "polygamous" than white families of the same economic class. Diligent and sexually conservative, black families that stay together tend to advance rapidly. The average income of intact black families with children rose during the 1970s to 90 percent of the income of comparable white households, from 71 percent at the beginning of the decade.[7] But other black households have stagnated and the overall gap between black and white family incomes has not narrowed in two decades.

It is chiefly in the ghetto that the black family is disintegrating. As early as 1965 Moynihan, then an assistant labor secretary in the Johnson administration, explained why in a report so glaringly true that it all but blinded most analysts who read it:[8] The black family was breaking down because female jobs and welfare payments usurped the man's role as provider, leaving fatherless families that tended to repeat themselves from generation to generation.

This is the source of the tangle of pathology in the ghetto: the dissolution of the ties that bind men to their children. It is sexual revolution—against the usual sources of child support, the expected roles of men and women, and the sanctity of marriage.

The breakdown of monogamy produces unproductive and disruptive men. Lacking the masculine assurance to submit to female patterns of sexuality, they try to impose male patterns on the women. In the ghetto, with few socialized men available, the women often give in, beginning families without responsible fathers.

The problems of young black boys are typical of all fatherless children.[9] As studies by Harvard sociologist Thomas Pettigrew have shown, fatherless black children of both sexes "experience unusual difficulty in differentiating the roles of men and women."[10] Like other fatherless youths, the black boys are less responsible, less able to defer gratifications, less interested in achievement, more prone to crime, and even, as other studies have shown, lower in I.Q. than boys from intact families of either race. Examination of prisoners and veterans has indicated that the pattern of sexual insecurity persists, with the fatherless men scoring higher on indices of femininity while behaving in a compulsively aggressive way, often in all-male gangs.[11] Girls from fatherless families, meanwhile, tend to reproduce their own childhood experience, associating more closely with their mothers than with their husbands—and giving more affection to their girls than to their boys. But because of more stable female sexual identity, girls in general suffer much less damage than boys in broken families.[12]

These boys, already unsure of their role and undisciplined by a father, then move on to ghetto schools, where many of the teachers are women struggling to maintain order, and most of the best pupils are girls. The boys learn once again that the world of regularity, responsibility, and achievement is a realm of women. Unless the boys excel in sports, the schools offer almost no mode of specific male affirmation. Success in the classroom usually means psychologically awkward competition with female students and resistance to peer pressures from rebelling boys, all in schools that are largely restricted by law from either effectively punishing or evicting delinquents.

This pattern of the ghetto would not be so damaging if the young men could easily undergo the later stages of socialization: love, marriage, and family responsibility. But the fatherless males, predictably enough, are very low in what Pettigrew calls "marital aptitude." Because they are unsure of their male identities, they feel constrained to prove them continually. They are unwilling or unable to love, court, and marry women.

A basic problem is economic. Sociologists are rather casual when they report that black women workers earn 80 percent as much as black males, while white women earn only about 58 percent as much as white men.[13] Yet when the impact of welfare is added—and the earnings of married black men are subtracted—it becomes clear that in the ghetto the male role as chief provider has as much as evaporated, and that the unmarried ghetto male is too poor in relation to women to be needed by them.

The social relationships of the community thus no longer revolve around the male as leading provider and the female as procreator, ultimately joining in monogamous love and marriage. Rather the woman is both provider and procreator, and the man and woman join only in male-oriented copulation that leads nowhere—except on occasion to an illegitimate child.

The usual response to ghetto problems is to demand the creation of more jobs. But this remedy fails to confront the reality of a male youth culture nearly immune to all the blandishments of established society. Jobs alone have never sufficed to break through the single male bias for street life, the peer-group pursuit of short-term excitements, the easy money of petty crime, and the easy women who succumb to the rhythms of young men. Entry-level jobs are unpleasant, often less appealing at first than the swashbuckling life as a "free-lance," hanging out and raising hell with males and freeloading off welfare women.

Men do not submit to the lifelong disciplines of the provider role unless they feel they have to. Except for brief stints on the job, often ending with complaints of "racism" and "hassles" when the employer demands hard work, the boys of the welfare culture stay clear of the labor market as much as possible. In Boston, for example, the overall joblessness rate dropped to 3 percent during the job boom of the mid-1980s without bringing significant numbers of young ghetto males into the work force. During the last 20 years the U.S. led the world in job creation—generating 35 million new jobs and employing a record share of all adults—while ghetto unemployment grew steadily worse. During that period, middle-class blacks acquired a net 4 million skilled jobs, getting new skilled work at a pace between three and five times as fast as whites, while the millions of unskilled jobs opening up were resolutely shunned by poor blacks.[14]

In general, taming the barbarians of any race requires not only that work be made available but also that women be largely unavailable without marriage. It requires not only jobs but jobs and upward mobility linked to the deepest drives of young men, channeling their sexuality into families and their aggressions into the provider role.

At a minimum, to break through the resistance of these black youths requires preferential male-oriented policies. But, largely intimidated by the equal-rights agencies, governments and corporations across the country show more interest in feminizing male jobs like policeman, fireman, and construction worker than in creating a world of work attractively male in spirit.

Ghetto boys need special treatment; they need intense, tough training of the sort the military often can provide, with male affirmations designed to overcome their masculine rebelliousness and their disadvantage in relation to ghetto women. A job program that provides genuinely equal opportunities for ghetto boys and girls will only reinforce the girls' economic edge. As shown in a comprehensive statistical study, federal job-training programs universally fail to improve the economic condition of men, black or white. But "with remarkable consistency," the same programs "all resulted in positive and significant employment and earnings gains for women."[15] With the boys resisting any environment in which they are excelled by women, the girls in general increase their advantage.

Women's entry into the work force, however, poses no problem in itself. Whether on farms or in factories, in households or in offices, most women in all societies have always worked hard. Indeed, by improving the adaptability of the work force and easing the formation of new companies, their overall efforts have helped create jobs for men. The spontaneous choices, aptitudes, and group biases of men and women normally tend to segregate the work force by sex, creating many categories of male-oriented jobs regardless of how many women work. The danger arises when all the available entries into the established order are feminine, and when, as Elliot Liebow's study indicates, work itself, along with legality and marriage, are identified as female domains.[16] This is the problem in the ghetto, and current policies only make it worse.

One of the few successful movements for the socialization of truly indigent young black males is the Black Muslims. The Muslims have learned the key lesson well: that the first step in restoring a poor community is to reinforce moral codes by religious observances and to rectify the sexual imbalance bred by poverty. Because the males are clearly dominant in a Black Muslim group, they can afford to submit to long-term patterns of female sexuality. They identify with their children and hence with the community and its future.

The result is that like the Depression-era followers of the similarly patriarchal cult of Father Divine, the Muslims created a network of small businesses, comparable on a lesser scale to the entrepreneurial accomplishments of Jews and Chinese (who also use patriarchal religions to affirm their males). Also like the Jews, Chinese, and

Catholics, the Muslims succeeded in establishing schools that actually teach poor black children to read and write at the white grade level.[17] In addition, like the patriarchal cults and fundamentalist religions now conspicuous among poor whites,[18] the Muslims managed to overcome addiction and make ex-convicts into law-abiding citizens. It is unfortunate that it is a movement of racial extremism that hit on this clear imperative of social regeneration. But as long as the rest of the society fails to recognize the need to reestablish the male, the field will be open for the fanatics.

The most surprising fact about our ghetto tragedy is the way we doggedly refuse to understand it—and the way we endlessly perpetuate it. It should be clear to any sentient observer with a smattering of anthropological and psychological insight that the worst parts of the ghetto present a rather typical pattern of female dominance, with women in charge of the family and male gangs away on the hunt. Workable in a few primitive societies with garden and game, this system brings unremitting tragedy in the tenements, and on the streets, of our modern cities.

In the absence of agricultural support, the women and children become dependent on government. The welfare bureaucracy supplants the matriarchal garden and displaces the husband's game. Expelled from the family, he becomes an outlaw under the sexual constitution and a threat to his women. Lacking familial motivation and psychological stability, he cannot persist responsibly at work even when he can find it.

Inevitably he turns to—or creates—a world of men: sports or music, if possible; crime, drugs, and revolutionary policies more probably—but predictably and necessarily a realm where males command, where he can find external symbols of the internal necessities of his sex. In the absence of socialization by women—the civilizing familial processes of love and procreative sexuality—he follows the usual impulsive circuits of male sexuality. It is a familiar drama, fraught with violence, anger, and yearning, enacted on the black stage and on the blacker street, sung in a thousand blue voices, celebrated in a thousand "soul" rituals, proclaimed and transcended in the art of jazz.

But the essential pattern should not be seen as a special propensity of blacks. It is sometimes imagined that the gynocentrism of many poor black families is a strength—the secret of black survival through the harrowing centuries of slavery and racism. In a sense, of course, this is true. In any disintegrating society, the family is reduced to the lowest terms of mother and child. The black family has long rested on the broad-shouldered heart of the black woman.

Yet this secret of black survival is also a secret of ghetto stagnation. It is quite simply impossible to sustain a civilized society if the men are constantly disrupting it. Whether among blacks or whites, male socialization through love, family, and work is indispensable to social peace and prosperity.

The drama of the unsocialized black has become the commanding motif of American culture. Driven to the wall, threatened with emasculation, surrounded everywhere by formidable women, the black male has summoned from his own body and spirit the masculine testament on which much of American manhood now subsists. Black jazz is the most important serious American music, acknowledged around the world if not in our own universities. Our rock culture finds its musical and rhythmic inspiration and its erotic energy and idiom in the jazz, gospel, dance, and soul performances of blacks. The black stage provides dramatic imagery and acting charisma for both our theaters and our films. Black vernacular pervades our speech. The black athlete increasingly dominates our sports, not only in his performance but in his expressive styles, as even white stars adopt black idioms of talk, handshakes, dress, and manner. From the home-plate celebration to the touchdown romp, American athletes are now dancing to soul music. Black men increasingly star in the American dream.

This achievement is an art of the battlefield—exhibiting all that grace under pressure that is the glory of the cornered male. Ordinarily we could marvel and celebrate without any deeper pang of fear. But as the most vital expression of the culture—widely embraced by a whole generation of American youth—this black testament should be taken as a warning. For much of it lacks the signs of that submission to femininity that is the theme of enduring social order. It suggests a bitter failure of male socialization. By its very strength, it bespeaks a broader vulnerability and sexual imbalance. Thus it points to the ghetto as the exemplary crisis of our society.

CHAPTER 9

Supporting Families

A man in the home is worth two in the street.

MAE WEST

Far from a racial problem, the crisis of the ghetto is an American tragedy: a part of a far broader disorder of American politics and culture. For just as our poverty programs disrupt black families and our established media disparage sex roles, so the broad drift of American social policy undermines work and marriage. The most direct pressures come from welfare incentives for family breakdown and tax penalties for male providers. Both poor and lower-middle-class families are the victims of a partly inadvert war by America's elites against the indispensable sanctions and sacrifices of life in families. As a result, more and more families are becoming bitter toward welfare.

No one begrudges money for the blind and disabled, and the sight of a deserted mother and child strikes deep emotional chords. Yet it is this welfare effort—Aid to Families with Dependent Children (AFDC)—that qualms and frightens nearly every lower-class man. He does not resent the subsidized women and children themselves. It is the notion of the male deserter, lovin' and leavin'—in the glamorous pattern of every male fantasy hero—that makes the lifelong husband and worker, with after-tax earnings little greater than welfare, feel like a cuckold. He remembers all the sexual opportunities forgone, all the payments dutifully made, all the disciplines arduously observed, and the image of the fugitive fathers tears at the very ligaments of his identity.

He feels that the social contract by which he has ordered his life has been broken. The society that entwined his sexuality in social cords—reaching from the depths of his psyche into the womb of a woman, and then into the future of mankind—has betrayed him. It has failed to maintain the civilization to which he has given his life as a man. It has used his money to subsidize the primal mode of male behavior that he painfully relinquished.

It is difficult for the financially comfortable to appreciate the psychological impact of money on the poor. The liberal looks at welfare payments and sees them as pitifully low. He cannot imagine how this amount of money appears to a man required to submit to forty or even fifty or more hours of drudgery a week to earn only slightly more after taxes. If his wife is restive, he sees welfare as a positive invitation from the state for her to dissolve the marriage. If he is restive, he finds the benefits—and the example of other unchastened deserters—an implicit moral exemption.

In any event, the welfare payment, from the point of view of the poor, is anything but negligibly small. It is the chief single source of funds in the community; it is free and can be augmented by unreported part-time or criminal income, more difficult to come by if one is working full time. It provides leisure time, one of the prime goals for which most men work long hours and years. It brings free medical and legal services, often vitally needed in poor communities. It often leads to public housing and other special aid. It is, in fact, the dominant economic influence in the lives of the indigent. It is not surprising that so many millions of lower-middle-class Americans, black and white, working hard for relatively low rewards, look with the greatest cynicism on welfare payments.

This is not a new problem, but as a society we have forgotten much of what we once knew about its most fundamental truths. Writing in the 1930s, Edwin Wight Bakke described the sexual constitution of welfare and its impact on white families. "Consider that the check normally goes to the woman and is often accompanied by female social workers. The man, already suffering from his failure as provider, is further demoralized by becoming dependent on two women, one of them a stranger. He is reduced to an errand boy to and from the welfare office."[1]

Some fifty years later, in 1979, a conference of experts on the U.S. welfare system was held in a small darkened room off Clinton Avenue in the midst of what passes for a ghetto in Albany, New York. Nothing much has changed; welfare still erodes the sexual constitution of society.

In the room were five men, as mild-mannered and soft-spoken as any assemblage of prominent sociologists. All but one had been convicted for violent crimes. One had raped a white girl. One had shot at a police car. All bore ugly scars from repeated knife fights on the streets and in the dives around Clinton Avenue.

Like so many academics, the men were gathered to offer criticism of a book they hadn't read. Although they pretended to have studied it carefully, all but one had previously revealed, in the face of street signs or bureaucratic documents, that they "didn't read too good." But all had copies of *Visible Man,* which had been based on hundreds of interviews with them, their families, and their friends, in Albany, Greenville (South Carolina), and New York City. The chief reader in the group was eager to speak. "One chapter really said it all," he declared, "The Welfare Trap. That's what it is, a trap. It's got us all." At that point, all the other men in the room, separately and in chorus, chimed in: "Yeah, the welfare trap. That's what it is. The trap. And we're in it. Yeah."

This assertion would have been entirely mystifying to the collection of real sociologists, learned in the details of the welfare system, who gathered in late 1984 in a sumptuous conference center in Williamsburg, Virginia. Like Senator Moynihan in the years after his initial report, they were busy showing that welfare has no substantial role in promoting family breakdown, illegitimacy, crime, or unemployment. They would have pointed out triumphantly that none of the five men could have been trapped by welfare because none was even on welfare at the time. In any case, the experts would have contended, welfare benefits available for able-bodied men are "meager to nonexistent in nearly all jurisdictions."[2]

Other academic analysts at Williamsburg denied any important connection between the rise of welfare and the incidence of illegitimacy and family breakdown. They showed that between 1972 and 1980, the number of black children in fatherless households rose nearly 20 percent, but the number of black children on AFDC actually fell by 5 percent, and AFDC payments, with food stamps, dropped some 22 percent adjusted for inflation.[3] They compared low- with high-payment states and found no significant difference in fatherless families.[4] They hemmed and hawed and fiddled with the data, and called for more aid and more research.

How can welfare be a trap for men who are not on the rolls? How could welfare have increased family breakdown during a period when the real value of the payments was decreasing? How can welfare cause illegitimacy if there is no correlation between the level of benefits and the rate of births out of wedlock or the number of fatherless children on the rolls? The sociologists are very sure they know the answer: welfare and associated programs are virtually irrelevant to the problems of the ghetto. The liberal politicians sigh with relief and continue their efforts to enlarge the welfare state.

How would the experts on Clinton Avenue respond to the experts in Williamsburg? They would begin with ready and contemptuous agreement that they are not on the welfare rolls. In fact they would declare that no man worth his snot would sign up for welfare. But they were trapped by welfare, nonetheless, because their women were in the program. For example, the Clinton Avenue room where they met was paid for by Aid to Families with Dependent Children. With sufficient effort, it could be determined that each of the men had lived with a succession of welfare mothers over the years. When one woman tired of him—or he tired of the woman—he would try to maneuver into another welfare apartment with another welfare mother. If she already had a man, dangerous tensions would arise. In fact, much of the violence in the ghetto erupts during the periods of transition in this game of musical beds, when a man who has lost his place with one woman seeks to find another bed, often that very night. Not only are the men dependent on welfare, but many of the scars from ghetto crime stem directly from that dependency.

The other skeptical questions of the sociologists all reflect the idea that the behavior of human beings responds to the kind of computations of relative benefit levels they perform in their regressions. The differences in AFDC and food-stamp payments from state to state or year to year are dwarfed by a sevenfold overall rise in real benefits over three decades.[5] This rise involves some seventeen programs. The *relative* shift in incentives against work and marriage tended to be greater in low-income, low-benefit Southern states than in the North, where welfare programs had long been more generous and wages were higher. In virtually no state could a typical ghetto man easily earn enough to compete with the benefit package available to a mother of small children.

The sociologists at Williamsburg compare cash benefits with the minimum wage and cite incentives for work and marriage. They ignore the value of leisure time, Medicaid, and a host of other programs, and they ignore the value of sure income acquired without work compared to the unsure earnings and onerous effort entailed by menial jobs. In other words, Senator Moynihan and the experts in Williamsburg, for all their familiarity with the statistics of poverty in America, had scarcely a clue to its reality on Clinton Avenue or in Harlem.

Particularly quixotic is their concept of the sources of illegitimacy. To all the Williamsburg sociologists the astonishing rise in illegitimacy among the poor in recent decades is a great mystery, one of the points on which more research is required. But any of five experts in Albany could have told him about "liberation day." Nearly all teenaged girls in the ghetto know—and many of them celebrate—this day of emancipation.

Consider a ghetto household. Much of its income over the last decade has come from welfare. Therefore the man is only sometimes present, and is only sometimes the real father of more than one of the children in the apartment. He is drinking beer and watching television. Periodically he gets surly and drunk and picks an argument with the woman. The teenaged boys are out of control; some have knives or even guns which they flaunt in a terrifying way. Tensions are rife.

If you were a troubled teenaged girl in a typical white suburban family, you might dream of running away with your boyfriend. But middle-class culture would probably prevent you from doing it; both you and he have too much to lose. If you are a fifteen-year-old girl in the ghetto, doing poorly at school, fighting with your mother, afraid of the men in the house, you will also want to escape, and you will know that it will be possible on liberation day.

On your sixteenth birthday, the government will offer you a chance for independence, in an apartment of your own: free housing, medicine, legal assistance, and a combination of welfare payments and food stamps worth several hundred dollars a month. It may not seem much to a sociologist, but it is a package hugely beyond the pittance allowed you by your mother and far beyond the earnings capacity of any of your male acquaintances. It is all offered on one crucial condition. You must bear an illegitimate child. After three children, the payments in New York State will rise to $8,333, an amount 45 percent higher than the after-tax earnings of a full-time job at the minimum wage. If you are that fifteen-year-old girl, what do you do? Do you go for it? Or do you go through a rigmarole of inserting diaphragms or taking pills?

Welfare experts might tell this girl that she could marry the father of her child without jeopardizing her benefits. But the AFDC program for families with unemployed fathers is hopelessly complicated and subject to withdrawal according to the caprice of bureaucrats and the reported earnings of the man, who may well be only temporarily employed.

The one safe, sure, and simple way for the girl to win liberation in an apartment of her own is to bear an illegitimate child. It is not surprising that, in the face of such an overwhelming inducement from the state, millions of young women have indeed launched such children into the welfare culture. As this behavior becomes accepted in welfare communities, it is adopted by many girls, black and white, on or off welfare, without calculation or deceit, as a simple reflection of a way of life.

It is currently the American way of life among the poor. With illegitimacy rates near 90 percent in many inner cities, the problem is now spreading more rapidly elsewhere in the society. Everywhere in America unemployment, illegitimacy, divorce, and separation find fuller favor in the laws of the land than does raising children in an intact family. Nonetheless, the effort of the sociologists to exonerate welfare as a special cause of the ghetto crisis was statistically deceitful.

One much-quoted Williamsburg paper, by David Ellwood and Lawrence Summers of Harvard, focused on eight years just after the tremendous AFDC surge in the late 1960s and early '70s. During the period they chose, between 1972 and 1980, the percentage of children in female-headed families rose much faster than the percentage on AFDC. The paper concluded: "If AFDC were pulling families apart and encouraging the formation of single-parent families, it is very hard to understand why the number of children on the program would remain constant throughout the period when family structures changed the most."[6]

It is not children, however, who choose to go on welfare. Liberation day applies chiefly to potential teenaged *mothers* making their decision to have their first illegitimate child. Contrary to the implication of Ellwood and Summers, throughout the late 1960s and the 1970s the movement of women onto AFDC led and dominated the overall rise in female-headed families. Between 1969 and 1979, the number of black families on AFDC rose 104 percent, 28 percent faster than the 81 percent rise in the total number of female-headed black families.[7] Even in the years between 1972 and 1980 chosen by the Harvard researchers, when the number of black *children* on AFDC declined, the number of black *mothers* in the program rose nearly 40 percent. Among black teenagers 82 percent of all births were illegitimate in 1980.[8] But during the late 1970s, a saturation effect occurred, and illegitimacy rose faster among blacks outside the welfare culture. Meanwhile, despite a steep rise in abortions and rapidly expanding contraceptive services focused on this group, a Princeton study found that the 1980 fertility rate of black American teenagers, though declining at last, was the highest among 32 populations studied in developed nations, 37 percent ahead of the next highest group, the Arab Israelis.[9]

AFDC played the key role in creating the environment in which this record was achieved. But the process of family breakdown in America cannot be fully comprehended without also studying the impact of changes in tax structure and other government policies.

Since 1950, all increases in personal taxation have fallen on married couples with children. While mothers of illegitimate children receive massive benefits, and single or "child-free" couples have faced no increase in average taxation, taxes on couples with children have risen between 100 and 400 percent, depending on the number of offspring.[10] A key reason is the evaporation of the child deduction, which would be worth some $6,000 today if it had risen apace with incomes and inflation since World War II.[11] Meanwhile the costs of bringing up a child have risen rapidly. According to estimates by the Department of Labor, the birth of the first child requires a family to increase its income 26 percent to preserve its childless standard of living, while two children require 46 percent more than the childless level. After 10 years, as the children grow up, family income must double in real terms.[12]

In the lower middle class, black and white, this collision of needs and taxes has created a crisis of conscience in which financial incentives clash sharply with the moral duties of paternal support. With welfare the only source of income that rises after the birth of children, lower-middle-class families are torn between the needs of their children and the maintenance of their marriages.

Aggravating the plight of the married woman with children is the campaign to end "discrimination" against females. It turns out that the most sophisticated computer analyses of sex discrimination can find only one large group of males significantly benefiting from "sexism"—only one group earning more than their "credentials" and education would seemingly justify: men with high-school education or less, and with large families to support. That this group, which includes most lower-middle-class husbands, outearns female college graduates seems an outrage to academic researchers and bureaucrats who are at least to some degree paid according to their credentials. But in the economy at large, the greater motivation and persistence of men with families—working overtime and often taking more than one job in their struggle to overcome the adverse economics of child support—generates income and productivity far beyond the "worth" of their credentials.

Congress, however, has devoted little of its famous "compassion" or reforming concern to families raising children. It has successively eliminated first the so-called "singles penalty" and then in 1981 the "marriage penalty" chiefly affecting two-earner couples without children. And it has enacted an array of programs that further penalize women who try to raise their children at home.

In a particular absurdity, Congress has sought "workfare" programs, focusing job-training funds on welfare recipients. An attempt to lure welfare mothers away from their children and into the work force, it seemed to suggest that, having deprived the black family of fathers, the Congress wanted now to take away the mothers as well.

Central to "workfare" is the provision of subsidized day care. It not only enables the government to force poor women into the work force, it presses all women to leave their children and take jobs. Far from being a neutral program, evenhandedly extending options of motherhood and job, subsidized day care is a massive multibillion-dollar federal endorsement of one option: the uninterrupted career. Swinging the heavy club of free money, the day-care program tells every young mother that the government wants her to remain on the job. It even makes families with mothers at home pay taxes to support her "liberation."

All these campaigns focusing on giving women jobs, or training them for nontraditional work, or rendering them free of the need for men or the needs of children deepen the crisis of the black family and of all American families. The cumulative result has been simple and overwhelming: irresponsible fatherhood and out-of-wedlock births have been legitimized and marital procreation, especially beyond two children, has been made a violation of the new constitution of sex.

In designing new social approaches, first of all we must decide what we want them to do. What we should want is in essence what Senator Moynihan had in mind in 1964 when he wrote the Moynihan Report. We should want to restore work and family as instruments of male socialization among the poor. We should try to establish the conditions in which large numbers of families can stay together and move up. This is already happening—despite all obstacles—among millions of poor people today, black and white. It is even happening among those most afflicted of blacks who turn to the Black Muslims. It is happening among the hundreds of thousands of young black couples from indigent backgrounds who are now earning as much or more than their white counterparts. It is happening among hundreds of thousands of Chinese and Cubans, Lebanese and Caribbean blacks, Koreans and Mexicans, from equally poor families, who manage to resist the myth of easy money, the government blandishments for broken families, and the short-circuit economics of the unsocialized male. But these processes of social progress are leaving millions behind in the familial ruts of stagnation. To overcome the prevailing antifamily pressures, we must deliberately work to restore the sexual constitution.

Viewed from this perspective, the limits of public assistance become clear. We must abandon the idea of completely eliminating poverty by distributing money to the poor, in accordance with formulas artfully designed to repress costs and enhance work incentives. There is no way it can be done. Welfare reform cannot eliminate poverty because as it approaches an "adequate" level, it necessarily subverts the male role as provider and promotes family breakdown. Family breakdown in turn bars escape from dependency.

The negative income tax idea and most of its derivatives that try to lift all families above a particular income level are falsely conceived. They are based on a static and statistical conception of poverty, as a problem of individuals lacking money rather than families lacking providers. There is no alternative to integrating the poor into the larger society through general programs aimed at strengthening all American families.

As a younger man, Moynihan called such programs "unities" because they solve different problems at once and bring different constituencies together. Tax cuts are a unity, because at best they can foster economic growth, reduce inflation, and raise government revenues, while bringing together both labor and business constituencies. The young Moynihan urged enactment of a scheme called child or family allowances. Consisting of a monthly payment to every family for every child, the plan would simultaneously counteract the shift in the tax burden onto families with children and counteract the welfare incentive for family breakdown and illegitimacy. It could be financed at first without expanded appropriations by converting the current child deduction, earned income-tax credit, day-care tax credit, and the relevant portion of AFDC into a child-allowance fund.

Such allowances are an extraordinarily flexible instrument. In France and Japan—the nations with the most fully developed programs—they have strengthened families and prevented poverty from becoming chiefly an affliction of children. The allowances can be used to defray child-care expenses without forcing mothers out of the home. They can be adjusted to raise benefits for intact families. They can be reduced, as in the French "single income" device, if both parents work. The allowances can be diminished for later children, on the grounds that the marginal cost goes down. Or they can be increased for the first two, because it is then that the mother faces the strongest pressure to leave work. All these adjustments, and many more, are used in various countries.[13]

By reinforcing the man's efforts as provider, the program tends to keep him in his marriage. By compensating for the greater burdens of raising children, the program can help keep mothers in the home, rather than out pursuing menial work that hardly pays for day care. By ending the assumption that every wage by itself must support a family, child allowances tend to reduce pressure to increase the minimum wage in ways that reduce employment for young people. Although no program alone can abolish poverty, this one can greatly alleviate it in the places where money itself can do the most good, particularly in those vulnerable families headed by a man who works full time but still cannot lift his children from privation.

The payments will relieve the resentment a mother in a working family feels at the welfare recipient's trips to Puerto Rico and will reduce the husband's envy of the welfare mother's nonworking boyfriend. The government would no longer massively favor illegitimate children over legitimate ones; the teenaged mother could marry the father of her child even if he is working at some menial job, without losing all public support.

With the nearly complete collapse of poor families in America, the argument for child allowances is far stronger today than ever before. It is no panacea; Sweden, for example, swamps its child allowance with contrary incentives for illegitimacy and family breakdown. But the program is a crucial first step toward a sensible welfare and tax system that will support families rather than subvert them.

Although the Williamsburg sociologists and economists will never acknowledge it, the U.S. does not suffer significantly from a problem of race or of poverty. Our problem is far worse: a crippling plague of broken families. The best way to alleviate it is to offset the influence of perverse welfare and tax incentives through economic growth and child allowances. There is no other way.

Ironically, however, the sociologists are correct on one important point. They are right that the wreckage of the ghetto and beyond cannot be explained or solved by economic incentives and support systems alone, particularly those focused on the ghetto itself. Together with the punishing combination of tax penalties and welfare benefits, the lower-middle-class family, black or white, must try to steer its children through a treacherous cultural arena in which traditional roles and disciplines are under continuous attack. Teachers, textbooks, television programs, and films all tend to show heavy feminist influence. Sex-education courses take fornication for granted, deny the differences between the sexes, and even arouse unnecessary fears of homosexuality in normal boys. Contraceptives are distributed widely without parental consent. Religious values of abstinence and sacrifice give way to "values clarification" and feel-good moral codes. The only clear moral imperative conveyed by the usual text in social studies is the bogus "crisis" of overpopulation and the need for small families.

Since these pressures pervade the society, mobilizing against them can be a new "unity," joining all races and creeds across the country. What is needed is a broad effort, embracing churches, schools, and businesses as well as government, to restore the primacy of family values. Out-of-wedlock births should be delegitimized again, and marriage with children restored to its necessary centrality in our national life.

Most crucial of all is the role of the churches. Several sociological studies have shown that churchgoers have sharply lower levels of illegitimacy and divorce than others in the population. The problems of the American poor are most fundamentally moral and spiritual. As Margaret Mead insisted, stable families—with long time horizons and a resistance to the buffeting of life's inevitable troubles—ultimately depend, in all societies, on the reinforcement of religious beliefs and ceremonies.[14] Without a strong religious culture a secular bureaucracy, with its rationalizing ethic, erodes the very foundations of family life and thus creates the very moral chaos it ostensibly combats. The effort to inculcate ethical behavior without religious faith seems one of the great fiascoes of the modern age. If the established churches are truly concerned with the problems of poverty, they will abandon their current tendency to serve as shills for the demoralizing materialism of the welfare state and return to their paramount role, giving moral and spiritual guidance to the poor, and to all American society.

PART THREE

THE ECONOMY OF EROS

CHAPTER 10

Sexual Politics

The 1980s saw what was one of the greatest miracles in the history of American politics and the climactic triumph of one of the supreme political leaders ever to emerge in America. That leader was a woman and though she is well known today, she has never achieved the honor and celebrity of her many inferiors. The national newsmagazines have never granted her a cover story or a full appreciation. The dimensions of her achievement are still not understood, even by the conservative publications that gave her their moderately enthusiastic support. The newest history texts pay heavy credit to her adversaries but scarcely acknowledge her epochal role.

None the less, when the histories of this era are seriously written, Phyllis Schlafly will take her place among the tiny number of leaders who made a decisive and permanent difference. As much as Martin Luther King, Earl Warren, John Kennedy, Lyndon Johnson, and Eugene McCarthy on the left and Ronald Reagan, Barry Goldwater, Robert Bartley, William Buckley, and Jack Kemp on the right, she changed the political landscape of her country. In fact, by the measure of the odds she faced and overcame, Schlafly's achievement excels all the others'.

Schlafly's ten books suggest the scope of her activities. *A Choice Not An Echo* sold 3 million copies and helped spark both the Goldwater movement and the Reagan candidacy. Her works on military strategy spurred the campaign that finally triumphed with Reagan's adoption of the High Frontier defense scheme. But the centerpiece of her achievement was the victory against the Equal Rights Amendment, a mobilization against all the most fully established and prestigious forces in American life.[1]

Opposed to her were ninety percent majorities in both houses of Congress, every live American president and president's wife, every major state governor except an ambivalent Ronald Reagan, all leading mayors, both political parties' platforms and leadership, every major newspaper, magazine, and television network, the League of Women Voters, all the old line Protestant denominations, the national and World Councils of Churches, several leading Catholic and Jewish organizations and publications, and huge majorities of the American public as registered by all public opinion polls. The ERA forces, moreover, combined their overwhelming numbers with fanatical determination, continual use of government funds and agencies, and the same complete dominance of the media that still today keeps Schlafly from receiving her due.

Within months, this coalition pushed the amendment through thirty-five state legislatures, just three short of the necessary three-quarters. For seven years the American political establishment unleashed a relentless bombardment of the remaining legislatures. Congress appropriated $5 million for the International Woman's Year, the bulk of it devoted to the ERA campaign, and gave scores of millions to other entities involved in the ratification drive. All Federal departments and agencies were ordered by the President to apply "every resource of the Federal government" to the cause. As an Interior Department memo put it: "This is not to be considered a partisan issue," but part of an anti-discrimination effort "which Federal employers are now obliged to support." During the climactic year of 1978, President Carter himself travelled with his wife to Illinois, Schlafly's home state, in the week before the scheduled vote, to implore the state legislature to pass the Amendment. But for the 13th straight time, the legislature refused. By the official deadline for ratification in 1979, the tally revealed a net loss of one state since Schlafly's effort began to gain momentum in 1977.

But the proponents would not give up. In a blatantly illegal action, in defiance of the constitution and the powers of the states, Congress extended the ratification period by an additional thirty-nine months and prohibited all rescisions during that time. In

November 1979, before the Congressional vote, 36 women's magazines, from *Ms.* to the *Ladies Home Journal*—with a combined circulation of 60 million and varying views on almost everything—chimed in lockstep with articles for ERA. Then the Carter administration lavished yet more money and mobilized the federal government anew in yet another massive drive for passage. But once again the opposition held firm; by the end of the extension no further states had passed the amendment and it was at last allowed to die.

By this time, the mood was beginning to turn. In 1980 a Republican platform, for the first time, actually came out against the amendment, despite a frenzy of protest. The Republican candidate Ronald Reagan continued to oppose it. But Reagan was never a leader in stopping ERA. Even in radio messages criticizing the law, he would spend most of his time asserting his fervent support for "equal rights." Then, amazingly, he would turn over the microphone to his daughter Maureen and give her equal time to speak in behalf of the amendment. No national political leader had any substantial impact on the outcome.

There was only one significant leader of the anti-ERA effort and that was enough—for it was Phyllis Schlafly. She won in part because she is one of the country's best speakers and debaters and its best pamphleteer since Tom Paine. She won because of her indefatigable energy and willpower, mobilizing women in state after state where the Amendment was contested. But most of all she won because she understood what was finally at stake in feminism. She was defending both the sexual and legal constitutions of the United States from their most serious attack of this century.

Essentially the ERA would have granted to the federal bench, long dominated below the Supreme Court level by the some 400 liberal appointees of the Carter Administration, nearly carte blanche to redefine the relations between the sexes in America. Voluminous testimony before Senator Orrin Hatch's subcommittee of the Judiciary Committee showed that, among many other significant effects, the Amendment would likely have: 1) eliminated all rights of wives and mothers to be supported by their husbands, except to the extent husbands could claim an equal right; 2) eliminated all laws in any way restricting the rights of the gay liberation movement publically to teach, proselytize, or practice their sexual ideology; 3) forced sexual integration of all schools, clubs, colleges, athletic teams, and facilities; 4) forced the drafting of women and the sexual integration of all military units; 5) threatened the tax exemption of most religious schools; and 6) compelled the use of government funds for abortions.

Even more extreme interpretations are perfectly possible in the courts. Indeed, some skeptics point out that feminists are now gaining from judges much of what they lost in the legislatures, that liberals are now attaining the ERA's goals through judicial interpretations of the 14th amendment and through novel extensions of the civil rights act. This is true to a great extent. But the ERA battle was always a struggle not only to stop a specific law, but also to halt the momentum of the sexual revolution. The battle will never be over. But Phyllis Schlafly, though still unique, no longer stands alone. Her example has created a new feminine ideal and a new constituency of the country's conservative women who know what is actually at stake in the smarmy rhetoric of feminism and should be able to repeat their victories.

The sexual revolutionaries had the support of "public opinion" as registered by the polls and of political opinion as asserted by politicians. But Schlafly tapped the support of private opinion: the real personal convictions of the men and women who voted again and again in referenda and in elections and finally even in legislatures against the sexual revolution. As repeated surveys by Stanley Rothman and S. Robert Lichter have shown,[3] private opinion diverges widely from establishment opinion on every major sexual question, from special gay rights to adultery.

In this sense, the defeat of the ERA was merely a symbol of a larger infrastructure of opinion that upholds our family life and our democratic processes. ERA was only one of many issues on which deeply ingrained conservative views prevailed in recent years against all the fevered movements and fashions of the time.[4]

Despite some public opinion polls and Supreme Court decisions to the contrary, voters have repeatedly rejected liberalization of abortion laws. Except in cases of rape, incest, or risk to the mother's life, substantial majorities continue to oppose abortion.[5] Yet the feminist demand for "control over our own bodies" seems eminently justifiable to virtually every media authority. The tragic results of covert abortion mills, coathanger surgery, and Mexican "vacations" are well known. Unlike most poll questions, moreover, on which most respondents know little and could care less about the topic, abortion is a matter on which significant public opinion actually exists, an issue on which people have relatively strong and considered beliefs. Since the knowledgeable elites have influence far beyond their numbers, the tenacity of public opposition suggests a resistance profound enough to demand explanation.

What is it about these so-called social issues—embracing matters as varied as gun control, abortion, and busing—that leads substantial majorities of voters to violate, and vote against, the considered views of perhaps 90 percent of the American intelligentsia. The answer is that all these issues directly impinge on that sensitive psychological terrain, involving sexuality, children, and the family, which underlies the sexual constitution of the society. Unlike many intellectuals whose lives are devoted to legal and scientific abstraction, most of the people still instinctively recognize that preservation of the sexual constitution may be even more important to the social order than preservation of the legal constitution. They recognize that no laws can prevail against the dissolution of the social connections and personal motivations that sustain a civilized polity. They acknowledge, with Carl Jung, that though the society can resist epidemics of physical disease, it is defenseless against diseases of the mind. Against "psychic epidemics," our laws and medicines are virtually helpless.[6]

The relationship of each of these issues to the sexual constitution, though perhaps not immediately clear, is psychologically profound. Guns are a good example. The United States is a nation of households, most containing a man who deeply feels his responsibility for defending his family—and who fears that his ability to do it is diminishing in modern society. The ultimate nightmare of almost every man is to witness helplessly the rape of his wife. Only somewhat less threatening to the very core of male consciousness is the possibility of the violation of his home.

The role of protector of wife and children is as old as the family nexus itself, as old and deeply ingrained as the role of provider. A move by the state finally to incapacitate the man in this responsibility—and usurp him—undermines the validity of the family itself and the man's part in it. In this role, the gun is not a mere symbol. It does objectively increase the man's capacity to defend his household.

In addition, a gun is an emblem of the male as hunter. This, according to many anthropologists, was the primordial role of the evolving male *homo sapiens*. In *Men in Groups*, recently revised and republished, Lionel Tiger contends that the male propensity to work in all-male teams originated in these early expeditions.[7]

Today men across the land continue to hunt compulsively, despite a possibly declining need or appetite for the available game. They early give their male children guns and ceremoniously teach them the rules of their use. As anyone who has undergone this paternal instruction knows and remembers, it is a portentous event, conducted in the atmosphere of an initiation rite.

The obstinate refusal of many males to support gun control is not chiefly a product of conditioning by the weapons industry. Rather, millions of men fear gun control because they are losing life-control; they are losing the sense of a defined male identity and role in the family. They cling to these weapons and persist in their hunts as totems of masculinity, as rites and symbols of their continuing role as protector and provider in the family.

In this sense, the guns have a virtually religious import, and gun restrictions pose a serious psychological threat. Unless this erosion of the sexual constitution is recognized as a major social problem—for which realistic solutions rather than utopian incantations must be provided—gun control, however desirable, will remain politically difficult and practically unenforceable outside a police state.

The sexual dimensions of the abortion issue may be more obvious, but they are little better understood. The usual assumption is that opposition to abortion on demand stems from a puritanical aversion to premarital sex, combined with a religious superstition that feticide is murder. The real reasons, however, may be significantly different. Beyond the significance of anti-abortion sentiment as a repudiation of sexual liberation in general, it may be seen as a symbol of resistance to the erosion of male sexuality.

When the women demanded "control over our own bodies," they believed they were couching the issue in the least objectionable way. But as Norman Mailer pointed out at the time, they were in fact invoking one of the most extreme claims of the movement and striking at one of the most profound male vulnerabilities.[8] For, in fact, few males have come to psychological terms with the existing birth-control technology; few recognize the extent to which it shifts the balance of sexual power further in favor of women. A man quite simply cannot now father a baby unless his wife is fully and deliberately agreeable. There are few social or cultural pressures on her to conceive. Male procreativity is now dependent, to a degree unprecedented in history, on the active pleasure of women.

The psychological consequences of this change are greater than they might at first appear. Throughout the centuries, men could imagine their sexual organs as profoundly powerful instruments. If they performed a normal amount of sexual activity—"spread their wild oats"—they could assume that they would cause a number of women to bear their children. Male potency was not simply a matter of erectile reliability; it was a fell weapon of procreation. Women viewed male potency with some awe, and males were affirmed by this response.

This masculine attribute is now almost completely lost. The male penis is no longer a decisive organ in itself. Thus the feminist demand that women have control over their own bodies accentuated an unconscious recognition that males have almost completely lost control of procreative activity. Women are only marginally dependent on men—women can conceive a baby artificially or in one passing encounter. But a man cannot validate his procreative powers, his role in the chain of nature, without the active, deliberate, and now revocable cooperation of a woman. A man's penis becomes an empty plaything unless a woman deliberately decides to admit a man's paternity. This change in the sexual balance between men and women is still being absorbed by the society. People resist legal abortion on demand out of a sense of justifiable conservatism toward continued changes in the sexual constitution.

Busing, sex education, and high school birth control often represent a drive by the state to take children from families and expose them to ideologies and social movements—or use them in social experiments—fervently opposed by the parents themselves. The parents' response—"not with my kid, you don't"—is a serious threat to the public schools. But the public school programs are a serious threat to the integrity and discipline of the future generations on which the nation's economy and stability depend.

The national elites remain largely incapable of offering programs of communal affirmation and male socialization that would in any way reduce crime, violence, and narcotic escapism, divorce, abandonment, and sexual disorder. So they advocate programs of adaptation—no fault divorce, sex education, free pills and condoms for teenagers, methadone clinics and outreach centers for addicts— which collectively worsen the crisis of the sexual constitution.

Neither liberals nor establishment conservatives have any real remedies. Liberals would make the problems far worse by subsidizing them with expanded welfare, daycare, unisex job training, and other feminized government programs that richly earn the disdain they receive in street society. But many conservative men are little better. Lacking the guts to rebuff the upper-class feminist ladies, they go along with most of the feminist agenda, which still prevails in Washington bureaucracies under the Reagan administration. They fail to show the resolution and decisiveness needed to develop a complex of new social policies designed to strengthen families and socialize men. Thus the problems keep getting worse, and the people, demoralized and confused, show a rising and justifiable contempt for the world of politics.

Enhancing that contempt is the effort of feminists to emasculate the political order itself. One of the most notable concerns of the moderate wing of women's liberation is equal representation in politics. In 1984, the movement induced the Democratic party to nominate for Vice President a woman with no apparent qualifications for the office, and the Republicans to pad out their convention schedule with little-qualified female speakers. Displaying indifference to American democratic principles, the movement has managed to get both political parties to accept the idea that a truly representative national convention would be half female. Although willing in practice to accept somewhat smaller proportions, both parties required every state to make a good faith effort to achieve a delegation composed 50 percent of women.

Such disguised quotas bear the implication, radically inimical to any democratic process, that the electorate consists of separate, homogeneous, and identifiable groups, each best represented by one of its own kind. Such a conception of American voters is obviously wrong. Women vote for men most of the time; young people vote for their elders; blacks vote for whites and whites for blacks. The woman's movement ranks high among the groups from whom women seem least likely to choose their representatives.

Indeed, the demands themselves symbolize feminists' incomprehension both of the requirements of democracy and of the ultimate relations between men and women in every society. Again and again—on ERA, abortion, employment quotas, and all-male clubs and associations, from the military to the Little League—the feminists turn to the courts for coercive solutions when voters refuse to give them what they want. But coercive solutions are necessarily enforced by male power and ultimately hostile to women's interests in politics. A social system based on physical force, even if disguised by court orders, will eventually become a patriarchy far more oppressive than any democracy dominated by men. It is only a democracy, spontaneously devoted to the rule of law and the restraint of male force, that can easily accommodate a feminist movement or ensure female suffrage.

The "moderate" demand for quotas in politics undermines these democratic protections. Politics has been chiefly a male domain in all societies ever studied by anthropologists and historians. Women everywhere, unless hectored by feminists, tend to turn to men for leadership. Male dominance in politics is part of the sexual constitution of all civilized societies. This does not mean imposition of any limits whatsoever on the extraordinary women who often rise to key positions by their own efforts and on their own merits. But it means that the effort forcibly to feminize our affairs violates profound human propensities. By preventing governance from conforming to human nature, sexual liberalism, necessarily using arbitrary quotas to overcome natural resistance, provides a perfect opening for the familiar excesses of abstract ideology and totalitarianism.

Politics is ultimately based on force, and the most effective wielders of force are groups of men. If young men are estranged from the leadership of society, any society faces a threat from its young men. Today in America the best example is the ghetto, where youths readily express far more respect for the Mafia than for any American public institution and where the women and elderly all too often cower in their apartments for fear of the hoodlums who rule the streets. But throughout history, alliances between military officers and male groups of mesomorphic thugs have always emerged when the established leadership lost its hold on the public.

To replace the legitimacy of the vote with the legitimacy of the warrior group has always been the essential fascist and revolutionary idea. The Nietzchean exaltation of tribal values against the effeminacy of democratic ideals, the celebration of the hunter against the domesticated man of the city and farm, the legendary rule of a male bond of blood in tribal Germany, the mystical worship of war and the warrior brotherhood, all served the Nazi stormtroopers as legitimizing myths. Similar ideas have informed all the most destructive regimes in history, from Mussolini to Mao, from the Japanese warlords to communist cadres.

In any primitive tribe, rule by male fighters is the most natural form of government. Not only do they command force, but they exert a moral appeal as well. The idea that the men who risk their lives to preserve and protect the state earn the right to rule it always offers a seductive alternative to the sovereignty of passing majorities of voters. When this idea prevails among large numbers of young men, democratic constraints are helpless against it.

The history of the twentieth century confirms the continuing potency of the warrior dream against all the codes and sanctions of democracy. Dictators and demagogues, juntas and caudillos, tyrants and revolutionaries, all supported by young men in military or paramilitary groups, always pose the greatest threat to civilization and peace.

Fascism is the political counterpart of the social breakdown of monogamy into the disorders of polygyny, homosexuality, and female-headed families. The release of large numbers of young men from the bonds and disciplines of marriage and family always leads to a threat to social stability. The punk rockers and soccer rioters of mid-eighties Britain reflect the loss of male roles through high tax rates and resulting levels of joblessness. The breakdown of law and order and the demoralization of the courts and police in U.S. cities suggests the utter impotence of the superstructure of government when the infrastructures of sexual discipline collapse.

Without a stable family order, in which adult men civilize the young men, terror necessarily rules. No array of daycare centers, police powers, social welfare agencies, psychiatric or drug clinics, special schools and prisons can have any significant effect. William Tucker's fine new book *Vigilante* vividly shows the imbecile bathos into which our legal system has already fallen as a result of the decline of the stark mandate of justice into the weasels and waffles of social liberalism.

At a time when millions of young men are slipping beyond the reach of democratic institutions—indeed, outside the social order itself—the drive to emasculate our politics threatens the foundations of democracy itself. Democracy is not so secure a system that in a serious crisis it can easily survive the loss of the instinctual appeal of male leadership. A state in which the police and other governmental authorities are heavily in female hands would not last a week. The very emergence of such a state would itself signify either the massive estrangement of men from politics or the degeneration of democracy into some court-ruled system of quotas.

It is part of Schlafly's genius to have persistently linked the concerns of family with the reform of education, the conservative revival of our politics, and the rehabilitation of our military. From her concern with the national defense to her defense of the nation's families, she espouses a fully coherent vision of the American predicament. A society of families both constrains male aggressions and channels them toward the protection and support of family and society.

With the breakdown of families, the economy also declines, as the long term efforts of male providers give way to short term and predatory economic behavior. An emasculated state neither can defend itself against male outlaws and exploiters, muggers and terrorists, hijackers and assassins, nor can achieve the economic growth to finance the welfare programs and police efforts required by a culture in chaos. As in the ghetto, the defection of men from family responsibilities leaves the women helpless to handle their teenaged boys and the police impotent to control them. The youth bully and terrorize the women and the weak.

Similarly in the international arena, an emasculated politics is incapable of sustaining an effective national defense. Rather than defending society, the young men attack it and exalt macho foreign potentates and desperadoes. Again the captivation of ghetto and other youth by Third World thugs and enemies of America illustrates the contempt that an emasculated politics and economics earns from its young men—and young women as well.

By joining the two issues of national defense and family defense, Phyllis Schlafly has tapped the energies that spring from the eloquent assertion of any long suppressed, evaded, and fragmented set of primal truths. All politics is on one level sexual politics. Defending the sexual constitution, she is clearly America's leading exponent and protector of democracy and capitalism.

The best sign of the continuing health of American society is the regular emergence of political leaders in unexpected places who are willing to commit themselves to a new defense of the values of civilization. Under perpetual assault from the forces of decadence and decline, protectionism and sloth, the American system still summons vibrant new tides of resistance and revitalization.

Our businesses and technologies are renewed by immigrants from around the world and by American entrepreneurs from rural and religious backgrounds. Our families are restored by forces of regeneration from both fundamentalist Protestant and traditionalist Catholic churches. Our politics find new resources of American redemption in the rise of moral majorities, immigrant patriots, tax rebels, conservative educational entrepreneurs, and pro-family campaigners.

Even to conservative intellectuals, some of these forces seem crude: too passionate, too fundamental, too foreign, too cultic, too populist, too unsophisticated, too lower middle class, altogether alien to the established schools and churches that for decades have purported to uphold tradition while in fact selling out and flaking out before every new fashion of decadence and socialism. The idea that America might find renewal from a melange of movements of evangelical women, wetbacks, Dartmouth Review militants, South Asian engineers, Bible thumpers, boat people, Moonies, Mormons, Cuban refugees, fundamentalist college deans, Amway soap pushers, science wonks, creationists, Korean fruit pedlars, acned computer freaks and other unstylish folk seems incomprehensible to many observers who do not understand that an open capitalist society is always saved by the last among its citizens perpetually becoming first.

In America, no one is required to go to the Liberty Baptist Church or watch the 700 Club. But the movements that these institutions represent and promote provide the best hope for American democracy and peace, capitalist prosperity and progress. Ironically enough, it is the so-called reactionaries who offer the best prospects for continued American leadership in the world economy in the new era of accelerating technological change. Just as the nuclear families of Western Europe unleashed the energies of the industrial revolution, so the new miracles of modern technology are created and sustained by the moral discipline and spiritual incandescence of a culture of churches and families. In families, men and women routinely make long term commitments and sacrifices that are inexplicable and indefensible within the compass of secular hedonist values. Modern society, no less than any previous civilization, rests on the accumulated moral and spiritual capital embodied in the rock of ages.

CHAPTER 11

The Perils of Androgyny

To the sexual liberal, gender is a cage. Behind cruel bars of custom and tradition, men and women for centuries have looked longingly across forbidden spaces at one another and yearned to be free of sexual roles. The men dream of nurturing and consoling; the women want the right to be tough and child-free. Today it is widely believed that the dream of escape can come true at last.

This belief leads to a program of mixing the sexes in every possible way, at every stage of life. In nurseries and schools, in athletics and home economics, in sex education and social life, the sexes are thrown together in the continuing effort to create a unisex society. But the results are rarely as expected, and the policies are mostly founded on confusion.

Some of the confusions arise in the schools, where the androgynous agenda has made the greatest apparent headway and its effects can best be studied. It turns out that what seems elemental to many expert educationists is actually bizarre from the long perspective of history and anthropology.

Until recent years, for example, most American parochial schools have kept strict sexual segregation. The boys and girls joined chiefly on ceremonial occasions—assemblies and graduations. Even the playground was divided into male and female territories. The restrictions were lifted only during carefully supervised dances, when young couples made their way chastely around the floor of the gym under the watchful eyes of nuns. Any unseemly body contact brought a swift reprimand: "Leave six inches for the Holy Ghost."

There is no room for the Holy Ghost any longer at most of our schools. The bodies and minds rub together from kindergarten to graduate study. The result is perfectly predictable. Sexual activity occurs at an increasingly younger age. In communities where the family cannot impose discipline, illegitimate children are common. Classrooms become an intensely sexual arena, where girls and boys perform for the attention of the other sex and where unintellectual males quickly come to view schoolbooks as a menace to manhood.[1]

All of this happens at a time when education is becoming increasingly important and the distractions of early sex are increasingly subversive to one's future. Our society enforces an ever longer period of objective latency before full participation is allowed, and at the same time refuses to grant its children the "latency period" of sexual separation provided in societies where marriage comes at age fourteen.[2] Boys and girls, often forced to write before their hands can manage a pencil,[3] are later thrust into sexual contact before their minds and bodies can deal with sexual emotion.

But there is "no turning back the clock," as they say. The few remaining sex-segregated schools dwindle in an ideological void— as a species that survives the death of its philosophy and rationale. The issue today is not the desirability of coeducation. Coeducation is about as universal in American schools as dissatisfaction with their performance. The issue is whether the remaining male or female schools should rapidly open their doors to both sexes and whether coed schools should proceed with their apparent agenda of integrating all their activities, from sex-education classes to athletics.

The abandonment of separate education, peculiarly enough, has occurred without any visible national debate. Prestigious prep schools like Exeter and Groton, eminent women's colleges like Vassar and Sarah Lawrence, and male institutions like Yale and Princeton have all quietly adopted coeducation as if it were inevitable. New elementary schools are universally coed. Many coed schools provide excellent educations, but the reasons for the movement seem to be less academic than financial and ideological. No one seems to have been able to offer cogent answers to the question, "Why not?" The Holy Ghost, needless to say, is no longer much consulted.

Yet, regardless of whether one considers the trend as ultimately desirable, most of the assumptions that impel it are demonstrably fallacious. A shift to coeducation is in fact "unnatural" by most anthropological criteria. In the evolutionary scheme, it represents a radical change in the learning environment for both boys and girls, who mature in very different ways and phases.[4] Its effects in grade school are drastically different from its effects in college. And whatever the benefits, many of the problems of America's schools—and disorders of the society—are attributable to the presumption, rare in all other human societies, that boys and girls should be thrown together whenever possible.

Let us begin with a few simple, crucial, and apparently unmentionable facts about a typical high-school classroom. First and most important, most of the boys and a good number of the girls are thinking about the opposite sex most of the time. If you do not believe this, you are a dreamer. The only thing about a classroom more important to adolescent boys than whether girls are present is whether or not it is on fire.

Imaginative advocates of coeducation will tell you that the boys are learning to regard the girls as "human beings" rather than as sexual objects. What in fact the boys are learning is that unless they are exceptionally "bright" and obedient, they will be excelled in their studies by most of the girls.[5] Unless you are imaginative, you will see that this is a further drag on their already faltering attention to Longfellow's *Evangeline*. Clearly in a losing game in masculine terms, the boys react in two ways: They put on a show for the girls and dominate the class anyway, or they drop out. Enough of them eventually drop out, in fact, to disguise the otherwise decided statistical superiority of female performance in school.[6] But they do not drop out soon enough to suit educators for whom aggressive boys are the leading problem in every high school.

Adolescent boys are radically different from adolescent girls. The boys, for example, are at the pinnacle of sexual desire and aggressiveness. In school, what they chiefly need is male discipline and challenge, ideally without girls present to distract them. Girls, on the other hand, are less aggressive and sexually compulsive at this stage and are more willing to study without rigid policing and supervision. Thus a classroom that contains both boys and girls will hurt both. The boys will be excelled and demoralized by the girls; the girls will be distracted and demoralized by the boys. Both sexes will be damaged by the continuous disciplining that the rebellious and unsuccessful boys require.

The cost is a system which is experienced by many boys as oppressively feminine in spirit and in which, as Patricia Cayo Sexton has elaborately documented, the most "feminine" boys tend to excel. The problem begins in the first grade, when many of the boys are a full nine months behind the girls in digital coordination, and the emphasis is on penmanship.[7] Mrs. Sexton believes that the striking aversion to writing shown by so many boys throughout their education may stem from their frustrations as six-year-olds when their hands are physically unready to write.[8] She contends that such patterns continue throughout a school career.

Mechanical and technical interests and skills, predominantly masculine, are downplayed in favor of the feminine realms of writing and high culture. The educational utility of the boys' preoccupation with sports and automobiles is universally neglected. The boys are not shown how to compute batting averages or taught the physical principles involved in a carburetor. Instead school consists almost exclusively of sitting down quietly for long periods among adolescent girls, at the behest of a female teacher, and reading and writing materials of little interest to most adolescent boys.

The result, according to Mrs. Sexton, who assembled reams of testing data to prove it, is that the most feminine boys prevail in school and tend to go on to college and into the best jobs. Meanwhile the most aggressive and masculine—the ones who cannot sit in one place for more than ten minutes without severe nervous strain, relieved only by dreams of cars and football games—these boys tend to drop out and take the lowest-paying work.

This pattern leads to tensions of sexuality and social class that are played out continually in the writings of sexual liberals. But their paradigms of victimization are no less valid when reversed. Some of the dropout males, for example, end up at construction sites whistling "oppressively" at upper-class feminist women as they amble by, their breasts jouncing loosely in their shirts. "Gee whiz, these brutes are treating us as *sex objects!*" say the feminists in their books and magazines, pamphlets and speeches. But a working man—committed to a lifetime of tough and relatively low-paid labor in support of his family—cannot feel himself the oppressor of women who seem to embody everything the world has denied to him: options, money, style, easy sex, freedom.

The tensions also affect the men who remain in school and prevail under coeducation. Not only are they harassed as "grinds" and "apple-polishers" by the more masculine boys, but they are often alienated from their masculine natures and from technical experience. Their sexual anxieties sustain billion-dollar markets in porn and prostitution. Baffled by a car battery or blown fuse, disdainful of the blue-collar life, and ignorant of the labor and business of the world, they tend to obsess themselves with odd resentments and conspiracy theories, abstract ideas and symbols.

As Mrs. Sexton writes, "In academic life, words are enshrined to the point that many feel all wars are settled, and all deeds accomplished, through arguments and speechmaking. The academy is often merely a repository of disembodied words . . . but there is hardly an act, deed or object in sight. That students should get restless about this condition and that they should be grossly inept at linking words with deeds should not startle us."[9]

Moreover, she explains, "If we block normal outlets of aggression, we may turn it inward. When we pacified the bopping gang of a decade ago, its members turned to narcotics and self-mutilation. And middle-class hippies (also without aggressive outlets) followed in the same path, adding their own variations."[10]

"We have much to overcome and destroy," Mrs. Sexton continues, ". . . floods and famine, illiteracy, anomie, unrewarding work, abuses of power, obsolete social institutions, the imminence of nuclear war. With so many enemies, we need a great deal of fighting spirit. It would seem wiser, both inside and outside our schools, to permit as much aggression as possible, but to direct it away from street fights and into combat with the real enemies of man."[11]

The mechanical interests that lead many boys to putter endlessly with automobiles, computers, and other technology represent no lesser intellectuality than the more verbal orientation of the others. But potentially valuable technical skills are lost and intellectual powers squandered or turned against the society because the educational system does not know how to deal with masculinity.

Surprisingly, to imaginative educators, both the verbal and the mechanical boys have less trouble in all-male institutions. Contrary to the widespread notion, homosexuality is rare at most one-sex prep schools and military academies. Boys with masculinity problems are reinforced by an all-male environment, while less intellectually competent though virile students are not so estranged from education by their failures. Competition with females is destructive to males in any arena, but nowhere is it so damaging as among impressionable adolescents preoccupied with their intense but inchoate sexuality.

Nonetheless, enough boys are surviving school with their masculinity intact to deeply distress the liberationists. It has become clear that in order to extirpate "sexism," it is necessary to attack it at the root. Beyond the effects of coeducation itself, the educationists want to give boys a "head start" in emasculation. Thus the movement is striking at the early stages: nursery school, kindergarten, and the lower grades. Exploiting their great strength in the teaching profession, particularly at the elementary level, the feminists want to remove every vestige of sexual differentiation from textbooks and class activities. They are succeeding widely, and, from Sesame Street to Main Street, few parents seem willing or able to resist.

The National Education Association has adopted a militantly feminist position, and many teachers across the country are turning elementary school into an even more destructive experience for little boys than it long has been. The liberationists seem to imagine that the sexuality of children is some kind of ideological playground. They should recognize the terrible damage that sexual confusions can cause in young boys.

What is at stake, for example, in the frequent proposals for a qualified merger of male and female athletics in high schools is nothing less than the integrity of one vital remaining process of male socialization. Mrs. Sexton, among countless other observers, has described the vast importance of sports in the lives of many boys. "Fish like to swim, and boys like to play games," she writes. Speaking of Sioux Indian youths, she quotes an observer: "The unselfconscious devotion and ardor with which many of these young men play games must be witnessed to be appreciated even mildly."[12] Sports are possibly the single most important male rite in modern society.

Whatever their detractors may say, sports embody for men a moral universe. On the team, the group learns to cooperate, learns the importance of loyalty, struggle, toughness, and self-sacrifice in pursuing a noble ideal. At a period in their lives when hormones of aggression are pouring through their bodies in unprecedented streams, boys learn that aggressiveness must be disciplined and regulated before it can be used in society. They learn the indispensable sensation of competition in solidarity.

The entrance of a large number of teenage girls, at a time in high school and junior high when they tend to be larger than boys, would be disastrous for all the slow developers. Leaders in Outward Bound physical programs for ghetto children, for example, find that the best athletes perform as well—if in a different spirit—with females present. The smaller, shyer, and less developed boys, however, are completely daunted by the girls and refuse to make a resolute effort. In addition, the lessons of group morality are lost. The successful boys, those who work with and encourage the others in all-male groups, simply show off for the females in mixed assemblages. Nor do the girls benefit. Some of them do quite well, but their performances seem directed more toward the boys than to the real values of the undertaking.

In joint athletics, girls subvert the masculinity of the weaker or slow-developing boys without gaining significant athletic reward themselves. The girls who could actually play on an integrated high-school team would be exceedingly rare. But the girls, nonetheless, would disrupt and deform the most precious rituals of young boys.

Athletics provide lessons relevant to many of the confusions and contradictions of American feminism. On the one hand, feminists make fervent demands for a separate realm for women, with prizes and other rewards equal to those received by far superior male athletes. In other words, for far inferior performances Martina Navratilova and Evelyn Ashford must receive prizes equal to John McEnroe and Carl Lewis—equal pay for unequal work. On the other hand, feminists make equally fervent appeals that exceptional girls—during the prepubescent stage when girls are as strong as boys—be admitted to boys' sports such as Little League baseball. High-school girls' teams, however, cannot be opened to the boys unable to make the first-string male teams, because by that route the girls' teams would disappear. Yet scarce athletic moneys must be equally divided between male and female teams.

The victims of such practices are male athletes unable to make the men's teams in their early years but far superior to the women on the women's teams that are displacing men's junior varsities on many campuses. Lacking funds and required to increase spending for girls' sports under Title 9 of the Education Amendments of 1972, schools and colleges reduce spending on boys. In high schools in several progressive districts of California, for example, girls' participation rates have more than tripled—from 12 percent to 37 percent—but boys' participation has dropped from 76 percent to about 50 percent.[13] In other words, millions of potential male athletes are losing opportunities to athletically inferior women, exclusively by reason of sex. Some of the excluded boys, who might have had satisfying athletic careers as their bodies matured, instead turn to alcohol, drugs, and crime.

The women who succeed in sports, however, usually do not embody or dramatize the power of women or their athletic ability. Unlike men, who succeed in athletics largely in proportion to their manliness—by perfecting their male bodies—women succeed by suppressing their femininity and imitating men. The most extreme case is female bodybuilding, in which most of the women take male hormones and create bodies that parody the masculine ideal. But throughout track and field and in many other Olympic tests of speed and strength, women prevail chiefly by virilizing themselves.

The Eastern Europeans specialize in such transformations. By extinguishing every hint of femininity, for example, Jarmila Kratochvilova, the marvel of women's track, can run almost as fast as a male adolescent. But her achievement is flawed as an athletic performance because it is less a natural and beautiful fulfillment of the female body than a perversion of it. Through such perversions Communist nations usually "win" the Olympics. But in the past several of their female record-breakers have turned out later to be chromosomally male.

Many other sports, with a greater stress on grace and timing, require much less physical or hormonal deformation. Female tennis players often display great feminine grace and appeal and bring a different dimension to the game. But however spectacular the performance of a Navratilova or a Billie Jean King, their lesbianism casts a pall on their skills as somehow unnatural and masculine in spirit.

Lionel Tiger and other anthropologists who emphasize the hunting origins of male *homo sapiens* offer plausible explanations for most of the specialized faculties of the male body. Its running and throwing skills, its ability to reach a pitch of violent activity for brief periods, all derive from the experience of the chase. The tendency to bond with other males in intensely purposeful and dangerous activity is said to come from the collective demands of pursuing large animals. The female body, on the other hand, more closely resembles the body of nonhunting primates. A woman throws, for example, like a male chimpanzee. She cannot run as well as men. But she has more long-range stamina and durability, particularly in the water, and, perhaps in compensation for limitations in pure strength, she has attained greater grace and beauty. Because her musculature is more internal, she can perform prodigious physical feats without breaking the aesthetic lines of her body with corrugations of bulging muscles. When she doesn't strain and struggle against her being to fulfill the standards of male physicality, she reaches greater kinesthetic perfection. She can achieve triumphs of her own at least the equal of male athletic exploits.

Consider, for example, women's gymnastics, a sport once obscure in the United States but universal in its appeal. The great performers achieve a synthesis of grace, agility, humor, beauty, flexibility, and stamina that reaches a level of sinuous poetry. Their dives and leaps and spins all fuse in a continuous calisthenic stream (in the true sense of the term—*kalos* and *sthenis*—beauty and strength).

Men, on the other hand, might leap higher, suspend themselves longer, and whirl faster. But they cannot touch the dazzling artistic integrity of the female performances. Their bodies seem less flexible and somehow excessively muscled, their effort too visible; and though they may do more, as often happens in aesthetics, even in athletics, more is less. In a pursuit of calisthenic grace, the men find themselves in a predicament suggestive of the female sprinter or weight lifter. They are working counter to their physical endowment. And when they assume a pose of elegance, it often seems narcissistic. All that male musculature burdens the terms of the art.

Like gymnasts, female divers and figure skaters have no apologies to make to the men in their fields—let alone to high-school freshmen in Keokuk. The female body, when trained calisthenically, attains a flexuous grace, a perfection of sensuous form and movement that finds no male counterpart.

Outside of the serious competitive arena, women can bring this kind of grace and style to a great many recreational sports. In general, women will do best by transforming athletics into calisthenics—by finding the aesthetic dimensions of a physical art and, by dint of the integrity of their performance, establishing it on their own terms.

In this sense athletics offer a metaphor of the entire dilemma of liberation. Jarmila Kratochvilova and her teammates enter the athletic realm on male terms. The sad irony is that, for all their effort, they gain not liberation but bondage to the male conditions of the activity. By submitting to male values, they symbolically affirm male superiority and betray the higher possibilities of their sex.

The lessons of athletics extend throughout the educational system. Boys and girls grow up in different ways and with overlapping but different potentials. Thus virtually every primitive society divides the children and teaches the sexes separately. Most provide the boys with dramatic initiatory rituals, needed because male lives lack distinct and dramatic stages like those found in the unfolding of female sexuality. In very few cases are the boys and girls thrown together more than two years before their marriages. These divisions may well promote the development of a confident masculinity and of a rich and successful later sex life.

In the United States and Western Europe girls and boys are expected to traffic together intimately for years before they can marry. They are subjected to intense sexual distractions and competitions during the critical stages of their educations. They are brought up in a society where sex is continuously advertised and propagandized.

The result is that boys and girls are driven into periods of sexual experimentation and stress unparalleled in either length or intensity by any other societies. One aspect of sex is drastically downplayed, however, and that is the most important, fundamental, and sexually differentiated part—procreation.

Thus the American system of increasingly far-reaching sexual integration vividly teaches the lesson that boys and girls are sexually similar and that sex is a matter of exchanging pleasures between them in a reciprocal way. This approach is inimical to durable love and marriage. The boys do not learn to venerate the procreative powers of women, and the girls stunt their own consciousness of a more elaborate sexuality. Thus, in effect, despite the feminized regimen of many schools, in sex itself—the domain of women—masculine patterns prevail and both sexes are diminished.

The advocates of sexual integration, moreover, seem ready to stop at virtually nothing—not sex education classes, not sports, not even, so it seems, the ultimate male arena of military combat.

CHAPTER 12

Women in Combat

Helmeted young women charging over beaches under fire with bayonets fixed, teenage girls occupying oil fields in an energy crunch, Marine coeds bunking down on bivouacs in combat zones, female pilots shot down and captured behind enemy lines. Such images may seem sheer fantasy—the farthest shores of radical feminism or an arresting montage for a futuristic film. Until recently, in fact, the military services and many sexual liberals dismissed the idea of warrior roles for women as "unthinkable." But today, when the subject comes up, the word more often chosen, by high officials in the Pentagon and by outside observers, is "inevitable."[1]

Current law for the Navy and Air Force still prohibits—at least formally—the use of women in "combat roles." The same undefined prohibition has been assumed by the Army but never made explicit in law. In recent years, however, many Pentagon observers have come to believe that, because of growing personnel shortages, the United States cannot maintain an adequate combat force in any of the services without using women more widely and flexibly.[2]

Experts downplay the onetime fantasy of women warriors by citing the changing nature of warfare and military technology. Women may indeed serve in "combat," it is suggested; but combat will no longer entail use of bayonets and physical force. Instead, battles will occur on some high technology computer-scape well beyond the reach of conventional weapons. In the future, combat will be a video game; there will be no front lines.

127

The issue of women in battle, however, cannot be so easily rationalized or evaded. Conventional combat remains common in a world where many modern weapons are too destructive to use. Most actual military and police activities, as opposed to happily hypothetical nuclear wars, entail the direct threat or application of personal and physical force, whether against rioters, prisoners, terrorists, or guerrilla armies. All the once unthinkable fantasies of combat women, moreover, are already a daily agenda of learning in training camps across the land, where women do indeed dig foxholes, fix bayonets, fly planes, and serve on ships under "fire."

Congress has approved the assignment of women to a wide variety of near-combat naval vessels. Initial classes of women flying fighter-style jets have been graduated from Air Force courses. And thousands of female soldiers serve in Europe, driving supply trucks and performing maintenance operations in logistical units that would bring them deep into combat areas in the event of war (although at any one time 20 percent are either pregnant or nursing infants).[3] The changing policies have brought forth, and then allowed to be constantly revised under pressure, an array of new rules prohibiting "relationships" between persons of different ranks and different sexes; and the classic training exercise called the "slide-for-life" was restricted by the Army after a twenty-year-old recruit fell to her death when her grip gave way on the high rope. The military is trying in many earnest ways to accommodate the female presence.

Pentagon officials claim that they plan no abrupt changes regarding the use of women in combat which might endanger "the national security." Nevertheless, they do entertain the idea—as one of the Joint Chiefs of Staff said—that "women may prove to be even more effective, more aggressive than men," and they ask for more flexibility in deploying them.

In addition, the military is under constant pressure from Equal Opportunity officers. A new alliance between Pentagon personnel administrators and policymakers and the women's liberation movement has emerged, pushing the United States military into a position where women will be so fully and flexibly involved in our armed services organizational structure that, in a war emergency, it will be very difficult—if not impossible—to separate them out.

In an interview, two leading figures in the new confederation of professional feminists and military men explained this change of attitudes. The feminist was lawyer Kathleen Carpenter, formerly special counsel for employment practices at Norton Simon Inc., who served as Deputy Assistant Secretary of Defense for Equal Opportunity when these policies were formed. The military man was Comdr. Richard Hunter. In recent years, he has emerged as one of the Pentagon's leading experts on personnel matters.

Both Commander Hunter and Ms. Carpenter believe that the differences between the sexes are no more important, and possibly less important, than the differences between the races. "When I came into the military, blacks were treated about the way women are now," Commander Hunter said. He and Kathleen Carpenter see the matter as a simple problem of civil rights.

Although Commander Hunter acknowledged that there were some differences in physical strength, Ms. Carpenter demurred. "Tests show," she said, "that while men have greater upper-body strength, women have greater midsection strength." The military is changing its task structure, she maintained, to make better use of female midsection strength. This restructuring of jobs, she added, "enriches the work experience for all."

A background study entitled "The Use of Women in the Military," produced under the leadership of Commander Hunter, offers two reasons for the growing urgency of introducing women into the battle forces: "First is the movement within the society to provide equal economic opportunity for American women. Second, and more important, use of more women can be a significant factor in making the all-volunteer force continue to work in the face of a declining youth population."

The Hunter study stresses that the scores of female recruits are 20 percent higher than men's in the Armed Forces Qualification Test and that more of the women have high-school diplomas. Responding to Army objections that "we should err on the side of national security" until all doubts about female performance are dispelled, the report asks: "Is recruiting a male high-school dropout in preference to a smaller, weaker, but higher-quality female erring on the side of the national security, in view of the kinds of jobs which must be done in today's military?"

The stepped-up recruitment of women, however, is required neither by the alleged personnel shortages nor by the other needs cited by the military. The all-volunteer force has done well statistically—attracting male recruits of "higher quality" with better education and test scores for longer average enlistment periods than at any previous time in the twentieth century. Moreover, both the Korean and Vietnam wars were fought under far more stringent manpower conditions than U.S. forces face in the foreseeable future. In the 1950s, for example, the supply of young men was only double the military demand; through the 1990s, supply will run between four and five times the projected demand. Increasing rates of immigration, legal and illegal, will tend to expand further the number of eligible males.

The presence of women in the American armed services is already greater than in the military forces of any other country, including the Soviet Union or Israel. The United States Army already employs women more extensively in combat-related areas than any other national force. All services are already recruiting women at a rate that is causing serious management and mobility problems, particularly among the one-third of servicewomen who are married to servicemen and among the increasing numbers of military women with small children.

But even if expanded use of women were desirable to relieve recruitment and attrition costs and to fill certain technical needs, removal of the combat exclusion would remain unnecessary and unwise. The proposed change is based primarily on a simple idea: that women could be used more efficiently if they were less restricted to traditional roles. This assumption is false even on narrow grounds of personnel management. Although attrition rates for women are sometimes lower than for men, this advantage is totally lost when women move away from traditional kinds of work. The female attrition rate is higher than the male rate in the combat-oriented Marine Corps, and between two and five times as high wherever women work in nontraditional fields. In fact, for both men and women, attrition rates soar when conventional sex roles are ignored in the delegation of military assignments. The Brookings Institution study "Women and the Military" conceded in a footnote: "Of all the women who entered the electronic-equipment repair specialty. . . only 24 percent remained [three years later] whereas the comparable figure for males was 49 percent. In maintenance, the corresponding proportions were 10 percent for women and 47 percent for men."[4] These low rates of female retention covered all nontraditional areas, and they are not improving with time.

Conversely, in the administrative, clerical, communications, and medical areas, among secretaries, nurses, and the like, male attrition rates were nearly double those of females. It seems clear that, at least in the military, most men and women prefer traditional work.

The military, in general, is going too far in "objective" and rationalistic personnel policies that defy common sense. Its tendency to view personnel "quality" almost entirely in terms of education and test scores could conceal a new form of bigotry, perhaps unintentional but certainly real. This is the fallacy of assuming that the most easily measurable of human qualities are more important than the unmeasurable ones. It may be coincidental that prominent among the victims of the new bigotry are the same dropout male youths who have always suffered, but the result is no less discriminatory. It is discrimination in favor of female credentials and test scores and implicitly against male aggressiveness and physical strength, discrimination in favor of quantifiable abilities tested in classrooms and against the intangible qualities tested in combat.

Almost every study of productivity in American industry or of success in the economy, as well as of courage in combat, has shown that the intangibles of character—enterprise, aggressiveness, drive, willingness to risk—are much more important than the measurable quotients of classroom ability.

The argument that advanced technology requires a more highly educated work force is also familiar in civilian life. Yet studies by Lester Thurow of M.I.T. reveal that the vast majority of all work skills are learned on the job, and that more advanced technology often reduces rather than enhances the need for outside education since the necessary skills are incorporated into the machines. Many of the technical industries of Europe and Asia that compete successfully in American markets make heavy use of poorly educated aliens who do not even know the language of the country in which they work.

No major military force in the world approaches the educational level of the American armed services. It may well be that the Pentagon should create new inducements—and suspend certain military disciplines and promotion requirements—to aid in the recruitment of highly educated specialists in certain fields. But this has little to do with the general matter of increasing the proportion of recruits with high-school diplomas, or of introducing women to combat roles.

The hard evidence is overwhelming that men are more aggressive, competitive, risk-taking—indeed more combative—than women. In fact, even feminist scholars Carol Jacklin and Eleanor Maccoby (Maccoby is chairman of Stanford University's department of psychology) acknowledge decisive biological differences between the sexes. In their voluminous and authoritative text on the subject, *The Psychology of Sex Differences*, they sum up their argument: "(1) Males are more aggressive than females in all human societies for which evidence is available. (2) The sex differences are found early in life, at a time when there is no evidence that differential socialization pressures have been brought to bear by adults to 'shape' aggression differently in the two sexes. (3) Similar sex differences are found in man and subhuman primates. (4) Aggression is related to levels of sex hormones, and can be changed by experimental administrations of these hormones." [5]

Another male trait—manifested in every human society but just as hard as aggression to measure in an exam—is aptitude for group leadership. Partly a result of greater aggressiveness and larger physical stature, partly an expression of the need to dominate (perhaps based on the neurophysiological demands of the sex act itself), males in all societies ever studied by anthropologists overwhelmingly prevail in positions of leadership and hold authority in relations with women. Goldberg's rigorously argued *The Inevitability of Patriarchy* refutes every anthropological claim that there has ever existed in human affairs either a society where women rule, or a society where final authority resides with them in male-female relations. [6]

Similarly, on the admittedly less crucial matter of physical ability, no pettifoggery about midsection strength can dispel the facts of greater male size and power. As the Hunter study concedes, "Women have about 67 percent of the endurance and 55 percent of the muscular strength of men. Even when size is held constant, women are only 80 percent as strong as men." An Army study conducted at West Point showed that young women improve their strength less than half as much as men under the same regimen of physical training.[7] Testosterone is a hormone not only of male sex drive and aggression but also of protein synthesis.

Bureaucracies that ignore these facts of life in favor of narrow criteria of test scores and schooling may create in time the same kind of demoralization, restlessness, and drive to early retirement that is often found in the American system of Civil Service and indeed the same kind of disgruntlement and dissatisfaction that Kathleen Carpenter found in the military services and ascribed to inadequate pay and benefits. (Both modes of compensation are more generous in the military than in other branches of government.)

The increasing tendency to use academic testing methods for all personnel and promotion systems is turning untold thousands of jobs in the military and elsewhere into dead ends for all but those adept at taking tests—dead ends for all the slow-learning leaders, all the dropouts with ingenuity, inspiration, and charisma, all the reasonably intelligent and exceptionally ambitious men who have excelled in every test of combat but who know they will never rank high in a rote-administered Civil Service-type exam.

Each service plays a special part in this debate. Does the naval leadership really mean it when it claims, as did former Navy Secretary W. Graham Claytor, Jr., that 85 percent of all shipboard roles require no particular "physical dexterity"? Perhaps the former secretary ought at least to have acknowledged that, in the heat of battle, crises often arise in which Navy personnel must switch jobs suddenly and perform different and more onerous roles, sometimes entailing acute physical stress and risk of injury (i.e., combat).

The Marine Corps has always especially prided itself on "building men," and has traditionally attracted recruits eager to meet the challenges of stressful and blatantly virile training. But the new military, in the typical "to get along, go along" spirit of bureaucracy, has forced a steady softening of this regimen. Even without the Equal Rights Amendment, the Army has made women eligible for more than 95 percent of all job listings, announcing that "unit commanders are authorized to employ women to accomplish unit missions throughout the battlefield. . . ." At the discretion of the Secretary of the Army, women continue to be prohibited from "engaging an enemy with an individual or crew-served weapon while being exposed to direct enemy fire, a high probability of direct physical contact with the enemy's personnel and a substantial risk of capture." Beyond that technical statement, anything goes.

But if the Congress can enact a law allowing female midshipmen to undergo temporary training on ships not on combat missions, it can enact a law barring women cadets from foxholes and other battlefield positions, even while in training. With Equal Opportunity officers attached to all large military units, any sensible barriers will be subject to erosion unless they are explicitly and unmistakably written into statute.

Similarly, in the Air Force, 94 percent of jobs, including many noncombat pilot roles, are now open to women. If the combat restriction is removed, the Air Force will soon open all its jobs to women. But even assuming that female pilots were of equal ability in the air, many would be captured by the enemy and face—with the obvious sexual variations—the same stresses and exploitations that men know in P.O.W. camps. Is there good and sufficient reason for the United States to expose women to such danger and abuse?

The advocates of change—from the *Defense Management Journal* to the Brookings report and various internal analyses for the Defense Department—regard current problems as merely transitional. As the entire society moves toward liberation from the "irrational" constraints of sex roles, so it is believed, everything will work out famously. Commander Hunter is very hopeful about the promise of radical sex-role training in nursery schools, and Kathleen Carpenter sees inspiring progress in private industry. Jeanne Holm, a retired Air Force major general, maintains: "[The change] is inevitable . . . because that's the direction our culture is going."

All such assumptions are profoundly doubtful. Other countries have made similar efforts to force abandonment of sex roles. The result has been not an inevitable progression toward androgynous societies but—as with the Israeli kibbutzim—a return to traditional roles.[8] The Soviet Union made great changes after the Revolution, and again after the heavy male losses of World War II. Yet today the status and earnings of women, their university attendance levels, and their work in nontraditional fields have all reverted to earlier patterns.

Symbols are important in society. The Pentagon should consider whether it wishes to become a mere bureaucracy, on the order of the Department of Health and Human Services, or whether it would not do better to build on its classic role as a focus of male patriotism and a strong force in the socialization and enhancement of young men. There is deep evolutionary symbolism in the warrior mystique, the chivalric tradition, the aggressive glory of the martial style. In its pursuit of the favor of a basically antimilitary counterculture that, needless to say, will protest and picket in case of war, the Pentagon may not realize how close it has come to losing its supreme and most motivating assets.

Moreover, like most other wars in human history, the campaign against sex roles is in reality dominated not by women but by men. It joins two fundamentally conflicting forces. On the one hand, there is the powerful and basically anti-individualistic movement toward ever more fully rationalized bureaucracy, governed by objective and quantifiable standards. On the other hand, there is the essentially individualistic movement of militant feminism, which advocates a society without sex roles in order to promote personal fulfillment. These forces actually have little in common, yet they reinforce each other. The feminists, with their rhetoric of equal rights, lend to the bureaucrats a tone of moral inspiration which their policies would otherwise lack, while the bureaucrats lend to the feminists an air of tough-minded practicality. The consequence, however, will be a rationalized, still-male-dominated military bureaucracy that gives short shrift to the feminist critique of an excessively competitive, violent, and hierarchical world.

The ancient tradition against the use of women in combat embodies the deepest wisdom of the human race. It expresses the most basic imperatives of group survival: a nation or tribe that allows the loss of large numbers of its young women runs the risk of becoming permanently depopulated. The youthful years of women, far more than of men, are precious and irreplaceable.

Beyond this general imperative is the related need of every society to insure that male physical strength and aggressiveness are not directed against women. All societies teach their men to avoid physically fighting with women and, most often, to avoid competing face to face with them. All civilized societies train their men to protect and defend women. When these restraints break down—as in tribes like those studied by Colin Turnbull[9] and the Mundugumor, described by Margaret Mead[10]—the group tends to disintegrate completely and even to become extinct.

The military services, however, are unanimous in asserting that successful use of women in battlefield units depends on men overcoming their natural impulses to treat women differently and more considerately. The consequence of this latest demand for equality would be nothing more or less than a move toward barbarism.

Nevertheless, the serious subject of women in combat roles has been treated, even at the top, in a strangely lighthearted spirit. Instead of confronting the realities of battle conditions, advocates evoke cheery images of paneled offices and glistening machinery and intent young women peering through microscopes or programming computers. There are visions of strapping young corporals reacting instantly in crisis to melodiously trilled female commands; of boys and girls who hear always—through the roar of hormones during long months at sea—the cool voices of orderly bureaucracy and cooperation. Above all, the arguments advanced for expanding the warrior role of women are as pleasantly devoid as Disneyland of any vulgar mention of sex . . . or war.

Before we move ahead on this matter, however, we should consider the idea that combat is not family entertainment—that it is a real possibility, not chiefly a job opportunity. While the Soviet Union's nearly all-male armies grow to a size three times ours and terrorists pursue American prey around the world, it would be unfortunate for American leaders to give the impression that they regard combat chiefly as an obstacle to women's rights.

CHAPTER 13

The Jobs Front

Between the physical world and the strobe-lit stage of the media—between fact and phantasmagoria—American families struggle for footing in the valley of the shadow. Monsters lurk in the darkness; we are afraid. We turn to the experts, seeking guidance and light, but every map they offer seems only to lead us deeper into the slough. We consult the Networks, but they throng the shores of the deep, broadcasting variations on the Loch Ness News.

Stalking now into view is a unisex chimera. You can't miss it. From TV green room to blue movie, nursery to news central, now looms the amazing story of the "sexual revolution in employment." Proclaimed and embodied by blond priestesses of network news, at once fiercely female and strangely sexless, and celebrated from the thrones of talk-show kings, it emerges in alternating news reports and prime-time fictions that melt together in our minds in an almost inseparable flow of images.

In the media parade, sultry detectives belted in karate follow firepersons glossy with bright red lipstick; Charlie's Angels and Rather's maidens race after police cars; mascaraed West Pointers march on with hard-hatted construction queens and hod carriettes, glamorous dealers in corporate leverage, lesbian mayors, women dunking basketballs, and space cadettes actually tumbling in space; vengeful call girls flaunt their guns on "The Streets of San Francisco" and the streets of New York—all interspersed with homosexual magnates and middle linebackers, men finding new fulfillment in nursery and needlepoint, and epicene authors and psychologists of every imaginable sex bemoaning the tortures of being a man or a woman, or not. Before this vivid show in *son et lumière,* our own very lives somehow pale to inconsequence. Our very bodies fade away in our minds, replaced by the strange creatures on the screen and their manic messages of change.

But surely this time the change is real. Drastic shifts in sex roles do seem to be sweeping through America. Though allegedly hobbled by sex discrimination, women everywhere seem to exhibit career patterns increasingly like men's. If feminists continue to complain that the movement toward employment equality is painfully slow, sociologists offer endless data to prove that it is inexorable. Even the careful statisticians at the Department of Labor project nearly equal male and female job-force participation and similar performance by 1995.[1]

The evidence mounts, and prophets climb it to declaim new sermons from its heights. Since 1890, work-force involvement by women between the ages of twenty-five and forty-four has soared from 15 percent to 60 percent, with the pace of change tripling after 1950.[2] Since World War II, even married women with children under age six have joined the fray, with the proportion of these young mothers in the work force rising from under 10 percent to over 50 percent by 1983.[3] Peter Drucker, the shrewdest of social analysts, declared, "We are busily unmaking one of the proudest social achievements in the nineteenth century, which was to take married women out of the work force so they could devote themselves to family and children."[4]

At the same time, the portentous media tales will show that women are crowding into nontraditional jobs. Between 1960 and 1986, the female share of professional jobs increased from 38 to over 50 percent and women's share of management jobs doubled from 14 percent to more than one-third.[5] Since 1970, reported sociologist Andrew Hacker in *The New York Times Magazine,* the proportion of female packinghouse butchers rose by one-third; nearly 80 percent of new bartending jobs went to women; the share of women lawyers rose from 2 percent to 15 percent; and the female share of banking and financial-management jobs surged from 9 percent to 38 percent.[6]

Altogether, Hacker and other analysts contend, women are displacing more and more men at work. While female employment soars, male work-force participation plummets. Between 1960 and 1984, the proportion of adult men in the work force dropped from 86 percent to 78 percent. Some 58 percent of all men now retire before age sixty-five compared to 36 percent as recently as 1970.[7] By 1995, the Labor Department projects, only 65 percent of men aged fifty-five to sixty-four will remain in the labor force.[8] Perhaps more significant in the long run is the substantial drop in employment and rise in unemployment among young men, particularly young blacks, which has also paralleled female entry into the work force.

The future apparently promises yet more displacement of men from high-paying work and more movement into lower-paid, traditionally female occupations. Girls now outperform boys in high school. Women comprise some 52 percent of all college undergraduates and a steadily rising share of all holders of advanced degrees, including close to one-third of all degrees in law, business, accounting, and medicine.[9] Meanwhile, the number of male flight attendants rose from virtually none to over 10,000, male voices became common at Directory Assistance, men began stripping on stage before ogling secretaries, TV journalists, and reporters from national magazines, and in a 1983 poll 21 percent of all married men declared they would prefer to stay home and care for the children if they could.[10]

In addition, many pundits contend that the evolving American economy will increasingly favor women throughout the job market, from clerical roles to the highest echelons of management. Not only is male physical strength increasingly irrelevant to most jobs, but male aggressiveness and drive are also alleged to be counterproductive in the age of information and services. The prevailing fashions in business leadership, epitomized by *In Search of Excellence*[11] and the best-selling texts on Japanese management, stress "soft" personal skills, intuitive guidance through communication and consensus, not the rigid hierarchies and controls favored by the macho businessmen of the past. The information and service sectors, according to a popular theory, will offer ever wider opportunities to women as time passes and these industries increasingly dominate the economy. Indeed, some analysts assert, feminine skills will tend to prevail over male aggressiveness in all the major businesses of the future.

With more than 50 percent of all women at work, with divorces and separations soaring, and with many men in flight from job and family, reference to the classic pattern of male provider and female housewife prompts only smirks and titters from audiences of college students, Congressional aides, and other knowledgeable folk during the mid-1980s in America. The feminists may have failed to pass the Equal Rights Amendment, but they seem to have achieved the much more important goal of transforming the lives and attitudes of American men and women. Even if women do not quickly gain power in America's executive suites and boardrooms, so it is said, they are setting the styles for the future and their attainment of near-equality in business is only a matter of time. The saga of sexual revolution is repeatedly told in the media, it would seem, largely because it dramatically continues to unfold. Every year's statistics break the previous records and ever more graphic images arise to signal the passing of the sexual concepts of masculine and feminine on which Americans have based their lives and expectations.

Now if you are an ordinary man or woman and the changes are real, the trend looms as a monster indeed, initially titillating perhaps, but finally menacing the future of your children and the settled habits of your own home and marriage. But closer scrutiny shows this "revolution"—for all its statistical weight and anecdotal pervasiveness—is just another shadow in the Loch Ness News.

A reader, after all, may be excused for remaining skeptical toward the story of a historic change in human behavior that after being featured in the media for twenty years can still be presented as a scoop. The accounts of major change in the roles of men and women in America in fact stand as a prime example of the pitfalls of statistical sociology and journalistic hype. There are many changes buffeting American life, but a transformation of sexuality is not among them. Despite massive contrary incentives from government policy, women in this century have not increased their work effort or contributions to family income.[12]

Much of the statistical change in job patterns cited in the stories of sexual revolution reflects instead the industrial revolution. As recently as eighty years ago, most American families were engaged in agriculture; this proportion has dropped to 3 percent. That is truly a revolution, and it has transformed everything else, including the official statistics of women in the work force. Female entrance into market employment has in fact merely lagged behind women's departure from farms. On farms, moreover, as every farmer knows, women did not restrict themselves to the kitchen and boudoir. Women in agriculture worked very hard beyond the hearth and cribside, commonly performing an array of jobs requiring far more onerous physical labor and longer hours than their current work.

Work-force participation by single women has not increased since 1950.[13] The key to the statistical change on the jobs front is the proportion of married women in the work force. But like their grandmothers on the farm, the vast majority of married women seek part-time or seasonal work convenient to their homes. Only 35 percent of all women between twenty and sixty-five, and 39 percent of women between the ages of twenty-five and forty-four, held full-time year-round jobs in 1983.[14] In intact families, only a little more than one-fifth of the wives worked full time all year, and women in intact families earned only 16.5 percent of the total family incomes.[15] Between 1960 and 1980, women earners in intact families actually reduced their incomes as a share of married men's, from 40 percent to 38.1.[16] Women show no signs of significantly encroaching on the man's role as principal provider.

American women perform full-time work chiefly as they always have: when they are forced to, usually by the desertion, divorce, death, or scarce earnings of their husbands. Women also are living some 12 percent longer than men and have a longer potential span in the work force after their children grow up. The influx of women into jobs reflects in part the greater number of divorced and single women and in part the abrupt decline in childbearing after the post-World War II surge of fertility—not any basic change in the motives and roles of men and women.

Contrary to most statistical analysis, women do just as well as men in getting what they want from their education and their jobs. They simply have different goals and priorities. Necessarily playing the central child-care role, women do not seek income as the top priority in their work. Commendably enough, they demand jobs near their homes, mostly part time and flexible, or with clearly defined hours—and they get them.

The increase in female education and credentials does not portend increased female competition for male jobs. Women do not compete in the same way. A study by the Institute for Research on Poverty at the University of Wisconsin—a liberal group financed largely by the government—demonstrates a drastic difference between the two sexes in their use of "earnings capacity," defined in terms of age, education, credentials, experience, location, physical health, alleged discrimination, and other determinants of potential earnings.[17] The Institute study showed that married men of working age use 87 percent of their earnings capacity, while comparable married women use only 33 percent. Thus married men exploit their earnings opportunities 2.3 times as much as married women.[18]

More significant, though, was the difference in the pattern of work performed by the two sexes, depending on their marital status and earnings capacity. Married men with the most earnings capacity also exploited it most effectively, working longer hours and more resourcefully the more education and credentials they possessed. By contrast, the more earnings capacity commanded by married women the less they used it. In other words, the more education and credentials possessed by a married woman the less likely she is to work full time all year at a highly demanding and remunerative job. While the earnings capacity utilization rates of married men rose from 84 to 94 percent from the bottom to the top tenth of earnings capacity, the earnings capacity utilization of married women dropped nearly one-third, from 35 percent to 24 percent, or to a level about one-quarter of their husbands'.[19]

The Institute based its study on data from the early 1970s, but later statistics confirm the general pattern, with the absolute and percentage gap between male and female earnings rising dramatically as age and schooling increases. In 1983 women with graduate education earned little more than men with four years of high school, even with both working full time all year round.[20] But the female college graduates and graduate-degree holders were far less likely to be working full time at their most remunerative possible employment.

A Harris public opinion poll shows that these data reflect basic differences in attitudes between the sexes. Unlike working men, who overwhelmingly prefer full-time jobs, working women express a preference for part-time work by a 47 to 17 percent margin. The women with the highest earnings capacity—managerial, professional, and executive women—preferred part-time work by a 51 to 19 percent margin.[21]

A 1982 Harris poll indicated that 39 percent of women would prefer to work only at home and another 14 percent would prefer to do only volunteer work, making a total of 53 percent who do not want to be in the job market outside the home at all. Since another 32 percent want part-time work only, this survey indicates that just 12 percent of all American women desire full-time employment in the labor force outside their own household.[22]

By the mid-1980s, women in large numbers were using entrepreneurial activity to fulfill their preference for work in the home. From knitting mittens to selling real estate and writing software packages for personal computers, women were increasingly launching small businesses in their homes. Between 1972 and 1982, the percent of self-employed women workers in nonagricultural industries rose from 25.6 percent to 31.8 percent of the total number of self-employed in this category[23] and in 1984 and 1985 women were actually forming sole proprietorships faster than men. Once again, though, the statistics do not suggest any female usurpation of the provider role. The average net income of female-operated businesses in 1980 was $2,200. The average net income of the most common such firm—a retail establishment—was $497.[24] Moreover, the average earnings of all female-run firms were dropping in relation to the earnings of similar male-run companies.

Such figures confirm the persistence of traditional sex roles. Women seek education and credentials chiefly in order to gain more time with their families, while men seek these qualifications in order to earn larger incomes and provide for their wives and children. Female physicians, for example, see 38 percent fewer patients per hour and work 22 percent fewer hours than male physicians;[25] female lawyers see fewer clients than male lawyers; female professors write fewer books and research papers than male professors.[26] In general, women in their prime earning years are by various measures between seven and eleven times more likely to leave the work force voluntarily than men are, and have only half as much experience in their jobs.[27] As has been demonstrated in several econometric studies, such differences in behavior amply explain the difference between male and female earnings without any recourse to claims of discrimination.[28]

Census data from November 1981 show no signs of significant blurring of work-force roles. Although the number of male secretaries and telephone operators was increasing, their share of the total was actually dropping.[29] Although women were more frequently interviewed by the media after they took masculine jobs, they usually left them quickly. The share of women construction workers, truck drivers, and other blue-collar employees scarcely rose at all. Federal contractors and firms such as the phone company under court order to hire women in unconventional roles almost universally failed to meet their quotas because of female resistance. Although local governments were forced to relax their physical standards and hire a few female firepersons and police officers, in general the revolution of sex roles in employment was still chiefly a media event by 1986.

The thesis that future economic and technical trends will decisively favor women in jobs is also highly questionable. It is true that male physical strength is becoming less important in the age of information and service industries. But men's distinctive aptitudes are not entirely physical. Male domination in the sedentary intellectual game of chess is virtually as great as the male lead in lifting weights. All but two out of the hundreds of international grand masters named over the years have been men despite millions of female competitors in the Soviet Union.[30] In work requiring similar feats of concentration and abstract reasoning, men now hold the vast majority of all the more exacting high-technology jobs in America, and this pattern seems likely to continue. In high-school computer classes and computer camps for teenagers, boys continue to outnumber girls between three and four to one and outperform them by a still larger margin.[31]

The reason for these gender differences in aptitude and performance is the difference in genetic endowment and psychological propensity between the sexes. Just as girls from earliest childhood consistently excel boys in all tests of verbal aptitude, male aptitudes are better adapted to advanced technology, with its abstract and mathematical base. In a study of 9,927 exceptional students by researchers at Johns Hopkins, the mathematical portion of the Scholastic Aptitude Test was administered on six different occasions between 1972 and 1979 to seventh- and eighth-graders with equal preparation. The authors' talent search found 32.5 percent more boys than girls, though the girls exceeded the average for their sex by a greater margin than the boys did. Overall, 7.8 percent of the boys, but only 1.7 percent of the girls, scored over 600 out of the 800 possible points, and all the scores over 760, including all the 800 scores, were by boys.[32] Contrary to the view that the large male edge in mathematics is socially conditioned and will tend to disappear as time passes, the male lead is most overwhelming among the best mathematicians—among scholars of both sexes who concentrate on mathematics throughout their student careers.

Nor do modern management trends especially favor women. In most job and business rivalries, male aggressiveness and technical aptitudes will remain crucial for the foreseeable future. Japanese management theory may seem to favor female approaches, but women are virtually absent from actual Japanese management. In fact, women's work-force participation has risen little in Japan since 1970. Japanese firms in the forefront of high technology are completely male-dominated. In general, in the U.S. and around the world, the more advanced the technology and the more entrepreneurial the industry the fewer women rise to commanding positions.

Trends in manufacturing, moreover, suggest no major shift in favor of female employment in lower-level jobs. The male mechanical aptitudes that still give men between 95 and 99 percent of all jobs in mechanics, repair, machinery, carpentry, construction, and metal crafts[33] will remain vitally important in the service economy. In addition, these aptitudes are readily convertible into skills in the maintenance of computers and other electronic appliances.

The assembly-line roles currently performed by women in technical manufacturing firms, however, are likely to continue to move overseas or give way to automation and robotics. Similarly, the computer revolution, striking at routine clerical functions, will tend to counteract the sexual revolution in employment in service firms. Although women will continue to play vital roles throughout the economy, nothing in the current direction of technical progress seems likely to give them a substantially greater role outside the home than they have today. In fact, the technology of computers and telecommunications may well accelerate the current return of cottage industries and home offices which allow women to remain near their children.

Current female contributions in the job market, like the historic female role in agriculture, chiefly complement rather than compete with male work. The alarmist view that women entering the job force will take jobs from men resembles the notion that immigrants take jobs from citizens. The job market is not a zero-sum game, with a limited number of slots distributed from above. Entrants into the job market create employment in several ways. They invent jobs for themselves and others, and they contribute to the flexibility, efficiency, and adaptability of the work force.

New workers of any sex cannot be employed for long unless the value of their service is greater than the value of their pay. They must produce more than they consume—in other words, create new wealth. Entrants to the job market generate new wealth that flows into other parts of the economy, creating new jobs for others. They launch new industries in the U.S. and allow other industries to stay here rather than move overseas. They foster business expansion that reverberates throughout the job market. For example, new office workers, chiefly female, feed demand for office builders, office-machine designers, computer repairers, office maintenance crews, and office-equipment entrepreneurs, all mostly male, in ever-widening circles of supply and demand impossible to follow or quantify but central to the success of capitalist economies.

During the very period that women and immigrants flooded the U.S. job market, the U.S. economy proportionately created more jobs for men than any other major economy in the world. During the decade of the 1970s, while the European economies created no net new jobs at all, the U.S. economy generated some 19 million new jobs, some 7 million of them for men, including most of the higher-paid full-time slots. While the female entry continued in 1983 and 1984, the U.S. created 7 million new jobs, nearly half of them for men, with steadily increasing real wages and rapid productivity growth. In 1985, over 60 percent of the adult population was employed, a peacetime record.

Contrary to the impression that men are rapidly leaving the work force, male participation rates have scarcely declined at all in the prime earning years between twenty-five and fifty-four.[34] The decline came among older men and was caused not by female employment but by government policy. Despite gains in health and longevity and improvements in working conditions, benefits for retirement and disability rose twice as fast as wages and salaries throughout the 1970s.[35] In addition, conditions for granting these payments were drastically liberalized.

Meanwhile, tax rates on incomes rose rapidly through inflation and through social-security levies to pay for the early retirements. As the supply-siders say, if you tax something, you will get less of it; and if you subsidize something, you will get more of it. During the 1970s, the U.S. increased taxes on work and increased subsidies for disability and retirement.[36] That early retirements and disability claims soared while work effort declined among the eligible elderly was a simple and predictable effect of policy. The decline in employment among young men was also not attributable to female entry into the job market. Here the situation was more complex, but the chief factors were government policies that favored extended schooling and tax and welfare policies that caused families to break down, depriving young men of role models and male disciplines.

Regardless of the intentions of government officials, women refuse to behave like men in the work force. Even in November 1980—the final year of a Democratic administration under constant pressure to hire and promote women—only 7 percent of the employees in the top three GS ratings were women, while more than three-quarters in the bottom grades were.[37] In fact, the pattern of employment in the federal government would suffice to justify an antidiscrimination suit if it were a private institution. Yet the federal government is not discriminating against women any more than private companies are. Women quite simply and commendably are discriminating in favor of their own families.

Similarly, women in Israeli kibbutzim have increasingly insisted on the maintenance of traditional roles. Despite a fervent initial commitment by the founders to socialist unisex theories, an intensive study covering some forty years, three generations, and 100,000 men and women showed that each successive generation moved more decisively toward traditional roles. Today the kibbutzim show the most distinct sex roles in Israeli society.[38]

It is often alleged that there are many women who are as "masculine" in a particular role as many men, and that many men display traits more "feminine" than many women. Therefore, it is said, the very concepts of masculinity and feminity are meaningless or irrelevant for particular individuals even if applicable to the "average." But no matter how nurturant a man may be, he cannot bear children; nor will their mothers be inclined to give him prime responsibility for child-rearing in the early years. Regardless of the existence of "feminine" men, all societies must depend mostly on women to perform these roles. The roles that women dominate will necessarily be seen as "feminine" and will thus inevitably feel uncomfortable even to many men who would otherwise perform them freely and well.

The fact that *many* women are more aggressive, physically strong, or technically adept than *most* men, moreover, makes relatively little difference in the organization of roles requiring these abilities. In each function or hierarchy of the society, women will not have to compete merely with average men. They will have to compete with those men whose aptitudes lead them to specialize in the particular task; in many economic activities, they have to compete with the best from the entire world. It does not help women chess players or wrestlers or mathematicians or microchip entrepreneurs or commodity traders that they are better at these activities than millions of men. What matters is that only a tiny number of women are willing or able to compete near the top male level in any of these fields.

Greater male commitment and aggressiveness mean that men will tend to dominate any roles not related to special female propensities and abilities. These roles will be felt as "masculine" even when women perform them. With roles constantly changing in all dynamic economies, some exceptional women throughout history have excelled in male activities. But these women are always seen and celebrated as exceptions, as prodigies. They pose no likelihood of widespread usurpation of men's places in the work force. Indeed their contributions foster economic growth and opportunity for men.

Although women are not taking jobs from men, the feminist movement is plunging many women into a strange state of suspi-

cion and resentment, fraught with illusions about the U.S. economic system and the possibility of radical change. Many otherwise
intelligent women, gulled by the media, continue to believe in
widespread discrimination as the source of all their trials. Regardless of how rapidly and spectacularly they rise, they continue to feel
uneasy, and by their very complaints about sexism reveal their own
discomfort in masculine activity.

A case in point is Karen Valenstein, an E. F. Hutton executive
featured on the cover of *The New York Times Magazine* and celebrated for some ten pages inside for her amazing achievements.[39]
Earning $250,000 a year at age thirty-eight as a First Vice-President
specializing in public utility finance, she told the *Times* she had
overcome enormous obstacles of sexism and hostility. "You have to
be 30 percent better than a man to make it," she claims. She fails to
explain why she—and her oppressed sisters—do not leave to form
their own firms and gain the benefits of this superiority for themselves. Jeane Kirkpatrick, a rather obscure professor promoted to
U.N. ambassador and national eminence by the Reagan administration despite being a Democrat, began whining about sexism and
discrimination when that same administration failed to put her in
charge of U.S. national-security policy. Feminist critics of Silicon
Valley continually speak of sex discrimination as the reason for the
dearth of women in the high echelons of these fiercely competitive
firms, as if they could afford to forgo any conceivable advantage in
their rivalry with the Japanese.

In their fantasies of discrimination, many essentially moderate
feminists advocate extreme and destructive policies that threaten the
prosperity and freedom of both sexes. Faced with the failure of their
campaign to change the essential behavior of men and women
through the ordinary processes of democratic capitalism, the feminists are now turning to judicial and legislative coercion. They are
urging measures that menace not only the sex roles on which the
family is founded but also the freedoms at the very heart of free
enterprise. Perhaps most threatening are their proposals for "equal
pay for jobs of comparable worth," often called the leading feminist
issue of the 1980s.

"Equal pay for comparable worth" is an unexceptionable idea.
Because everyone supports it, it makes an attractive slogan. The
problem is defining the "worth" of a job beyond the willingness of

employers and consumers to pay for it. All the characteristics that the feminists claim are important—skill, effort, responsibility, working conditions, experience, educational requirements, and the like—are in fact irrelevant if consumers (or taxpayers) do not want the product at the price required by the "comparable pay."

The ability to build an elegant mechanical adding machine requires more training, skill, experience, and responsibility—and entails work under harsher conditions—than using a word processor or driving a truck. But building a mechanical adding machine is worthless, just as many jobs richly paid today (such as antidiscrimination lawyer) may well be seen as worthless in the future as tastes and technologies change. The idea that jobs have an intrinsic worth of their own is medieval in spirit and would return the world to the stagnant system of feudal guilds. Even the "contribution to institutional objectives," cited by some as an appropriate measure of worth, cannot be calculated objectively. That means it could only be calculated subjectively—and arbitrarily—by bureaucrats. Comparable worth would overthrow the right of workers to choose their own jobs, negotiate their own pay, and prove their own worth and grant this power to the state. It is indeed, as Michael Levin has put it, "the feminist road to socialism."[40]

Capitalism works because it allows the continual flow of creative contributions from the bottom, from new workers and new businesses relentlessly redefining jobs and products and testing them in the marketplace. Under capitalism any man or woman with a new idea, however unpopular or "unqualified"—even living in a foreign country that trades with the capitalist homeland—can challenge the special interests and privileges, the inappropriate job definitions and pay relationships, and the entrenched cells of fat and inefficiency that afflict an economy. A comparable worth system would be fatal to this process of renewal. In particular it would be deadly to the interests of the immigrants and outsiders, often devoid of credentials and initially illiterate in the prevailing language, who play vital roles in the entrepreneurial ventures that impel growth and progress around the world.

In place of a relatively free job market, comparable worth would require a federal bureaucracy to determine the appropriate pay for each job and each set of credentials and qualifications and to enforce the law throughout millions of businesses in the inevitable flux of economic change. Utterly subjective despite a show of scientific pettifoggery and precision, comparable worth evaluations would be open to endless litigation and challenge, and thus to arbitrary power. Like the system of apartheid that currently paralyzes South African employment with a Byzantine maze of rules and regulations, comparable worth would require endless interference in the job market, classifying every function as an ever-changing economy and channeling the appropriately credentialed men and women into the appropriate niches. The result would be stagnation. That so many feminists have endorsed the idea shows their complete incomprehension of the needs of a prosperous economy.

It is unlikely that many feminists have any idea of the totalitarian implications of their ideas. In practice, comparable worth could never be widely enforced even if it were enacted. It would probably bog down even in the federal government itself and would serve only to slow private economic growth and opportunity with another layer of particularly intrusive bureaucracy. Comparable worth is thus chiefly significant because it reveals the inner logic and agenda of more moderate feminist ideas.

Most feminist proposals seem designed to establish the working mother as the social norm by making it impossible for most male providers to support their families alone. The feminist attack on the social-security system for giving housewives a right to the husband's benefits after he dies; the subsidies for day care; the affirmative-action quotas for women who pursue careers outside the home—all such measures seek to establish the careerist woman as the national standard and incapacitate the woman who tries to care for her own children.

Allan Carlson has explained how a similar policy worked in Sweden.[41] Until 1965, Swedes spurned a quarter-century of feminist indoctrination and followed a social pattern similar to the U.S. Only a quarter of mothers of children under seven entered the work force and more than half of them held part-time jobs. Over the years, however, the Swedish socialists, under pressure from feminists led by Alva Myrdal, managed slowly to destroy the essential supports of the nuclear family. The entire present agenda of American feminism—from universal day care and family-planning programs to paternity leaves for fathers—was eventually enacted.

Carlson writes: "With the homemaker declared to be 'a dying race,' legal changes removed the special protections afforded women in marriage. Changes in Swedish tax law essentially eliminated the joint return for a married couple, and have left all persons paying the same tax, whether alone, married but childless, or married with children. . . ."[42] Moreover, marginal Swedish income taxes were increased to nearly 100 percent at modest income levels, making it all but impossible to support a family on one income by extra personal effort. "Swedish welfare policy was also altered to discourage maternal care of preschool children. Housing and tax benefits are effectively curtailed if families decide to care for their children and refuse to place them in day care centers [and these parents also lose] benefits such as free children's meals and diapers."[43]

By 1986 these policies had failed to induce Swedish women to perform men's roles or men to assume an equal role with children. But according to Carlson, laws were proposed to "force men to shoulder their responsibilities" in the home. School officials were ordered to "redouble their efforts to challenge conventional stereotypes" that after fifty years of feminist indoctrination still orient Swedish schoolgirls toward "traditionally female fields." Women still earn less than men throughout the economy and are virtually absent from the higher echelons of the established multinational corporations that utterly dominate the Swedish private sector.

Nonetheless, the Swedish policy was dramatically successful in several important ways. By 1984 the official "poverty line" for a family of four in Sweden was approximately 40 percent above the average annual wage. Therefore only the rich (chiefly families with sources of funds outside Sweden) could maintain a family on one income. The male role as principal provider was effectively abolished for most of the population. This policy, though, resulted not in more egalitarian marriages, but in the obsolescence of marriage itself.

Not only did the rate of illegitimacy rise to over 40 percent of all live births,[44] but the marriage rate fell to the lowest level ever recorded in world demographic data. Despite the world's most ambitious programs of sex education and family planning, despite the widespread issuance of free contraceptives, the abortion rate soared to a 1981 level just below the U.S. rate of 43 percent of all live births.[45] The Swedish people voted against the officially favored egalitarian marriage by mostly not marrying at all. The birthrate fell to a point 40 percent below the replacement rate required to maintain zero population growth.[46] Despite one of the world's best-educated populations and some of the world's most resourceful large companies, the Swedish economy foundered. With the industrial world's highest tax rates came also a governmental deficit in the early 1980s some three times as high as America's huge shortfall as a share of GNP.

The United States is enacting many of the policies that brought sexual suicide to Sweden. Despite the defeat of the Equal Rights Amendment and universal day care, the feminists are gaining their ends piecemeal. In particular, the decline in the value of the child deduction has shifted the tax burden massively onto families with children. Through court decisions in favor of comparable worth, through the infiltration of the schools by feminist texts and teachers, through the day-care tax credits and other subsidies for the two-earner family, and through the rapid erosion of the joint income-tax return and the housewife's right to social security, feminists are winning quietly by legal and legislative action what they cannot win in referenda.

The central lesson of the Swedish experience is the profound and irretrievable damage inflicted by a policy of driving mothers of small children out of the home and into the work force. Women in the home are not performing some optional role that can be more efficiently fulfilled by the welfare state. Women in the home are not "wasting" their human resources. The role of the mother is the paramount support of civilized human society. It is essential to the socialization both of men and of children. The maternal love and nurture of small children is an asset that can be replaced, if at all, only at vastly greater cost. Such attention is crucial to raising children into healthy and productive citizens. Moreover, the link of men through marriage to the support of particular children is crucial to male motivation and productivity.

The provider role of men not only gives the society the benefit of a lifetime of hard work oriented toward long-term goals. It also channels and disciplines male energies and aggressions that otherwise turn against that society. By contrast, full-time work by mothers of small children comes at a serious twofold cost: first, the loss of the immeasurable social benefit of the mother's loving care for her child; second, the frequent loss of the husband's full-time concentration on his career. The yield of the mother's job to the economy or the man's help in the home only rarely can offset these costs of her employment. The society will pay the costs one way or another: not only through tremendous outlays for day care but also through economic declines, population loss, juvenile delinquency, crime, mental illness, alcoholism, addiction, and divorce.

Together with the tragic breakdown of the American black family, the Swedish example should disabuse Americans of the illusion that it can't happen here. Family breakdown and demoralization can occur with frightening suddenness when government policy destroys the role of the male provider in the family. The alternative to traditional family roles is not a unisex family; it is sexual suicide.

CHAPTER 14

Sex and
the Social Scientist

To examine the bases of feminist claims and policies, it is often necessary to ponder the field of sociology. Contrary to the usual view, sociology can be fun. Indeed, in recent years sociological studies, particularly researches of a feminist bent, have even verged on becoming quite divertingly raunchy. In leading sociological journals, for example, one can discover the amazing fact that publicly supported colleges and universities in the United States today give courses in sexual behavior, featuring, as audiovisual aids, the regular display of movies with titles like *Ping-Pong Orgy* and *Western Lust*. These institutions also conduct and publish studies based on solar research at nude beaches, frequent visits to and interviews at houses of prostitution, and comparative surveys of pickup techniques at singles bars and bus stations (a study conducted at Harvard).

One of the most prestigiously raunchy of all social-science journals is called *Transaction/Society*, or just plain *Society*. It is, in general, a serious and valuable magazine, often even stuffy, published at Rutgers, New Jersey's state university, and now edited by the estimable Irving Louis Horowitz. From time to time, however, it deals with the subject of sex and goes altogether wacko.[1]

In recent years, for example, *Society* has offered in-depth studies on female weight lifting as a paradigm of social progress,[2] on women camping out with men on bivouacs as a plausible advance for the military,[3] on prostitutes in Nevada as social prophets, on

155

pornography as an educational tool, on rape and marriage, and on all the favored forms of sexual deviance. One is subtly given to understand that prostitutes themselves practice a kind of folk sociology, seeing through the sham and hypocrisy of the housewife's similar role; that pornography is useful in overcoming sexism; and that sexuality can be deviant only in the presumably sick mind of the beholder. In 1979, under the title "The Big Toe, Armpits, and Natural Perfumes: Notes on the Production of Sexual Ecstasy," the magazine offered ten pages of titillating excerpts from the leading sex manuals, followed by a few paragraphs of professorial punditry.[4]

Because sociology affects to be valuefree, no moral position is taken on most of these matters. But whether weight lifters or soldiers, men who display a natural resentment toward women invading their turf are gently derided. Masculinity is always a gaffe in the world of social science. In one article, the magazine also came out quite strongly against rape, because it is a crime that illegitimately discriminates between men and women. The article warned, however, that harsh enforcement of the rape laws is not the answer, because it would culpably discriminate against the perpetrators of the crime (who are no more guilty than other men), and in the process do blacks "an enormous injustice."[5] In general, though, *Society* does not explicitly violate its stance of benign objectivity toward the sexual phenomena it discusses, unless it is faced with some obvious and extreme evil, such as the nuclear family, which was revealed to be the source and locus of most violence in America.

Society does not confine its light to the pages of its magazine. It has also published many books. In one issue of *Society* were advertised eight expensive volumes. The first one was entitled *The Madam as Entrepreneur: Political Economy of a House of Prostitution*. This book, it says, "utilizes an interactionist perspective with data gathered via intensive personal interviews over a period of four years." The second book is entitled simply *Deviant Life-Styles;* as the advertisement hurriedly reassures us, it offers "no positive or negative judgments on the definition of deviance." Thus the voyeurism would be uncontaminated by boring theories or opinions, of the sort that ruins so much otherwise hard-core sociology with nearly impenetrable thickets of redeeming social value.

The same issue of *Society*, for example, contained an article on "Alternative Life-Styles" (sexual deviance to you) by a Dr. James W. Raney,[6] whose prose virtually groans under its burdens of professional certification and prestige. Dr. Raney serves not only as "senior research associate at the Center for Policy Research," but also as "founder and director of the Center for the Study of Innovative Life-Styles, and consultant to the University of Southern California Medical School and to Bowman Gray School of Medicine," among other listed institutions. In other words, he must be quite at home in the offices of HHS and the health-oriented foundations.

His article announces a "new age," the one in which we currently live. It is characterized, so he says, by the end of the family "as the basic unit of society" and by rampant and unprecedented sieges of what he calls "sexually open relating." Born yesterday like most in his trade, he thus finds novelty and revolution in the most venerable vices, even in the world's oldest profession. But before the article is over, he permits a drear paragraph of responsible deflation. He admits he doesn't know whether this revolutionary new age is waxing or waning. "Only time and national probability sample research will tell us how many people are involved . . . ," he writes. But we are not to give up hope, for "such research has been proposed and is now under consideration for federal funding." Of course.

It should not be supposed that for all its remorseless secularity— its treatment of religion chiefly as a mental illness or social disease— *Society* is entirely devoid of the voice of the Church. A typical Catholic contributor is Robert Francoeur, a scientist-theologian who has long pursued a dream of human reproduction by test tube as his own particular holy grail of liberation.

To Francoeur and his kind there seems nothing in the world quite so consummately divine as an American professor of sociology experiencing human growth and fulfillment and open sexual relating with a pretty coed on the pill, after several hours spent banishing all sex-role inhibitions by watching pornographic films. In *Society*, Francoeur writes: "Hopefully ten, twenty, or perhaps more years from now Americans will be comfortable enough with our sexuality that we will not need to use explicit sexual behavior films" in the classroom. But until then, he makes clear in his article, students in his course at Fairleigh Dickinson University will be required to attend a weekend workshop that he terms a "sexarama."[7]

It begins with soft-core openers—"a little lighthearted campy film on nudity," as he puts it—and then, presumably for the delectation of any fruit-lovers, or fruit, in the audience, continues with a short, depicting "a sensuous orange being peeled and eaten." Then our liberated theologian gets down to business: nine full hours of movies on "the varieties of sex, with male and female masturbation; male and female homosexuality, and a couple of paraphilias films—sado-masochism, beastiality [sic], and the like." After that comes "a brief discussion with the whole group of what is normal"; and—because Mr. Francoeur, remember, is a theologian—there follows, in a gruesome touch, "a comment by a priest."

"We close," writes Francoeur, "with a film of a 65-year-old man and a 58-year-old woman, with student reactions ranging over shock that their grandparents or parents might still copulate, really enjoy it, and be more innovative than the young experts are."

So much for "modern" theology. There seems to be something about the great leveler, sex, that transforms the most somberly learned social scientists, editing the most highfalutin magazines, into prophets of a fatuous sociology of wet dreams. Few of the articles, however, are so much fun to read. Social scientists, with few exceptions, write boringly as if their lives depended upon it, as their grants and salaries surely do. They must, after all, conceal all the unreported prurient interest that they earn on their government money.

What is interesting about these kinds of books and articles is the strange spectacle they afford, of high-ranking professors at prestigious state universities palling around with pimps and prostitutes, poring over pornography, sampling sessions of sexual therapy, investigating behavior at homosexual bars, attending orgies at Esalen—all, ultimately, at the expense of the American taxpayer, who supports what are humorously termed our institutions of higher learning.

All these expressions of the hunger for knowledge and enlightenment on our state-subsidized campuses pass without any protest by the federal government—provided, of course, that the student audiences are chosen with due regard for the inclusion of appropriate numbers of blacks, women, native Americans, and persons with Hispanic surnames; that the classrooms in which the pornography is exhibited are equipped with wheelchair runways; that dubbed versions are made available for Spanish-speaking students; that no discrimination is shown against persons with a history of alcoholism or drug addiction; that the faculty involved reasonably reflects the demography of the relevant human resource base; that all the textbooks and other publications used in this research are entirely free of language that tends to reinforce invidious sex-role or racial stereotypes; and, finally, provided that students required to attend these films and other educational exhibits are not made to pledge allegiance to the American flag or say any prayers.

This order of priorities—the condemnation of discrimination above all other offenses—escapes wild guffaws from serious people chiefly because it is affirmed solemnly by social science and its techniques. Although sociologists tend to scorn the proposition that sexual promiscuity or pornography is evil or destructive, they hasten to condemn discrimination at every turn of every essay that even touches upon the subject. Discrimination, even by sex, is regarded to be an unquestionable crime.

This attitude is not accidental. It expresses the deepest vulnerability of statistical social analysis and modeling. In explaining social behavior—whether productivity, crime, marriage, or fertility—the social scientist wants above all to avoid the murky domains of psychology and religion, affiliation and aspiration. Warped and webbed with familial and ethnic loyalties, sexual drives and religious commitments, unconscious compulsions and spurious public rationales, the behavior of the sexes in society would completely confound the social scientist without the use of heroic simplifications.

In general, the larger the data base the more statistically "significant" the results. But the way to enlarge the data base is to reduce the information base for each item and to eliminate the interconnections between members. Individuals become "monads," ball bearings that respond only to observable outside influences and that are governed only by measurable vectors of self-interest. Social scientists may readily acknowledge that many particular individuals behave in irrational and unpredictable ways. But the aggregation of many entities is assumed to nullify the singularity of each case. The singularities "wash."

The result is a science that attempts to understand the whole without a tenable theory of the parts. Whether in economics or sociology, this approach is absolutely necessary. The individual human brain still defies the explorations of neurophysiology. Even the ecology of a puddle of water is complex beyond the reach of modeling by biologists. The human ecology of a town—comprising hundreds of families, friends, churches, clubs, and businesses, linked in millions of ways, compounded by the endless intricacies of human character and personality, reflected in thousands of inscrutable minds—would totally elude the ken of the sociological or economic modeler.

Such apparently simple concepts as poverty or productivity or capital accumulation are actually complicated far beyond the measure of the social scientist. Poverty, for example, is primarily a matter of prospects and connections. An intact family of four—well below the "poverty line" and without high-school education, but with close links to relatives, good work disciplines, and maintenance skills—will look, act, and be essentially middle class, while a slovenly welfare family lacking these virtues will be essentially impoverished regardless of how much money it gets from the government. A happy pretty girl may be rich regardless of income; an alcoholic may be poor. A highly motivated young person preparing for a career in medicine, with close connections with friends and relatives, is wealthy. Yet poverty statistics will find him to be poor if he has little income.

The dynamics of any economic process respond more to family relationships and motivations than to measurable economic conditions. A rapidly rising company—or family—may at one point in time show a financial balance sheet identical to the balance sheet of a unit on the way to bankruptcy. The identity is spurious but in static terms exact. Similarly, marital status, personality, religious beliefs, morality, and motivation are incomparably more important than race, ethnic origin, or even short-term income in defining the prospects or social contributions of a person. Yet the sociologist pores endlessly over indices of race and ethnic origin while all the crucial factors elude him.

Since the average social scientist spends his life ignoring what is important in order to aggregate data, he sees concepts like "poverty lines," "comparable worth," "productivity," and "child-care facilities" as more significant than morality, family loyalty, religious belief, male solidarity, motivation, knowledge, and maternal love. He believes as a professional hypothesis that what is measurable and aggregatable is more important than what is not. This hypothesis can yield interesting observations about the economy and society. But unless the social scientist understands the limitations of his data, he will propose monstrous errors of policy. He will imagine that women can be combat marines or police officers without disrupting morale, or that girls can participate in male sports without demoralizing the underdeveloped boys, or that welfare benefits can rise to near the poverty line without expanding real poverty, or that the spread of promiscuity, divorce, pornography, and homosexuality are irrelevant to the health of an economy or society.

The requirements of the social-science model all too readily become the parameters of a social ideal. Measurable rationality, sexual homogeneity, environmental determinism, and credentialism all subtly change from heuristic simplifications to social goals. Slipping all too easily from the statistically convenient to the socially desirable to the politically imperative, social scientists begin advocating policies to fulfill their ideals. They support measures to assure that just as they are incapable of discriminating among job applicants with the same credentials and qualifications, no one else should discriminate either. They urge the teaching of the valuefree sociological view of sex to teenagers in schools. They assume that because the ties that bind the male group or the nuclear family or the Mormon church are irrational or "sexist," they are socially objectionable. But whether forming an army, a police force, a business, or a moral individual, this neutral approach is fundamentally misconceived.

Crucial to creating an army, for example, is evoking in soldiers the willingness to die for one another and their country. This is entirely irrational. No army that ignores gender dynamics or depends on rational emotions can succeed in its central mission. Crucial to creating a civilized society is inducing girls to say no to boys. This requires strong and usually religious rationales and sanctions that differentiate by gender. Valuefree sex education is a powerful invitation to premature sex.

Crucial to economic growth is the process of creating businesses. Yet such entrepreneurship consists precisely in making discriminations that cannot be predetermined statistically. Any large firm can perform market surveys and purchase computer time to ascertain anything about the marketplace that can be modeled at reasonable cost. Small businesses thrive in part because they can go beyond the measurable to exploit family ties, exceptional motivations, unusual ideas, bright intuitions, intense group loyalties, trust, and faith. In other words, businesses succeed by discriminating, by proving social science wrong or inadequate. It is a final offense that for these discriminations successful entrepreneurs tend to earn more than successful social scientists.

In revenge the social scientists attempt to impose their own visions by law, usually favoring socialism and other forms of rule by intellectuals. This approach offends democracy. For perhaps the most disabling flaw of mainstream social science is its blindness to the depth of human resistance to its vision of a better world. Universal in all human societies, so the anthropologists inform us, are patriarchy, religion, and private property. One can still find, of course, here and there in the ethnologies, a few tribes so primitive that they refuse to acknowledge or comprehend these human propensities. There are groups of nomadic bushmen who lack all possessions and thus may be said to transcend possessiveness; there are people with a religious impulse so stunted that they worship only the palpable shapes and materials within their own reach and view; there are tribes like Malinowski's famous Trobriand Islanders, who do not even understand the nature of sexual intercourse and its role in procreation; there are groups like the Malabar Nayars, who practice infanticide of females and then wonder why there are so few women that they can each command several husbands; there are groups that try female dominance and then wonder why the men spend all their time hunting.

Today such repressive and perverse societies are extraordinarily rare. There is, in fact, only one fully documented case surviving in the modern world of a tribe so abjectly retarded, or so mystically impervious to its own nature, that it simultaneously rejects and tries to abolish all three of these human characteristics—sex roles, religions, and property rights. That group, not even strictly speaking a tribe, is, of course, the community of social-science scholars in America.

In their venerable groves, private property—except possibly in the form of books—arouses particular indignation because it tends to lead to unequal patterns of wealth and income. The only inequalities generally regarded as justifiable in the social-science fraternity are those founded on certain favored forms of merit, often as measured by Ph.D. theses and other publications implicitly or explicitly attacking capitalism, in the name of a mystical process never clearly defined but believed by some to be associated with professional tenure. This mystical process is often called "Social Change." Social Change, it can be determined by long observation, is what is left over for the poor after liberal social scientists and bureaucrats are through feasting on government dollars.

Among the more advanced social scientists, however, there are two phenomena even more detested than capitalism. One is sex, to the extent that it depends on fundamental differences between the sexes; the other is religion, particularly if it implies a belief in a realm beyond the reach of social scientists, even those who use up-to-date techniques of national probability sample research. The most crucial characteristic of modern social-science methods, in fact, is an inability to register the differences between the sexes, or the existence of God.

Social scientists do, however, have a form of religion of their own. In general, when liberal sociologists bother to identify themselves in terms that go beyond their belief in dollars and Social Change, they call themselves "humanists." Humanists can be easily recognized by their blind faith in the possibility of overcoming some of the most universal and ineradicable characteristics of human beings: the inequalities among them; their piety; their acquisitiveness and competitiveness; their irrational bent for speculation and entrepreneurship; their persistent and universal sexual differences, both psychological and biological. The humanist vision calls for a cooperative, communal, egalitarian, secular, nonsexist, nonhierarchical, and rational society. This in fact, as C. S. Lewis contended in a famous essay, entails nothing less than the abolition of human nature.[8]

The different roles of men and women, the love that arises from them, the allegiance to one's own family, the worship of God, the possession and improvement of property, the production of wealth, the cultivation of excellence and beauty, the competitive masculine rituals of sport and play, the emergence of loyalty to kin and community, church and country, all are among the highest values of human life. Because they spring from human reality, they can be fulfilled in ordered freedom in a democratic society. Achieving economic planning, income equality, bureaucratic rationality, and sexual liberation—the retrenchment of religion and suppression of sex roles—requires a totalitarian state. And in the end, as communist regimes everywhere show, the result defies the ideal. For the ultimate source of cooperation, community, productivity, and equality in every society is the nuclear family that the humanist vision would erode or destroy.

CHAPTER 15

The Home Front

The family . . . is the native soil on which performance of moral duty is made easy through natural affection so that within a small circle a basis of moral practice is created, and then is widened to include human relationships in general. . . .

I CHING

Nearly a century ago, Karl Marx and Frederick Engels first anticipated and revealed to the world the secret dream of the sexual liberal. "In communist society," they wrote, "where nobody has one exclusive sphere of activity but each can become accomplished in any branch he wishes, *society* regulates the general production and thus makes it possible for me to do one thing today and another tomorrow, to hunt in the morning, fish in the afternoon, rear cattle in the evening, criticise after dinner, just as I have a mind, without ever becoming hunter, fisherman, shepherd or critic."[1]

The contemporary liberal would wish to banish male bias from the dream. Assigning to "society" the duties not only of "general production" but also of reproduction, the new dreamers would extend to women as well as men the life of a British country squire. Liberating both sexes from restrictive roles and moral codes, the dream would bring a new spirit of sharing—of jobs, bodies, vocations, and pleasures. People would be full "human beings" rather than oppressed men and women.

There are two serious problems with this arrangement, and unfortunately both are fatal. The first problem is that except in an abstract sense there is no such thing as "society." Both production and reproduction, therefore, will be left to particular human beings. The second problem is that there are no "human beings," just men and women. Since the nature of things assures that men will do most of the production and women most of the reproduction, we are back

165

where we started before Marx and his modern followers began their reveries.

The communal dream always fed on the vast ignorance of intellectuals like Marx about the production of wealth, and their aristocratic disdain for the lives of ordinary men and women. To Marx and Engels, the role of men seemed so simple that it could in due course be passed on to a few bureaucrats managing the machines of mass production. To the average sexual liberal, the role of women seems so routine that it can be assumed by a few bureaucrats managing child-development centers. To the current advocates of shared sex roles, both the work of the world and the duties of the home are so undemanding that they can be accomplished with part-time effort.

The truth is, however, that even beyond full-time duties nurturing infants, the mother's role imposes continual challenges. Raising several children is a project that exacts a constant alertness and attention that none of the sexual liberals remotely understand when they urge that "society" do it. With fewer children, kept longer within the household, the focus on each child is even more intense than it was in the past. The near-demise of extended families, though it was crucial to the industrial revolution, also increased the burdens of the mother alone.

As Midge Decter has observed, previously motherhood was regarded as inevitable: one didn't choose it; one accepted it.[2] Without any sense of other options, the responsibility for numerous children may even have seemed less onerous than the responsibility for a few today. In the past, sickness, mortality, slow-learning, and other childhood afflictions were taken for granted as a part of life. Today the mother is expected to control them. To the difficult tasks of caring are now added burdens of medical attention, psychological analysis, and early education. It is not a role that, in its continual and varied demands, men show any serious inclination to perform. Indeed most of the divorced men who gain custody of their children immediately surrender it again to new wives, girlfriends, day-care centers, or female servants.

The dimensions of the new mother's role are evident in the activities that go on in that center of American child care, the single-family dwelling in the suburbs. Ever since Betty Friedan's *cri de coeur* from Westchester County[3]—then perhaps the richest spot on the face of the earth—feminists have shed public tears for the women doing this crucial labor in the American suburbs. Isolated, unstimulated, sexually deprived, trapped by babies, frittering away their talents in boredom and drudgery, these women were seen as victims of male oppression in an exploitative capitalist culture. This description caught on widely, particularly among intellectuals in American universities.

Two sociologists, however, have actually taken the trouble to investigate in great detail the condition of these housewives. Herbert J. Gans examined Levittown,[4] which was widely regarded as the most alienating of all suburban environments, and Helen Znaniecki Lopata conducted 573 close and specific personal interviews around Chicago.[5] They concluded, like many subsequent observers, that people, particularly women, deeply enjoy suburban living, and that suburbanites tend to be among the happiest and least isolated Americans.

In general, Lopata and Gans both depict a panorama of social engagement, community concern, cooperative activity, and even, in many cases, cultural and intellectual animation: a realm of options that substantially exceeds those of either men or working women. Mrs. Lopata, for instance, found that suburban housewives, by a significant margin, were more likely than working women to be using their education in their lives, to be reading widely and curiously, to be maintaining close and varied friendships, and to be involved in community affairs. "The role of the housewife provides her a base for building a many-faceted life, an opportunity few other vocational roles allow, because they are tied down to single organizational structures and goals."[6] Working women normally looked forward to leaving their jobs. Gans found that only 10 percent of suburban women reported frequent loneliness or boredom.[7]

Women's activities are far richer in intellectual and social challenges than most academic writers comprehend. It is foolish to imagine that these complex roles and relationships can be abolished or assumed by outside agencies. The woman's role is nothing less than the hub of the human community. All the other work—the business and politics and entertainment and service performed in the society—finds its ultimate test in the quality of the home. The home is where we finally and privately live, where we express our individuality, where we display our aesthetic choices, where we make and enjoy love, and where we cultivate our children as individuals.

The central position of the woman in the home parallels her central position in all civilized society. Both derive from her necessary role in procreation and from the most primary and inviolable of human ties, the one between mother and child. In those extraordinary circumstances when this tie is broken—as with some disintegrating tribes—the group tends to sink to a totally bestial and amoral chaos.[8]

Most of the characteristics we define as humane and individual originate in the mother's love for her children. Men have no ties to the long-term human community so deep or tenacious as the mother's to her child. Originating in this love are the other civilizing concerns of maternity: the desire for male protection and support, the hope for a stable community life, and the aspiration toward a better long-term future. The success or failure of civilized society depends on how well the women can transmit these values to the men.

This essential female role has become much more sophisticated and refined in the modern world. But its essence is the same. The woman assumes charge of what may be described as the domestic values of the community—its moral, aesthetic, religious, nurturant, social, and sexual concerns. In these values consist the ultimate goals of human life—all those matters that we consider of such supreme importance that we do not ascribe a financial worth to them. Paramount is the worth of the human individual life, enshrined in the home, and in the connection between a woman and child. These values transcend the marketplace. In fact to enter them in commercial traffic is considered a major evil in civilized society. Whether proposing to sell a baby or a body or a religious blessing, one commits a major moral offense.

This woman's role is deeply individual. Only a specific woman can bear a specific child, and her tie to it is personal and unbreakable. When she raises the child she imparts in privacy her own individual values. She can create children who transcend consensus and prefigure the future: children of private singularity rather than "child-development policy." She is the vessel of the ultimate values of the nation. The community is largely what she is and what she demands in men. She does her work because it is of primary rather than instrumental value. The woman in the home with her child is the last bastion against the amorality of the technocratic marketplace when it strays from the moral foundations of capitalism.

In recent years, the existence of a distinctive feminine role in ethics has been discovered by feminists. Seeking to answer male psychologists who regard masculine defense of justice and equality as the highest level of moral development, female scholars have offered a contrary case for the moral perceptions of women. The leading work in this field is *In a Different Voice,* by Carol Gilligan of Harvard.[9] She postulates a uniquely feminine moral sense rooted in webs of relationship and responsibility, in intimacy and caring, rather than in rules and abstractions.

Gilligan's point is valuable and true and her book is full of interesting evidence for it. But contrary to her egalitarian vision, women's moral sense is not merely an equal counterpoint to masculine ideals. Stemming from her umbilical link to new life itself and from a passionate sense of the value and potential of that life, the woman's morality is the ultimate basis of all morality. The man's recognition of the preciousness and equality of individuals is learned from women and originates with the feminine concern for relationships, beginning in the womb and at the breast. This concern contrasts sharply with his own experience of hierarchy and preference, aggression and lust, and the sense of sexual and personal dispensability he experiences as a single man. Just as outside male activity is regarded in all societies as most important in instrumental terms, women's concerns are morally paramount, by the very fact that they are female, part of the unimpeachable realm of life's creation and protection.

What is true for individual moral issues is also true for the practical needs of a nation: the maternal role remains paramount. There is no way to shunt off child care to the "society" or to substantially reduce its burdens. If children lack the close attention of mothers and the disciplines and guidance of fathers, they tend to become barbarians or wastrels who burden or threaten society rather than do its work. Raising children to be productive and responsible citizens takes persistent and unrelenting effort. The prisons, reformatories, foster homes, mental institutions, and welfare rolls of America already groan under the burden of children relinquished to "society" to raise and support. In the sense of becoming self-sufficient, all too many of these children never grow up at all. To reproduce the true means of production—men and women who can uphold civilization rather than subvert it—the diligent love of mothers is indispensable. In fact, the only remedy for the "overpopulation" in female-headed families is the creation of a larger population of children brought up by two active and attentive parents.

Crucial to the sexual liberals' dream of escape from family burdens is zero population growth. Because each individual no longer depends on his children to support him in old age, many observers seem to imagine that children are less important than they were in the past. But substantially fewer offspring are a possibility only for a while in modern welfare states. No less than in the past, the new generations will have to support the old. The only difference is that now the medium is coercive taxation and social security rather than filial duty.

With some 15 percent of couples infertile and others child-free by choice, in order to raise enough workers to support the social programs of retirees, each fertile woman must still bear more than two children. In order to prevent a substantial decline in the quality of children—their willingness to work hard and contribute to society in the face of high taxes and a generous dole—women must devote long hours to raising and disciplining the new generation. The decline in the quantity of children demands a rise in the quality of their contributions to society—a rise in their diligence and productivity.

This female responsibility, as Gilligan observes, entails difficult sacrifices of freedom and autonomy.[10] Other researchers, notably Jessie Bernard, have noted that these sacrifices produce a significantly elevated incidence of emotional stress and neurosis among full-time housewives, particularly when their children are young.[11] Some of this anxiety clearly reflects the sharp rise in expenses and tax burdens incurred by families raising children. Some of the problem is simply hard and grueling work. Part of the distress, though, may derive from the media's widespread disparagement of traditional women. Margaret Mead found that women are most contented not when they are granted "influence, power, and wealth," but when "the female role of wife and mother is exalted." A devaluing of "the sensuous creative significance" of woman's role, she wrote, makes women become unhappy in the home.[12] But regardless of the source of this stress, Gilligan's point is correct. Women do make great sacrifices, and these sacrifices are essential to society.

Some theorists list sexual restraint high among these sacrifices. But women's sexual restraint is necessary for the fulfillment of their larger sexuality in families, which cannot normally survive the birth of children by men other than the family provider. In general, a man will not support a woman while she philanders.

Contrary to the assumption of most analysts, it is men who make the major sexual sacrifice. The man renounces his dream of short-term sexual freedom and self-fulfillment—his male sexuality and self-expression—in order to serve a woman and family for a lifetime. It is a traumatic act of giving up his most profound yearning, his bent for the hunt and the chase, the motorbike and the open road, the male group escape to a primal mode of predatory and immediate excitements. His most powerful impulse—the theme of every male song and story—this combination of lust and wanderlust is the very life force that drives him through his youth. He surrenders it only with pain. This male sacrifice, no less than the woman's work in the home, is essential to civilization.

Just as the female role cannot be shared or relinquished, the male role also remains vital to social survival. For centuries to come, men will have to make heroic efforts. On forty-hour weeks, most men cannot even support a family of four. They must train at night and on weekends; they must save as they can for future ventures of entrepreneurship; they must often perform more than one job. They must make time as best they can to see and guide their children. They must shun the consolations of alcohol and leisure, sexual indulgence and flight. They must live for the perennial demands of the provider role.

Unlike the woman's role, the man's tends to be relatively fungible and derivative. He does not give himself to a web of unique personal relationships so much as to a set of functions and technologies. Just as any particular hunter might kill an animal, so within obvious bounds any workman can be trained to do most jobs. The man makes himself replaceable. For most of his early years at the job site, individuality is an obstacle to earnings. He must sacrifice it to support his wife and children. He must eschew his desire to be an athlete or poet, a death-defying ranger or mountaineer, a cocksman and Casanova, and settle down to become a functionary defined by a single job, and a father whose children are earned by his work. Not his own moral vision but the marketplace defines the value of that work.

Extraordinary men transcend many of these constraints early in their careers and many men eventually rise to significant roles of leadership and self-expression. But even then jobs rarely afford room for the whole man. Even highly paid work often creates what Ortega y Gasset called "barbarians of specialization."[13] One may become a scientist, a doctor, an engineer, or a lawyer, for example, chiefly by narrowing the mind, by excluding personal idiosyncrasies and visions in order to master the disciplines and technicalities of the trade. In some cases, exceptionally successful specialization may bring some of the satisfactions won, for example, by the great athlete. Nevertheless, this process usually does not make a man interesting or whole. In fact, he is likely to succeed precisely to the extent that he is willing to subordinate himself to the narrow imperatives of his specialty, precisely to the extent that he forgoes the distractions and impulses of the full personality.

Among men, the term *dilettante* is a pejorative. Yet, because the range of human knowledge and experience is so broad, the best that most people can ever achieve, if they respond as whole persons to their lives, is the curiosity, openness, and eclectic knowledge of the dilettante. Most men have to deny themselves this form of individual fulfillment. They have to limit themselves, at great psychological cost, in order to fit the functions of the economic division of labor. Most of them endure their submission to the marketplace chiefly in order to make enough money to sustain a home, to earn a place in the household, to be needed by women. This effort most of the time means a lifetime of hard labor.

As with the woman's role, what is true in most specific cases is still more true on the level of general rules and expectations across the entire society. On forty-hour weeks the world dissolves into chaos and decay, famine and war. All the major accomplishments of civilization spring from the obsessions of men whom the sociologists would now disdain as "workaholics." To overcome the Malthusian trap of rising populations, or to escape the closing circle of ecological decline, or to control the threat of nuclear holocaust, or to halt the plagues and famines that still afflict the globe, men must give their lives to unrelenting effort, day in and day out, focused on goals in the distant future. They must create new technologies faster than the world creates new challenges. They must struggle against scarcity, entropy, and natural disaster. They must overcome the sabotage of socialists who would steal and redistribute their product. They must resist disease and temptation. All too often they must die without achieving their ends. But their sacrifices bring others closer to the goal.

Nothing that has been written in the annals of feminism gives the slightest indication that this is a role that women want or are prepared to perform. The feminists demand liberation. The male role means bondage to the demands of the workplace and the needs of the family. Most of the research of sociologists complains that men's work is already too hard, too dangerous, too destructive of mental health and wholeness. It all too often leads to sickness and "worlds of pain," demoralization and relatively early death. The men's role that feminists seek is not the real role of men but the male role of the Marxist dream in which "society" does the work.

"Women's liberation" entails a profound dislocation. Women, uniquely in charge of the central activities of human life, are exalting instead the peripheral values—values that have meaning only in relation to the role they would disparage or abandon. In addition, sexual liberals ask society to give up most of the devices and conventions by which it has ensured that women perform their indispensable work and by which men have been induced to support it. As a result, in many of the world's welfare states that have accepted the feminist vision, the two sexes are no longer making the necessary sacrifices to sustain society.

Shunning the responsibilities of family support, men are rejecting available jobs and doing sporadic work off the books and stints on unemployment insurance. Shunning the role of wife and mother, many women are forgoing marriage. Consequently many Western nations are far overshooting the mark of zero population growth. With the average couple bearing scarcely more than one child, most of Northern Europe now shows a fertility rate about 60 percent of the replacement level.[14] If this rate continues, dictated by the pressures of excessive welfare programs, it would mean near-extinction of the genetic stock within four generations. To a less but still dangerous degree, the same pattern is evident in America. The U.S. also is under the replacement level of reproduction.

A nation may gain the illusion of a rising standard of living by raising and supporting fewer children. To paraphrase Allan Carlson, a society may consume for a while the ghosts of the unborn.[15] More specifically, we may eat the meals that would have gone to our prevented or aborted babies. But these gains are rapidly lost. In a vicious circle well known in Europe, smaller generations of workers find themselves devoting ever larger portions of their pay to supporting the child-free aged. Soon the young workers begin reducing their efforts in the face of rising tax rates and their wives themselves begin bearing still fewer children. This is the final contradiction of the welfare state. To the extent that it deters work and childbearing, it ultimately self-destructs.

There is a way out, however. It is to export the woman's role and import people through immigration. In more positive terms, this policy can be seen as extending the higher and more abstract role of motherhood and home into the world. In recent years, as much as a third of America's economic growth and technological progress has stemmed from such an opening of the arms of Lady Liberty to the refugees of socialism. For example, in California's Silicon Valley, the fount of the worldwide computer revolution, immigrants play key roles on assembly lines, in making major innovations, in performing laboratory research, and even in the entrepreneurial launching of major companies, from Intel in the 1970s to Tandon and Xicor in the 1980s. Immigrants may yet save the American social-security system.

The immigration option works to save the welfare state, however, only on one condition: the immigrants must stay off welfare. The dangers are clear from the U.S. experience with Puerto Ricans, who once showed far better family stability and work effort than American blacks. In two generations, the U.S. welfare state has turned hundreds of thousands of hard-working Puerto Rican families into fatherless units dependent on the state. European social democrats who prate about their compassion for the poor know well that they must mostly exclude their own poor and the world's real poor—i.e., immigrants—from welfare. If immigrants were allowed on the dole, they would throng from around the world to the welfare states of the West and bankrupt them. The choice is clear. The welfare state must either bar immigration or create a second-class citizenship.

The Europeans, and to a lesser extent the U.S. with its illegal aliens, are already in the process of creating such a two-tiered society. At the top will be the leisured peers with full entitlement to be supported by others. On the bottom are laboring newcomers: a new serfdom imported to save the child-free socialism of the rich. The assertion of a new morality of caring for the world thus leads to a rejection of the dream of equal justice at the foundation of the welfare state.

Rather than face the full implications of their policy, the Europeans have also been toying with the ultimate form of protectionism: not only barring the products of poor people overseas but also barring the people themselves. Several European governments have recently been paying some of their immigrants to leave. Before long, though, Europe will have to invite them back, but without full access to the benefits of socialism. With this decision will collapse the last pretense that socialism can provide equality or compassion for the truly poor, as opposed to the welfare state's entitled peers.

In an important essay, "Two Cheers for ZPG," Norman Ryder illustrates some of these ironies in the current stance of sexual liberals. "A collective commitment to population replacement," he writes, "is a defensible posture only if we assume that whatever it is that we are proud of must be transmitted biologically." He suggests that we fulfill our "thrust toward immortality . . . by efforts to ensure that future generations share our values, whether or not they share our genes."[16] As Carlson comments: "In the end, we learn that the final consequence of the existing welfare state is biological extinction. The grim humor lies in Ryder's belief that he could find self-respecting immigrants who would want to 'share values' with a decadent intelligentsia presiding over a self-inflicted genocide."[17]

Sexual liberalism is the cause, not the solution, of the problem of the West. But the error of the liberals comes not only in their fantasies of flight from work and children—not only in their illusion that full-time work and child care have declined in importance to modern society. They also deeply misunderstand what makes people happy. The pursuit of promiscuous sexual pleasures which many of them offer as an alternative to the duties of family leads chiefly to misery and despair. It is procreation that ultimately makes sex gratifying and important and it is home and family that gives resonance and meaning to life.

The woman's place is in the home, and she does her best when she can get the man there too, inducing him to submit most human activity to the domestic values of civilization. Thus in a sense she also brings the home into the society. The radiance of the values of home can give meaning and illumination to male enterprises. Male work is most valuable when it is imbued with the long-term love and communal concerns of femininity, when it is brought back to the home. Otherwise masculine activity is apt to degenerate quickly to the level of a game; and, unless closely regulated, games have a way of deteriorating into the vain pursuit of power.

It is the judgment of women that tames the aggressive pursuits of men. Men come to learn that their activity will be best received if it partakes of the values of the home. If they think the work itself is unworthy, they try to conceal it and bring home the money anyway. Like the legendary Mafiosi, they try to please their women by elaborate submission to domestic values in the household, while scrupulously keeping the women out of the male realm of work. But in almost every instance, even by hypocrisy, they pay tribute to the moral superiority of women.

In rediscovering for the secular world this feminine morality, rooted in "webs of relationship," Gilligan has written an important book. What she and the male moralists she criticizes do not see is that the self-sacrifice of women finds a perfect complement in the self-sacrifice of men. On this mutual immolation is founded the fulfillment of human civilization and happiness. For just as it is the sacrifice of early career ambitions and sexual freedom that makes possible the true fulfillment of women, it is the subordination of male sexuality to woman's maternity that allows the achievement of male career goals, that spurs the attainment of the highest male purposes. In his vaunted freedom and sexual power, the young single man may dream of glory. But it is overwhelmingly the married men who achieve it in the modern world. They achieve it, as scripture dictates and women's experience insists, by self-denial and sacrifice.

The fact is that there is no way that women can escape their supreme responsibilities in civilized society without endangering civilization itself. The most chilling portent of our current predicament, therefore, is the conjuncture of a movement of female abdication with a new biochemistry, which shines direct and deadly beams of technocratic light on the very crux of human identity, the tie between the mother and her child.

CHAPTER 16

The Sexual Suicide Technocracy

A book about men and marriage written during the last half of the twentieth century labors under a cloud. Now no larger than a man's hand, it promises to shadow all debate about human sexuality in decades to come. Now mostly confined to laboratories, it is emerging year by year to become a major force in the definition and prospects of the two sexes, of masculinity and femininity.

The cloud is biogenetic engineering, and it makes technically possible for the first time in human history a change in the very essence of sexuality. Often seen as offering a new liberation of women—and actually promising a series of impressive medical benefits—the new life sciences also pose grave dangers to both sexes.

The nature of the new technology has been scrupulously weighed and explored in a book by Leon R. Kass, a doctor who thinks like the best of lawyers and writes like the best of writers.[1] In a more purely literary mode, Edward Grossman's essay "The Obsolescent Mother"[2] has elegiacally captured the possible impact of the new techniques on the long, historic saga of childbirth in mystery and tumult. Other analysts range from the cogently premonitory to the wildly prophetic.

Progress in bioengineering enables the world to contemplate nothing less than a new stage of evolution, such as is intimated at the end of the movie *2001* and similar science fiction. But key developments may happen even before the turn of the century, for technological ventures into the space of woman, though less cinematically spectacular, are both more advanced and more portentous than any prospective adventures of astronauts.

The three approaches about which most is known are *in vitro* or test-tube fertilization; extracorporeal gestation (the artificial womb); and cloning, the exact reproduction or "xeroxing" of particular genotypes. Cloning poses the most obvious threat to human individuality, but the other two techniques also have far-reaching implications.

A clone is created by implanting the nucleus of a human cell, from any part of the body, into the enucleated cell of a female egg. This process, which can be repeated as often as eggs and wombs are available, creates genetic copies of the donor of the nucleus, identical twins in every way except age. It has the additional fillip of making possible the abolition of males, since the three necessary elements—a cell nucleus, an enucleated egg, and a womb—can all be provided by a woman. Successful cloning has already been done with frogs, salamanders, and fruit flies, and by a related technique, scientists have engineered a mouse with genetic material from six parents.[3]

Progress toward cloning feeds on a stream of recent successes related to *in vitro* fertilization, the conception of a child in a laboratory dish and the transmittal of the blastocyte or fertilized egg to the uterine wall. In 1978 the first human baby so conceived—Louise Brown—was born in England, and hundreds more have been born in America, mostly after procedures managed by Drs. Howard and Georgeanna Jones at their clinic in Norfolk, Virginia.[4]

The next step after test-tube conception—extracorporeal gestation and ectogenesis—is far more complicated. It entails in essence the creation of artificial wombs. The problems are being approached from both ends: the saving of increasingly premature babies and the extension of the life of blastocytes into the embryonic stages. The obstacles remain formidable, but impressive successes have been obtained with rats.

After reading the available literature, an apprehensive layman is left with the impression that it will be a very long time before artificial wombs for humans can be fabricated in number. But the creation of even a small number of elaborate and expensive devices would be ominous because it would relieve the scientists of the tiresome task of finding and managing available women. Clones, chimeras (human-animal hybrids), and other experimental "sports" might be generated and flushed at will.

Scientists can only guess at the likely chronology of new developments. Nobel Prize–winner James D. Watson, the discoverer of DNA structure, told Congress in the early 1970s his fear that cloning will be perfected for humans "within the next twenty to fifty years."[5] In other words, he doesn't know. But with *in vitro* fertilization a *fait accompli* and the artificial womb advancing steadily, the coming of clones seems perilously close.

Test-tube conception may seem a relatively limited step beyond the use of artificial insemination. That widely accepted practice has already given a few hundred medical students technical paternity over several hundred thousand children. Laboratory fertilization merely seems to extend relief to certain childless women that was previously available only if the sterility afflicted their husbands. The relief is decidedly better, moreover, since it allows the woman to retain full genetic maternity of her children.

Yet this seemingly innocent practice, which will ultimately help millions of childless couples to have babies, also poses many perplexing problems. Dr. Kass maintains that many of the women who can be helped by this technique also could be given a permanent cure by surgery on their oviducts (particularly if this operation were promoted as lavishly as the fertilization projects). Test-tube conception also potentially reduces the demand to adopt children. It advances the day when parents will be able to choose the gender of their child, either ordering a fetus of the preferred sex or aborting all undesired ones. And by circumventing the act of love, *in vitro* conception takes another small step toward dislodging sexual intercourse from its pinnacle as both the paramount act of love and the only act of procreation. It thus promotes the trend toward regarding sex as just another means of pleasure, and weakens the male connection to the psychologically potent realm of procreation.

In addition, the process offers human uses far beyond the circumvention of sterility. It makes possible a further disconnection between motherhood and pregnancy. Since the fertilized ovum does not have to be placed in the body of the real "mother," it can be farmed out to any willing woman—for pay. This is not a farfetched idea. Using artificial insemination, a woman in Michigan has already rented her womb to a friend, borne a child fathered by the friend's husband, and delivered it to the wife. The family has received thousands of inquiries from others.

With *in vitro* techniques rather than artificial insemination, a much more attractive result—full genetic offspring—could be achieved by such means. New, more partial and detached forms of motherhood become possible for busy or preoccupied women. The very role of mother and the profound biological tie with her child—enacted in the woman's most intense sexual experiences in child-birth—become optional. This development threatens to diminish further the perceived and felt authority of the basic connections of human life.

Individuality is far more deeply threatened, though, in cloning. The first clones will likely be done for a few rich experimenters or for the scientists themselves. But eventually the state would probably intervene to determine which persons were most suitable for copy-ing. If artificial wombs were achieved, the state could assume increasing control over the genetic future of the race. With govern-ment controlling both production and reproduction, the dreams of the social planner could at last be fulfilled. But it would not likely turn out as Marx envisaged in his idyll of the country squire.

Kass quotes C. S. Lewis's powerful tract, *The Abolition of Man:*

> If any one age really attains, by eugenics and scientific education, the power to make its descendants what it pleases, all men who live after it are patients of that power. They are weaker, not stronger. . . . The real picture is that of one dominant age . . . which resists all previous ages most successfully and dominates all subsequent ages most irresistibly, and thus is the real master of the human species. But even within this master generation (itself an infinitesimal minority of the species) the power will be exercised by a minority smaller still. Man's conquest of nature, if the dreams of the scientific planners are realized, means the rule of a few hundreds of men over billions upon billions of men. There neither is nor can there be any simple increase in power on man's side. Each new power won *by* man is a power *over* man as well.[6]

Few things ever happen much as predicted. Lewis's vision of a centralized power of reproduction might well give way to a messy proliferation of eugenic experiments and enterprises proceeding over centuries. But the long-run social implications remain dire for the human species as we know it.

In sexual terms, the nature of the change is easier to define. Although some analysts have predicted the liberation of women or the redundancy of males, the technology in fact most profoundly threatens women. Ultimately the womb could be made obsolete. Not only could the female body become a strange combination of otiose spaces and appendages, not only could the man's become the exemplary, utilitarian physique, but the power of women over men could gradually pass away. First, with time, her sexual powers would decrease. For if we break the tie between sexual intercourse and procreation, destroy the childhood memory of the nurturing and omnipotent mother, banish the mystique of the breasts and the womb and of the female curves and softnesses, we could remove as well much of the special attraction of heterosexual love. We may liberate men to celebrate, like the ancient Spartans or the most extreme homosexuals today, a violent, misogynistic, and narcissistic eroticism.

Millions of American men know something about the spirit and feasibility of such a masculine society, not even homosexual. The men who have been to war have told their story. Otherwise the epitome of male liberation is Marine Corps boot camp. In its classic form, it comprises twelve weeks without a moment of liberty, all devoted chiefly to the extirpation of feminine ties and sentiments in the assembled young men. From the moment the recruits arrive, the drill instructors begin a torrent of misogynistic and anti-individualist abuse. The good things are manly and collective; the despicable are feminine and individual. Virtually every sentence, every description, every lesson embodies this sexual duality, and the female anatomy provides a rich field of metaphor for every degradation.

When you want to create a solidaristic group of male killers, that is what you do: you kill the woman in them. That is the lesson of the Marines. And it works. Artfully exploiting the internal pressures of the group, the instructors manage to evoke a fanatical commitment from almost every recruit. They arrive as various and rebellious boys, swearing under their breath what they will do to any drill instructor who lays a hand on them. They end up, after twelve weeks of manhandling, often including violent physical abuse, gladly and voluntarily making large financial gifts to the instructors.

Under less intense control and training, homosexual impulses can arise in such a sequestered all-male group. In prisons, for example, the dominant men often demand and extort sexual services. But their victims, surprisingly—even when exclusively heterosexual in outside life—can sometimes feel a powerful psychological and even physiological change. Contrary to their every expectation, some may become willing partners in homosexuality.

The bonding process that occurs in the military, however, has no homoerotic content. It is a powerful example of the male ties that Lionel Tiger explored so fruitfully in *Men in Groups*.[7] The system has its uses in protecting a society from enemies or in abetting the performance of crucial group activities. But it can be deadly to individuality and civilization. It is deadly to the sentiments that women evoke from men: love, creativity, nurturance, commitment to the future. Above all, it is perfectly barren. The male group, separated from women, is the male solidarity. There is no real love, little individuality, and no procreative instinct.

The male group treats women exclusively as sexual objects. Pornographic movies near military centers reek with attacks on women, and one of the favorite stories told on return to the base from liberty is of the violent abuse of a whore. Mass rape has been frequent throughout the history of war. The alternative to the system of men and marriage is usually the system of men and misogyny. The men are freed to pursue their own sexual cycles in uncivilized groups of hunters.

This is the ultimate pattern that might unfold if the new bioengineering technology is devoted heavily to the agenda of "women's liberation." The women might be released from pregnancy, but the men would be released from marriage, and thus from the influence of female sexuality. The male physique, far inferior to the woman's in a sexual society, would become superior in a sexual-suicide society in which the state manages reproduction. The women's breasts and womb would lose their uses. The male body would become the physical ideal and lend symbolic authority to the male command of other instruments of power. The technocracy, a dominantly male creation in the first place, would remain in the hands of a male minority.

The system of marriage that tames men and evokes their love is the chief obstacle to this technocratic future. If marriage endures, the realm of the state and the development and use of the technology can be limited, while the maintenance of human individuality can be assured. If the family should widely break down, then the world of artificial wombs, clones, and child-development centers can become an important reality rather than a laboratory curiosity. Norman Mailer was thus most profound when he defined the movement of women's liberation as the fifth column of the technocracy. He might have added that it is also the fifth column of true patriarchy: the sterile solidarity.

Human biology, however, may well obstruct the biologists and their schemes of technocratic sex. Although ideologues persist in their dreams of transcending gender, the evidence of profound differences between the sexes has now been accepted even by many sexual liberals. Under normal circumstances, biology is destiny. Men and women grow up in different ways, seek different goals, and transcend their biological separation chiefly through the mystery of love and marriage. But the new circumstances are not normal. We can no longer retreat to automatic affirmations of biological destiny. We are approaching a time when our destinies can be bioengineered. The question is whether we apply these sciences to preserve and enhance the human species or to invade and transform the most profound and definitive domains of its sexuality.

In more immediate terms, the question is whether male or female sexual nature will prevail. More than ever before, society needs today a real feminist movement that asserts the primacy of female nature in marriages and families. Just as women tame the barbarians of each generation of men, women can save sexuality from the male barbarians of specialization who would socialize reproduction. While eschewing a Luddite effort to stop the progress of knowledge, a real woman's movement can rebuke the social planners of Marxism, who have been widely thwarted in their efforts to create a "new society" but are now proposing to engineer a "new man."

In this resistance, the new feminists should find many male allies. For whatever dreams of glory men may cherish for society or for other men, few indeed will wish a new biology for themselves or for their sons. Men enjoy being male, and being married.

CHAPTER 17

Why Men Marry

Men marry for love. But what does this mean beyond what they got in their lives as single men: the flash of a new face, new flesh across a room. The glimpse of breasts shifting softly in a silken blouse. The open sesame of a missing ring. The excited pursuit, the misunderstood meanings, the charged meetings. The telling touch of hands. The eyes welling open to the gaze. The scent of surrender. The pillowed splash of unbound hair. The ecstatic slipping between new sheets. The race. The winning. The chase and the conquest. . . and back on the road. Definitely back on the road. Free again. Strong again. For new women, new pursuit. What more is there in life—in love—than this?

Marriage means giving it all up. Giving up love? That is how it seems to the single man, and that is why he fears it. He must give up his hunter's heart, forgo the getaway Honda growl, shear off his shaggy hair, restrict his random eye, hang up his handgun, bow down and enter the cage. At bottom, what he is is hunter. No way he will be hubby.

And yet, he will. For years he lunges at women's surfaces, but as time passes he learns of a deeper promise. For years he may not know the reasons or believe them or care. The heart, it is said, has its reasons. They spring from the primal predicament of man throughout the history of the race: the need to choose a particular woman and stay by her and provide for her if he is to know his children and they are to love him and call him father.

187

In procreative love, both partners consciously or unconsciously glimpse a future infant—precarious in the womb, vulnerable in the world, and in need of nurture and protection. In the swelter of their bodies together, in the shape and softnesses of the woman, in the protective support of the man, the couple senses the outlines of a realm that can endure and perpetuate their union: a pattern of differences and complements that goes beyond the momentary pleasures of reciprocal sex.

Marriage asks men to give up their essential sexuality only as part of a clear scheme for replacing it with new, far more important, and ultimately far more sexual roles: husband and father. Without these roles, a woman can bear a child, but the man is able only to screw. He can do it a lot, but after his first years it will only get him unthreaded, and in the end he is disconnected and alone. In his shallow heats and frustrations, he all too often becomes a menace to himself and his community.

There are millions of single men, unlinked to any promising reality, dissipating their lives by the years, moving from job to job, woman to woman, illusion to embitterment. Yet they are not hopeless. Many more millions have passed through the same sloughs, incurred the same boozy dreams, marijuana highs, cocaine crashes, sex diseases, job vapors, legal scrapes, wanderings. They follow the entire syndrome and then break out of it. Normally they do not escape through psychiatrists' offices, sex-education courses, VISTA or Peace Corps programs, reformatories, or guidance-counseling uplift. What happens, most of the time—the only effective thing that happens, the only process that reaches the sources of motivation and character—is falling in love.

Love is effective because it works at a deeper, more instinctual level than the other modes of education and change. Love does not teach or persuade. It possesses and transforms. . . .

It is not just an intelligent appraisal of his circumstances that transforms the single man. It is not merely a desire for companionship or "growth." It is a deeper alchemy of change, flowing from a primal source. It seeps slowly into the flesh, the memory, the spirit; it rises through a life, until it can ignite. It is a perilous process, full of chances for misfire and mistake—or for an ever more mildewed middle age. It is not entirely understood. But we have seen it work, and so have we seen love. Love infuses reason and experience with the power to change a man caught in a morbid present into a man passionately engaged with the future.

The change that leads to love often comes slowly. Many of the girls a man finds will not help. They tend to go along with him and affirm his single life. But one morning he turns to the stranger sleeping next to him, who came to him as easily as a whiskey too many, and left him as heavy-headed, and decides he must seek a better way to live. One day he looks across the room over a pile of dirty dishes and cigarette butts and beer cans and sex magazines and bills and filthy laundry, and he does not see the evidence of happy carousing and bachelor freedom; he sees a trap closing in upon him more grimly than any marriage. One day while joking with friends about the latest of his acquaintances to be caught and caged, he silently wonders, for a moment, whether he really wishes it were he.

Suddenly he has a new glimpse of himself. His body is beginning to decline, grow weaker and slower, even if he keeps it fit. His body, which once measured out his few advantages over females, is beginning to intimate its terrible plan to become as weak as an older woman's. His aggressiveness, which burst in fitful storms throughout his young life but never seemed to cleanse him—his aggression for which he could so rarely find the adequate battle, the harmonious chase—is souring now. His job, so below his measure as a man, so out of tune with his body and his inspiration, now stretches ahead without joy or relief.

His sex, the force that drove the flower of his youth, drives still, drives again and again the same hard bargain—for which there are fewer and fewer takers, in a sexual arena with no final achievement for the single man, in which sex itself becomes work that is never done.

The single man is caught on a reef and the tide is running out. He is being biologically stranded and he has a hopeless dream. Studs Terkel's book *Working¹* registers again and again men's desire to be remembered. Yet who in this world is much remembered for his job?

Stuck with what he may sense as a choice between being trapped and being stranded, he still may respond by trying one more fling. The biological predicament can be warded off for a time, like Hemingway's hyena. Death often appears in the guise of eternal youth, at the ever-infatuating fountains: alcohol, drugs, hallucinogenic sex. For a while he may believe in the disguise. But the hyena returns and there is mortality in the air—diseases, accidents, concealed suicides, the whole range of the single man's aggression, turned at last against himself.

But where there is death, there is hope. For the man who is in touch with his mortality, but not in the grips of it, is also in touch with the sources of his love. He is in contact with the elements—the natural fires and storms so often used as metaphors for his passions. He is a man who can be deeply and effectively changed. He can find his age, his relation to the world, his maturity, his future. He can burn his signature into the covenant of a specific life.

The man has found a vital energy and a possibility of durable change. It has assumed the shape of a woman. It is the same form that has caught his eye and roiled his body all these years. But now there will be depths below the pleasing surfaces, meanings beyond the momentary ruttings. There will be a sense that this vessel contains the secrets of new life, that the womb and breasts bear a message of immortality. There will be a knowledge that to treat this treasure as an object—mere flesh like his own, a mere matrix of his pleasure—is to defile life itself. It is this recognition that she offers a higher possibility—it is this consciousness that he has to struggle to be worthy of her—that finally issues the spark. And then arises the fire that purges and changes him as it consumes his own death. His children . . . they will remember. It is the only hope.

The man's love begins in a knowledge of inferiority, but it offers a promise of dignity and purpose. For he then has to create, by dint of his own effort, and without the miracle of a womb, a life that a woman could choose. Thus are released and formed the energies of civilized society. He provides, and he does it for a lifetime, for a life.

The Faith
of Fathers

In the spring of 1981, I was asked to give a speech to the Forty-fifth Reunion of my father's Harvard class. The invitation came as a pleasant surprise and solved a difficult problem. For months I had been receiving in the mail various messages from my own Harvard class, which was also gathering for a reunion, and I had not yet decided how to reply.

It was the twentieth anniversary of my graduation from college with a head full of liberal and secular ideas. It had taken me most of the interim to recover the wisdom of my youth: the beliefs in God and family taught me, chiefly by my mother, as I was growing up on a farm in Massachusetts.

Now my Harvard class was preparing a set of reunion seminars that seemed to repeat all the liberal pieties I had finally learned to escape. I was invited to hear a collection of family therapists discuss the problems of sex roles, listen to a group of the usual experts discourse on the crisis of energy and population, and attend a lecture on the problems of the Third World by a speaker who believes they mostly spring from American capitalism. Although I could not exactly anticipate the contents of the sessions, I could clearly sense a serious agenda of liberal gloom and guilt about the condition of the world.

I was sure that the chief problem underlying all the complaints—about family life, population, energy, and the Third World—would turn out to be people like myself and my classmates. The enemy would be us—at least those of us who had gone forth in the world, started families, pursued careers, and launched businesses without constant pangs of remorse about ourselves and our children as burdens on an overpopulated earth.

Since I was not asked to contribute my own views on any of these subjects, I could see myself full of frustration, seething and fuming through my reunion, insufferable company for whatever innocent classmates might stumble into my path. Yet it was my Twentieth and I wanted to go, see my old friends, and enjoy old places and fond memories. It was a dilemma.

Then, about a month before the event, a member of my father's class called up. My father was a bomber pilot killed in the Second World War, and I never knew him at all. As a matter of fact, I never much allowed anybody to talk to me about him because I always felt somehow embarrassed; I felt that when they described his extraordinary virtues, somehow by extension they were praising me. Also, I had a stepfather later on, whom I loved, who I felt might be hurt by hearing too much about my own father.

So I was told little about him. I understood he had done a lot of writing, but all of it had supposedly been lost during the course of moves from one household to another. The only sample I did see was a once-famous front-page editorial he wrote for the *Crimson,* presumably to greet Franklin Roosevelt on his arrival at the tercentenary celebration of Harvard in 1936. It ended with an exhortation: "Let the presence of this man in the White House at the time of our great tercentenary celebration serve as a useful antidote to the natural overemphasis on Harvard's successes." The olympian tone and conservative spirit intrigued me, and I was eager to see more of his work.

The day after I received the first bound pages of *Wealth and Poverty,* which was well on its way to publication, I was told by my uncle that to his great surprise he had discovered in his basement a big box full of my father's papers. I eagerly went through them; at the top was a 175-page manuscript on economics that he was working on when he died. One of its themes was the importance of what he called "intangible capital." It corresponded nearly perfectly with the key message of *Wealth and Poverty*: that the driving force of a free economy was not material resources or even physical capital, but the metaphysical capital of family and faith. In fact, my father's work, if it had been completed, could very well have been entitled *Wealth and Poverty*.

The manuscript seemed to confirm a deep sense I carried with me throughout my youth that I was linked in an almost mystical way to this man I never knew. Family was not some arbitrary accident of parental pressure and example that ended with departure from the household. Its influence did not flow only from genetic information or home education. It did not end with distance or even death.

My father taught me no economics, and Harvard taught me scarcely more in the one introductory course I took and barely passed. Yet discovering the literature of the subject in my fortieth year, I tapped a new source of creativity and intellectual power that I never imagined I possessed. I like to think some of that inspiration came from the young man in khaki who climbed into a Flying Fortress at age twenty-six in the war against the Nazis and left forever behind him a two-year-old boy and an unfinished text of economics back home in a box.

Even denying a mystical tie, the family has always been important to me as an idea. Its values, its atmosphere, its experiences, its interests, its intellectual temper, its ancestral history, its hopes for the future, so it seemed to me, pervade every psyche and define every person, even in rebellion from its specific rule. I was a link in an unending biological chain, a genetic vessel cast forth into nothingness with a prayer, before the lieutenant boarded the plane for the final takeoff. But the survival and success of the link depended upon the persistence of love, first from my mother, and, in my case, from many friends and relations of my father as well, then from my wife and children.

Most achievement in the world, I believe, reflects the force of family, first the patience and patrimony of parents and relatives, then the inspiration and support of husband or wife, finally the challenge and responsibility of the next generation. Some children can thrive in the absence of all this; but the society as a whole depends on family connections to succeed. Their breakdown and decay brings the danger of sexual suicide.

That was the essence of my earlier book by that title and part of my message to the Class of 1936. But I also wanted to tell them what I had learned from their experience. My own class was listening to incantations of despair about the future. A general assumption of most such analysis is that current conditions are relatively unfavorable for the bearing of children, that rising populations are exerting dangerous pressure on dwindling reserves of natural wealth. The U.S., with a small percent of the world's people consuming nearly half of its so-called resources, is said to be the worst culprit of all.

A popular movement, anticipating the "me-generation," maintained that it was not only most pleasurable to live child-free, but also most moral and responsible. Together with economic pressures, that movement won a great triumph both in the U.S. and Europe, reducing the birthrate of the West by about one-half and greatly weakening the constraints of monogamy in sexual relations. In particular, the movement won a great triumph among my classmates, who drastically lowered their family size compared to the graduates of the 1950s.

Yet for all the pretense of intellectual analysis and patina of moral concern, it seemed to me that this despair about the future and spurning of children was in fact quite simply sick. To anyone with any historic imagination who conceives of what it was like to be in the Class of 1936, moving out of the Great Depression, moving toward the Second World War, the idea that the problems we face today are somehow extraordinary or especially difficult or unparalleled in human experience is obvious nonsense. As a matter of fact, it struck me that for my father to write militant testaments to capitalism between 1936 and 1941 was incomparably more bold and daring than for me today, with all the postwar experience behind me, to assert that capitalism is the crucial source of growth and progress. And it was quite apparent to me that if the timorous spirit of zero population growth had prevailed in the Class of 1936, the allies might well have lost the war from a sheer failure of will; in any case much of the Class of 1961 would never have been born to grow up and contemplate the terrible threats of acid rain and nuclear winter.

Couples who choose to go without children in the name of sexual pleasure or in the fear of resource scarcity reveal an incomprehension of the nature of the human predicament. Lewis Lehrman once summed up the answer to their concerns. Responding to a woman questioning his sense of responsibility in having five children, who would consume "precious natural resources," he said: "But Madam, don't you understand? Those children, themselves, *are* our most precious natural resources." Children are not the problem; being child-free is no solution. But free children, under capitalism, in families that give them roots in the past and horizons in the future— that give them faith and discipline and moral courage—afford most of the pleasures and solve most of the problems of the world.

This is not merely a polemical point. The trends of sexual suicide that I attack in the pages of this book have already had a dire effect on the economies of the West. Pervading the media, the churches, the schools, the universities—persisting even in the 1980s at Harvard— in a fervor of antinatalist faith, the belief arose and prevailed that growth was a problem, rather than the solution. Crucial was the notion, originating with Pastor Malthus, that populations consist mainly of mouths, not minds—that people will tend to consume more than they can produce.

This ideology led to massive family-planning and abortion programs that contributed heavily to a drastic decline in the population growth rates of the U.S. and Europe. Indeed, in the U.S., the number of American women between the ages of 30 and 34 who expected to have four or more children dropped from 55 percent in 1967 to 11.5 percent in 1982.[1] Overall, by the 1980s, the industrial nations of the West most capable of supporting and educating children were no longer reproducing themselves at the replacement level.

If we are lucky, the U.S. may end up solving the problem through massive immigration and capitalist growth. The Malthusian deficit will be closed by outsiders. But those fashionable moralists who do not stress the "problem" of overpopulation instead often contend that the world, and the moral order as well, are threatened by enterprise and growth. In fact, perhaps Britain's most eloquent critic of sexual revolution, E. J. Mishan, blames sexual excesses on capitalism.

In a recent essay in *Encounter* offering many of the same themes that *Sexual Suicide* first presented some thirteen years before, he wrote: "In pursuit of the economic growth imperative, traditional forms of propriety and good taste, of moderation and restraint, were inevitably subverted . . . A society in which increasingly 'anything goes' is also the kind of society in which virtually anything will sell. Thus for the economies of the West, at least, a permissive, indeed a promiscuous, society is a necessary condition for economic growth."[2] Dale Vree, editor of the Catholic intellectual journal *New Oxford Review*, also urgently argues that far from subverting capitalism, feminism and sexual hedonism are essential products of it.[3]

Both these views stem from the false assumption that capitalism is driven by consumer demand. By this standard, anything that excites the desire of consumers to spend is a positive force in economic growth. Since prostitution, divorce, pornography, adultery, fornication, homosexuality, and other forces of social dissolution all increase the purchase of market goods, as opposed to goods provided in the home, all may be said to enhance the rise of the GNP. Thus conservatives and socialists can sometimes come together on social issues. To the extent that both believe the engine of economic growth is driven by greed, they can see permissiveness as favorable to growth under capitalism.

In Britain, for example, the aristocratic Tory, dubious of men in trade, is often as antibusiness as any labor-union socialist. The libertarian, meanwhile, feeds their mutual doubts about capitalism by linking it to a licentious freedom that both abhor. Adding to the confusion is the fact that erotica, nearly always a product of private enterprise, is rare in Communist countries, and is one of the few untrammeled private ventures in the Scandinavian social democracies.

Nevertheless, all these views of capitalism are false. All partake of the view that the system is a kind of Faustian pact, a deal with the devil in which we gain prosperity by giving in to greed and avarice, selfishness and lust. Like most deals with the devil, such a transaction might bring a short-term payoff. But such deals also inflict deadly long-term costs. They subvert the moral and familial values on which all capitalist systems rely for their success.

Demand, whether avaricious or just, is impotent to impel growth without disciplined, creative, and essentially moral producers of new value. All effective demand ultimately derives from supply; a society's income cannot exceed its output. The output of valuable goods depends not on lechery, prurience, lust, and license but on thrift, sacrifice, altruism, creativity, discipline, trust, and faith. To the extent that pornography and promiscuity debauch the moral capital of the society—to the extent that they distract workers and entrepreneurs from the long-term effort to create new value—these sources of "demand" actually undermine economic growth.

By that measure, the sexual revolution clearly retards economic progress and prosperity. It distracts, demoralizes, obsesses, and depraves the men and women who must forgo immediate returns, sacrifice immediate pleasures, master difficult disciplines, and respond to the needs and desires of others if they are to create successful businesses. Capitalism has been incomparably the most productive economic system in the history of the world because it best evokes the effort and creativity—the moral quality and productive energy—of workers and businessmen who put the interests of others before their own gratifications.

Greed, in fact, impels people to seek first their own comfort and security. The truly self-interested man most often turns to government to give him the benefits he lacked the moral discipline to earn on his own by serving others. He follows his own hungers at the expense of his family and leaves them to the dole. Self-interest—and all its relations, from avarice to lust—leads therefore as by an invisible hand not to a soundly growing economy but to a rampantly growing welfare state. It leads to socialism, not capitalism.

Capitalism begins with the love of families for their children and the belief that any child may grow up and make huge contributions to his society. The history of capitalism is a saga of the last becoming first—of once-poor and unlettered entrepreneurs, often immigrants or outsiders, challenging the redoubts of established wealth and expertise. Most of the time these creative rebels are believed and supported at first only by their families. Their initial funds nearly always come from relatives. Capitalism begins at the mother's breast, with the feminine belief in the sanctity of every life, enshrined in the family and equal before God. Any system that does not uphold the value and freedom of individuals, however lowly, will miss most of the greatest technical and economic breakthroughs.

Giving, beginning within the family and extending outward into the society, is the moral center of the system. It does not succeed by allowing the leading capitalists to revel in riches; if they hoard their wealth the system tends to fail. It succeeds by inducing the capitalist continually to give his wealth back to the system in the form of new gifts and investments.

A key misconception of the Left is that giving is somehow simple and easy: you just stand on the street corner and distribute dollars, or you create a welfare system that redistributes money. But anyone who really considers the problem closely discovers that it is difficult to give without harming, that it takes intimate knowledge to give without taking in the long run. This is why families are the crucial instrument of overcoming poverty: because people who live with others and have direct responsibility for them, who bear children and thus have their lives descended into the future, can give in a productive and successful way. Distant institutions distribute dollars, but they cannot really give.

A capitalist business is a better instrument of giving than is a welfare state. The process of investment, oriented toward fulfilling the needs and desires of others, in cooperation with others in the firm, leads to a more altruistic way of life and result of effort than does many a public charity. The ultimate morality of the company is rooted in the morality of family—in the golden rule and the returns of giving.

Indeed, the essential capitalist act—the very paradigm of giving or investing without a predetermined outcome—is the bearing, raising, and educating of children. Above all, in advanced societies where child labor is rare, children entail a prolonged and precarious commitment of work and wealth, love and faith, with no assurance of future return. They require elaborate decades of expensive preparation before they can make their own contributions to the society, negative or positive; and all too often, at least in the view of the parents, they turn out wrong. (In fact, Ann Landers's famous poll suggested that 70 percent of mothers felt betrayed by their children and, given the choice, would not bear them again.)

Parents are the ultimate entrepreneurs, and, as with all entrepreneurs, the odds are against them. But all human progress—of businesses and families as well as societies—depends on an entrepreneurial willingness to defy the odds. It is in the nuclear family that the most crucial process of capitalist defiance and faith is centered.

Here emerge the most indispensable acts of capital formation: the psychology of giving, saving, and sacrifice, in behalf of an unknown future, embodied in a specific child—a balky bundle of possibilities, which will yield its social reward even further into time than the most foresighted business plan. In this venture, few mothers—and no societies—can succeed without enlisting the fathers.

Marriage is the key to the connection of fathers to this central process in the creation of life and the production of wealth. The golden rule and perennial lesson of marriage is: "Give and you will be given unto." It is the obvious message of motherhood. But societies thrive only to the extent that this maternal wisdom becomes as well the faith of fathers.

Notes

Chapter 1
THE NECESSITIES OF LOVE

1. A cross-cultural survey of 580 of the world's societies indicated that in one-quarter of them the father is only an occasional visitor with his children. George P. Murdock, "World Ethnographic Sample," *American Anthropologist* 59 (1957). Perhaps the most famous society where physiological paternity is not recognized is the Trobriand Island tribe discussed by Bronislaw Malinowski in *The Sexual Life of Savages in North Western Melanesia*, 2 vols. (New York: Harcourt Brace Jovanovich, 1929); and in *The Father in Primitive Psychology* (New York: Norton, 1927; Norton Library paperback, 1966).

2. Ashley Montagu, *Touching: The Human Significance of the Skin* (New York: Columbia University Press, 1971), pp. 181–82.

3. Karen Horney, *Feminine Psychology* (New York: Norton, 1967); idem, *New Ways in Psychoanalysis* (New York: Norton, 1939), and Erik H. Erikson, *Identity: Youth and Crisis* (New York: Norton, 1968), pp. 261–94.

4. Margaret Mead, *Male and Female: A Study of the Sexes in a Changing World* (New York: Morrow, 1949), quoted from the paperback (New York: Dell, 1968), p. 123.

5. Judith Hole and Ellen Levine, *Rebirth of Feminism* (New York: Quadrangle, 1971), p. 306.

6. Seymour Fisher, *Understanding the Female Orgasm* (New York: Basic Books, 1973), p. 187. (This book is a condensation of *The Female Orgasm: Psychology, Physiology, Fantasy*. New York: Basic Books, 1973.)

7. Nancy Chodorow, "Being and Doing: A Cross-Cultural Examination of the Socialization of Males and Females," in Vivian Gornick and Barbara K. Moran, eds., *Women in Sexist Society: Studies in Power and Powerlessness* (New York: Basic Books, 1971), pp. 173–98 and passim.

8. Mary Jane Sherfey, *The Nature and Evolution of Female Sexuality* (New York: Random House, 1972).

9. Robert Musil, *The Man Without Qualities* (New York: Putnam, 1965).

10. Midge Decter, *The New Chastity and Other Arguments Against Women's Liberation* (New York: Coward, McCann, & Geoghegan, 1972), p. 93; also pp. 61–105 and passim.

11. Clellan S. Ford and Frank A. Beach, *Patterns of Sexual Behavior* (New York: Harper & Row, 1951). This cross-cultural study indicates that the male is universally more responsive to visual stimuli (p. 95), more prone to masturbation (p. 257), and more likely to engage in homosexuality (p. 257). "In all animal species . . . males exhibit far more [initiatory foreplay] than do females" (p. 259). In many societies the man has to give a gift to the woman (p. 98).

12. Lionel Tiger and Joseph Shepher, *Women in the Kibbutz* (New York: Harcourt Brace Jovanovich, 1975), p. 7. "Kibbutz boys and girls who are reared together in the same children's house never marry each other, in violation of the sociological 'law of propinquity,' which holds that people marry people who are geographically near and with whom they share a set of life experiences. Using census data presented in this volume [*Women in the Kibbutz*], Shepher demonstrated that . . . out of some 3,000 kibbutz marriages over three generations, there was not one between men and women who had been together during the ages of three and six . . . The firm correlation with a maturation stage in the life cycle suggested to Shepher that it may be comparable to the imprinting which some biologists (most prominently Konrad Lorenz) have conceived to explain certain regularities in some animals' social behavior. [Shepher's] research strongly implies that some infrasocial process in individual growth inhibits men and women from engaging in sex and marriage if they have spent a particular, long period together as boys and girls." In any case, companionship alone surely did not lead to marriage in the kibbutz.

13. Robert Briffault and Bronislaw Malinowski, *Marriage: Past and Present* (Boston: Porter Sargent, 1956), p. 50.

14. Mead, *Male and Female*, p. 195.

15. Briffault and Malinowski, *Marriage*, p. 79.

Chapter 2

THE BIOLOGICAL DIFFERENCE

1. John Money and Anke A. Ehrhardt, *Man and Woman, Boy and Girl: The Differentiation and Dimorphism of Gender Identity from Conception to Maturity* (Baltimore, Md.: Johns Hopkins University Press, 1972).

2. Harry F. Harlow and Margaret Harlow, "Social Deprivation in Monkeys," *Scientific American*, November 1962; Harry F. Harlow, "Sexual Behavior in the Rhesus Monkey," in Frank A. Beach, ed., *Sex and Behavior* (London: Wiley, 1965).

3. Eleanor Emmons Maccoby and Carol Nagy Jacklin, *The Psychology of Sex Differences* (Stanford, Calif.: Stanford University Press, 1974). Jacklin and Maccoby hedge their findings with the usual academic waffling. But their voluminous and authoritative study, based on analysis of some 2,000 research tests and experiments involving several hundred thousand subjects, explicitly confirms the biological origins of the male advantage in aggression and presents telling evidence on all the other points of difference cited between the sexes.

4. B. Whiting, *Six Cultures: Studies of Childrearing* (London: Wiley, 1963).

5. Steven Goldberg, *The Inevitability of Patriarchy* (New York: Morrow, 1973). As Goldberg points out in an unpublished recent paper answering his critics, "A society may have a titular queen or a powerful queen serving in an hereditary position when no appropriate male is available; there were more female heads-of-state in the monarchical world of the first two-thirds of the sixteenth century than in the first two-thirds of the twentieth. Occasionally a woman will attain the highest position in her society, but this is unusual in every such society; moreover, when this does occur . . . the vast majority of the other upper positions are filled by males. A government may claim an ideological commitment to hierarchical equality and even that this commitment is being met. But the reality is always that the claim is not true; in China, for example, sixty-seven of the ministers are male and the other five ministerial positions are vacant. One may choose any society that has ever existed anywhere and find the same thing."

See also Robin Fox, *Kinship and Marriage* (Baltimore, Md.: Penguin Books, 1967), p. 31 and passim. Fox maintains that no marriage system can endure with a male presence unless the men exercise control.

6. Margaret Mead, review of *The Inevitability of Patriarchy*, *Redbook*, October 1973. Although Mead objected to Goldberg's argument on inevitability (she thought new technologies might eventually overcome male dominance), she endorsed the persuasiveness and accuracy of his research. On his central empirical thesis, she wrote: "It is true, as Professor Goldberg points out, that all the claims so glibly made about societies ruled by women are nonsense. We have no reason to believe that they ever existed . . . Men have always been the leaders in public affairs and the final authorities in the home."

7. Clelland S. Ford and Frank A. Beach, *Patterns of Sexual Behavior* (New York: Harper & Row, 1951).

8. George P. Murdock, "World Ethnographic Sample," *American Anthropologist* 59 (1957).

9. Naomi Weisstein, "Tired of Arguing about Biological Inferiority" (*Ms.*, November 1982), is typical of this mode of denial. Ms. Weisstein ignores the fact that in size and sexuality humans are among the most dimorphic of primates. Men and women differ more in physique and hormonal makeup, and probably in psychology, than chimps, gibbons, macaques, and other monkeys that Weisstein cites; she stresses the few species of primates with relatively large females. In addition, she implies that the critics of feminism deny virtually any influence of environment and culture. In fact, it is the thesis of this book that culture and environment are crucial to creating productive male roles, preventing male disruption of society, and inducing male submission to female values. If culture didn't matter, feminism and male chauvinism wouldn't matter either.

A recent presentation of evidence stressing the importance of the size advantage to male dominance and polygyny among primates is physiologist-anthropologist Jared Diamond's article on sexual differences in *Discover*, April 1985, p. 70 and passim.

10. Money and Ehrhardt, *Man and Woman*.

11. Corinne Hutt, *Males and Females* (Baltimore, Md.: Penguin Books, 1972). For a readable account of these and other studies, *see also* Maggie Scarf, *Body, Mind, Behavior* (Washington, D.C.: New Republic Book Co., 1976), pp. 19-35. For a more detailed explanation of the endocrinological material, see Seymour Levine, ed., *Hormones and Behavior* (New York: Academic Press, 1972), p. 73 and passim.

12. Hutt, *Males and Females.*

13. Ibid., pp. 52-56.

14. This is one of a long series of experiments and observations conducted at Yerkes Regional Primate Research Center, Lawrenceville, Georgia. Irwin S. Bernstein, "Spontaneous Reorganization of a Pigtail Monkey Group," *Studies of Social Behavior in (Large) Enclosures.* Proc. 2nd int. congr. primat., Atlanta, Ga., 1968, vol. 1 (New York: Karger, Basel, 1969), p. 111. *See also* Scarf, *Body, Mind, Behavior.*

15. Patricia Cayo Sexton, *The Feminized Male: White Collars and the Decline of Manliness* (New York: Random House, 1969; Vintage Books, 1970).

16. Thomas Pettigrew, *A Profile of the Negro American* (New York: Van Nostrand Reinhold, 1964), pp. 18, 20 (chart).

17. Robert M. Rose, Thomas R. Gordon, and Irwin S. Bernstein, "Plasma Testosterone Levels in the Male Rhesus: Influences of Sexual and Social Stimuli," *Science* 178 (10 November 1972), pp. 643-45. Rose has subsequently presented evidence that this phenomenon also applies to humans, with infantrymen in Vietnam, for example, registering very low testosterone levels under the stress of impending combat.

18. Ford and Beach, *Sexual Behavior.*

Chapter 3
AFTER THE HUNT

1. Margaret Mead, *Male and Female: A Study of the Sexes in a Changing World* (New York: Morrow, 1949), quoted from the paperback (New York: Dell, 1968), p. 168.

2. Lionel Tiger, *Men in Groups*, second edition with foreword by Desmond Morris (New York: Marion Boyars, 1984), p. 44 and passim.

3. Nancy Chodorow, "Being and Doing: A Cross-Cultural Examination of the Socialization of Males and Females," in Vivian Gornick and Barbara K. Moran, eds., *Woman in Sexist Society: Studies in Power and Powerlessness* (New York: Basic Books, 1971), pp. 173-98. *See also* Colin Turnbull, *The Mountain People* (New York: Simon & Schuster, 1972), p. 24-26.

4. Mead, *Male and Female*, pp. 118-19; Baldwin Spencer and F. J. Gillen, *The Arunta* (New York: Humanities Press, 1966), vol. 1, pp. 175-303. *See also* Bruno Bettelheim, *Symbolic Wounds: Puberty Rites and the Envious Male* (New York: The Free Press, 1962); and Theodore Reik, *Ritual* (New York: International Universities Press, 1946).

5. Mead, *Male and Female*, pp. 118-19.

6. David Pilbeam, "The fashionable view of man as a naked ape is: 1. An insult to apes; 2. Simplistic; 3. Male-oriented; 4. Rubbish." *The New York Times Magazine*, 3 September 1972, p. 30.

7. Tiger, *Men in Groups*, pp. 39–54.

8. E. A. Wrigley, *Population and History* (New York: McGraw-Hill, 1969), pp. 76–77.

9. Ibid., p. 116.

10. Peter Laslett, *Family Life and Illicit Love in Earlier Generations* (New York: Cambridge University Press, 1977).

11. In *Montaillou* (New York: Vintage, 1979), Emmanuel Ladurie shows the nuclear family well established in rural France in the fourteenth century.

12. Wrigley, *Population and History*, p. 13.

13. Ibid., p. 116–27.

14. Brigitte Berger and Peter L. Berger, *The War over the Family: Capturing the Middle Ground* (Garden City, N.Y.: Anchor Press/Doubleday, 1984), pp. 85–104. The Bergers present an array of further testimony confirming the Wrigley thesis. They write, "Recent research into the history of the family, both in Western Europe and North America, shows that the nuclear family, far from being a product of modernization processes . . . antedates these processes by centuries . . . in Western Europe, while Eastern Europe did indeed have the sort of extended family that Westerners have been so nostalgic about . . . It could well be that the nuclear family is a precondition, rather than a consequence, of modernization. This hypothesis, needless to say, would stand on its head many of the assumptions that sociologists have operated with since the 1920s" (p. 87).

Chapter 4
TAMING THE BARBARIANS

1. I first heard the concept of the generational barbarian invasion, as well as many other concepts in this volume, from Daniel Patrick Moynihan.

2. In 1983, according to census data, 8.9 percent of women in intact families earned half or more of family income, and fewer than one in 45 earned more than 75 percent of family income. Unpublished data from Current Population Survey, Bureau of Labor Statistics, 31 May 1984, Marital and Family Characteristics of the Labor Force, Table 30: "Contribution of wife's earnings to family income in 1983, by family income, work experience of wife, and age of husband." Even with husbands under age 25, wives earned only 31.6 percent of family incomes in two-earner families and less than one in ten earned half of family income in all intact families.

3. Isabel V. Sawhill, "Economic Perspectives on the Family," *Daedalus*, Spring 1977, p. 119. "One of the most dramatic and consistent findings has been the greater prevalence of marriage and the lower probability of divorce where women's wages or labor-market participation are relatively low." Vassar economist Shirley Johnson computes that each additional $1,000 of a woman's earnings increases her

likelihood of divorce by two percent. Quoted in Caroline Bird, *The Two Paycheck Marriage* (New York: Rawson, Wade, 1979), p. 13. Summing up the evidence, Bird concludes: "The more money a woman earns, the less likely she is to be married. The relationship cannot be denied . . ." *See also* similar findings, termed the "independence effect," cited by Heather L. Ross and Isabel V. Sawhill, *Time of Transition: The Growth of Families Headed by Women* (Washington, D.C.: The Urban Institute, 1975).

4. Quoted in E. J. Mishan, "Women's Lib—Was the Movement Really Necessary?" *Encounter,* January 1985.

5. Nena O'Neill and George O'Neill, *Open Marriage: A New Life Style for Couples* (New York: M. Evans, 1972; M. Evans paperback, 1984).

6. Margaret Mead, *Male and Female: A Study of the Sexes in a Changing World* (New York: Morrow, 1949; New York: Dell, 1968).

7. Ibid., pp. 116–17.

8. Ibid., pp. 114–15.

9. Ibid., p. 89.

10. O'Neill and O'Neill, *Open Marriage,* p. 145 (1972 edition).

11. Anne Steinmann and David J. Fox, *The Male Dilemma* (New York: Jason Aronson, 1974), p. 52.

12. Philip Blumstein and Pepper Schwartz, *American Couples* (New York: William Morrow, 1983).

13. Jane E. Brody, "U.S. Couples Surprisingly Conventional, Study Finds," *New York Times* news service, 10 October 1983.

14. Sawhill, "Economic Perspectives," p. 119.

Chapter 5
THE PRINCESS'S PROBLEM

1. Computed from data in U.S. Department of Health and Human Services, *Vital Statistics of the United States, 1979,* Volume III, "Marriage and Divorce" (Hyattsville, Md.: National Center for Health Statistics, 1984), Table 1-21 and Table 1-22. Includes divorced and separated in singles category.

2. Ibid.

3. Neil Bennett, Patricia Craig, and David Bloom, unpublished study, discussed in cover story, *People,* 31 March 1986, pp. 28–33. Since divorcees of this age have nearer a 30 percent chance of remarriage, the low rates of marriage for never-married women in their thirties suggests that some resist marriage, perhaps in part because of feminist ideology. The decline of feminism and improved public policy should increase marriage rates above the levels estimated in the study.

4. Computed from data in U.S. Bureau of the Census, *Current Population Reports,* Series P-20, No. 380, "Marital Status and Living Arrangements: March 1982" (Washington, D.C.: U.S. Government Printing Office, 1983), Table A and Table 1.

5. Ibid.

6. Computed from data in Department of Health, *Vital Statistics,* Table 1-21 and Table 1-22.

7. Andrew Hacker, *U.S.: A Statistical Portrait of the American People* (New York: Viking Press, 1983), pp. 112–13.

Chapter 6
THE BARBARIANS' REVENGE

1. U.S. Bureau of the Census, *Current Population Reports,* Series P-20, No. 380, "Marital Status and Living Arrangements: March 1982" (Washington, D.C.: U.S. Government Printing Office, 1983), Table A and Table 1.

2. Solomon William Polachek, "Women in the Economy: Perspectives on Gender Inequality," in *Comparable Worth: Issue for the 80's* (Washington, D.C.: U.S. Commission on Civil Rights, 1984), Vol. 1, Table 7, p. 43.

3. Ibid., p. 44–45.

4. U.S. Bureau of the Census, *Current Population Reports,* Series P-60, No. 146, "Money Income of Households, Families, and Persons in the United States, 1983" (Washington, D.C.: U.S. Government Printing Office, 1985), Table 45, p. 145. After age 55, according to 1970 census data, single women tend to outearn single men.

5. Irwin Garfinkel and Robert Haveman, with the assistance of David Betson, U.S. Department of Health, Education and Welfare, *Earnings Capacity, Poverty, and Inequality,* Institute for Research on Poverty Monograph Series (New York: Academic Press, 1977), pp. 29–32 and Table 3.3, p. 32.

6. Single men in 1982 had an unemployment rate of 17.7 percent compared to 13.6 percent for single women. *Handbook of Labor Statistics,* U.S. Department of Labor, December 1983, Bulletin 2175, p. 73.

7. Census Bureau, "Money Income, 1983," Table 45, pp. 145–52.

8. Ibid.

9. Jessie Bernard, *The Future of Marriage* (New York: World Publishing Company, 1972), pp. 295–316.

10. Ibid.

11. Ibid.

12. Morton Hunt, *Sexual Behavior in the 1970s* (Chicago, Ill.: Playboy Press, 1974). *See also* Joyce Brothers, Richard Koppenaal, and John Darley, interpreting poll data collected by Bill Johnson & Associates, Survey Research, Mt. Vernon, N.Y., 1985; and John Leo, "Sex in the '80s," *Time,* 8 April 1984, pp. 74–83.

13. Hunt, *Sexual Behavior,* pp. 211–13.

14. Harvey E. Kaye, *Male Survival* (New York: Grosset & Dunlap, 1974), p. 84. While Alfred Kinsey's 1949 report indicated problems with impotence in 1.3 percent of men under 35, a 1970 poll by *Psychology Today* reported one in three men with erectile difficulties, and John Leo of *Time* reported, "For sexologists these days, the new frontier is inhibited sexual desire . . .[which] accounts for 30 percent to 50 percent of the case load for many therapists." ("Sex in the '80s," 8 April 1984, p. 83).

15. U.S. Bureau of the Census, "Census of Population: 1980." Subject Reports, *Persons in Institutions and Other Group Quarters* (Washington, D.C.: Government Printing Office, 1982).

16. Computed from ibid., and from *Uniform Crime Reports* (Washington, D.C.: Federal Bureau of Investigation, 1980).

17. Ibid.

18. *World Almanac and Book of Facts, 1985* (New York: Newspaper Enterprise Association, 1985), p. 789. From *Uniform Crime Reports*, Federal Bureau of Investigation.

19. A. Wynne, "Trends in Youth Suicide, Homicide, Arrests, and Drug Use," testimony prepared for delivery to the U.S. House of Representatives, Select Committee on Children, Youth and Families, 20 July 1983.

20. Hugh Carter and Paul C. Glick, *Marriage and Divorce: A Social and Economic Study*, rev. ed. (Cambridge, Massachusetts: Harvard University Press, 1976), chapter 11, "Marital Status and Health," pp. 324-57; and Metropolitan Life Insurance Company, "Canadian Mortality According to Marital Status, by Sex [and age] (Death Rate per 100,000 during 1969-70)." *Statistical Bulletin*, August 1973. For supporting data from nineteenth-century Europe, including France, Switzerland, Italy, Prussia, Saxony, Baden, and other areas, see Emile Durkheim, *Suicide, A Study in Sociology*, trans., John A. Spaulding and George Simpson, ed. George Simpson (New York: The Free Press, 1966), pp. 178, 183, 196, 197, and passim. *See also* James J. Lynch, *The Broken Heart: The Medical Consequences of Loneliness* (New York: Basic Books, 1977), pp. 239-49, including evidence from Japan, p. 243.

21. Durkheim, *Suicide*.

22. Phyllis Chesler, *Women and Madness* (Garden City, N.Y.: Doubleday & Company, 1972), p. 328.

23. Census Bureau, *Persons in Institutions*.

24. Carter and Glick, *Marriage and Divorce*, pp. 340-41. *See also* Lynch, *Broken Heart*, pp. 239-49.

25. Carter and Glick, *Marriage and Divorce*, pp. 345-47.

26. John Bowlby, *Attachment and Loss* (New York: Basic Books, 1973).

27. Lynch, *Broken Heart*.

Chapter 7
CRUISING

1. Leon McKusick, William Horstman, and Thomas J. Coates, "AIDS and Sexual Behavior Reported by Gay Men in San Francisco," *American Journal of Public Health*, May 1985, p. 493.

2. Wardell Pomeroy, *Dr. Kinsey and the Institute for Sex Research* (New York: Harper & Row, 1972), p. 76.

3. Arno Karlen, "Homosexuality: The Scene and its Students," in James M. Henslin and Edward Sagarin, eds., *The Sociology of Sex*, rev. ed. (New York: Schocken

Books, 1978), p. 247. *See also* Arno Karlen, *Sexuality and Homosexuality* (New York: Norton, 1971), pp. 572–606.

4. Jeremy Cherfas and John Gribbin, *The Redundant Male* (New York: Pantheon, 1984), p. 132.

5. Karlen, "Homosexuality: The Scene," p. 228.

6. Ibid.

7. Karlen, *Sexuality*, pp. 526–28.

8. Paul Cameron, Day Proctor, William Coburn, Jr., and Nells Forde, "Sexual Orientation and Sexually Transmitted Disease," *Nebraska Medical Journal*, Vol. 70, No. 8, 1985, pp. 292–99.

9. Ibid.

10. George P. Murdock, "World Ethnographic Sample," *American Anthropologist* 59 (1957).

11. Karlen, *Sexuality*, pp. 232–36.

12. Ibid., pp. 239–42.

13. Ibid., pp. 468–74.

Chapter 8
GHETTO "LIBERATION"

1. Computed from data in U.S. Department of Health and Human Services, Vital Statistics of the United States, *Monthly Vital Statistics Reports*, "Natality" (Hyattsville, Md.: National Center for Health Statistics, 1985).

2. Computed from data in U.S. Bureau of the Census, *Current Population Reports*, Series P-20, No. 380, "Marital Status and Living Arrangements: March 1982," (Washington, D.C.: U.S. Government Printing Office, 1983).

3. Ibid. Reported in William Julius Wilson and Kathryn M. Neckerman, "Poverty and Family Structure: The Widening Gap Between Evidence and Public Policy Issues," *IRP Conference Paper* (Madison, Wisconsin: Institute for Research on Poverty, 1985), p. 6. This article is a revised version of a paper prepared for presentation at the conference on "Poverty and Policy: Retrospect and Prospects," 6–8 December 1984, at Williamsburg, Virginia.

4. Statistics computed from Census Bureau, "Marital Status 1982."

5. U.S. Department of Health and Human Services, Vital Statistics of the United States, *Monthly Vital Statistics Reports*, "Death Rates by Age, Race and Sex in the United States" (Hyattsville, Md.: National Center for Health Statistics, 1985).

6. Murray did regression equations on illegitimacy data from 1969–71, comparing proportion of population in poverty with illegitimacy ratios. Correlations were .75 for whites and .71 for blacks and the projected ratios for 100 percent in poverty were 62.2 percent for whites and 85.4 percent for blacks (personal communication, 16 October 1985).

7. Computed from data in U.S. Bureau of the Census, *Current Population Reports*, Series P-60, No. 146, "Money Income of Households, Families, and Persons in the

United States: 1983'' (Washington, D.C.: U.S. Government Printing Office, 1985), Table 14. *See also* Gordon Green and Edward Welniak, "Measuring the Effects of Changing Family Composition During the 1970s on Black-White Differences in Income," U.S. Bureau of the Census (Washington, D.C.: U.S. Government Printing Office, 1983).

8. The original Labor Department version is reproduced, with much interesting commentary, in Lee Rainwater and William L. Yancey, *The Moynihan Report and the Politics of Controversy* (Cambridge, Mass.: MIT Press, 1967). *See also* Daniel P. Moynihan, *Family and Nation* (Cambridge, Mass.: Harvard University Press, 1985).

9. For discussion of recent research on the syndrome of fatherlessness, see George A. Rekers, "Father Absence in Broken Families: The Effects on Children's Development," testimony 22 March 1983, published in *Broken Families*, Hearings before the Subcommittee on Family and Human Services of the Committee on Labor and Human Resources, United States Senate (Washington, D.C.: U.S. Government Printing Office, 1983), pp. 131-75.

10. Thomas Pettigrew, *A Profile of the Negro American* (New York: Van Nostrand Reinhold, 1964), pp. 18, 20 (chart). Pettigrew adduces a wealth of psychological studies indicating that a key problem of ghetto males is sex-role insecurity originating in fatherless families. But some of the femininity indices ("singing ambition") may be false for blacks.

11. Ibid., p. 16. *See also* Rekers, "Father Absence," pp. 138-41 and passim.

12. Rekers, "Father Absence," pp. 141-42.

13. Even this deceptive income advantage of black men over black women may be eroded by the campaign against sex discrimination (as measured by the government). See Ronald L. Oaxaca, "Male-Female Wage Differentials in Urban Labor Markets," Working Paper No. 23, Industrial Relations Section, Princeton University, 1971. This study suggests that the 20 percent income advantage of black males over black females is 94 percent attributable to sex discrimination, while the advantage of white males over white women was found to be only 64 percent attributable to bias. The bias is mostly if not entirely illusory. Such statistics are excessively dependent on appraisals of education, credentials, and experience rather than on actual job performance and competitive mobility, initiative, and aggressiveness in exploiting job-market opportunities. The black woman's educational advantage over black men thus skews the figures to show more sex discrimination. Nonetheless, the analysis suggests that the already grossly inadequate income advantage of black males over black females is very vulnerable to the campaign against sex discrimination, which necessarily focuses on "credentials."

14. See Charles Murray, "Some Reasons for Concluding that We Lost the War on Poverty," testimony prepared for delivery to the Subcommittee on Fiscal and Monetary Policy of the Joint Economic Committee, 20 June 1985. Murray used data from U.S. Department of Labor, *Employment and Training Report of the President, 1980* (Washington, D.C.: U.S. Government Printing Office, 1981), Table A-20. The "skilled" category includes all workers in the white-collar and "craft &

kindred" categories while "low-skilled" comprises workers in the nonfarm labor and service categories.

15. Laurie J. Bassi and Orley Ashenfelter, "The Effect of Direct Job Creation and Training Programs on Low Skilled Workers," *IRP Conference Paper* (Madison, Wisconsin: Institute for Research on Poverty, 1985), p. 14 and passim. This article is a revised version of a paper prepared for presentation at the conference on "Poverty and Policy: Retrospect and Prospects," 6–8 December 1984, at Williamsburg, Virginia.

16. Elliot Liebow, *Talley's Corner* (Boston: Little, Brown, 1967), pp. 55, 62, 86, 116–19, and passim. Liebow quotes Albert K. Cohen, *Delinquent Boys* (New York: Free Press, 1955, p. 138): "People do not simply want to excel; they want to excel as a man or as a woman, that is to say, in those respects which, in their culture, are symbolic of their respective sex roles. . . . Even when they adopt behavior which is considered disreputable by conventional standards, the tendency is to be disreputable in ways that are characteristically masculine and feminine."

17. C. Eric Lincoln, *The Black Muslims in America*, rev. ed. (Boston: Beacon Press, 1973), pp. 131–35.

18. Mary White Harder et al., "The Jesus People: Sexism Revived," *Psychology Today*, December 1972.

Chapter 9
SUPPORTING FAMILIES

1. Quoted in *The Negro Family, A Case for National Action*, as reprinted in Lee Rainwater and William L. Yancey, *The Moynihan Report and the Politics of Controversy* (Cambridge, Mass.: MIT Press, 1967), p. 63.

2. Quoted in Allan Carlson, "Poverty and Ideology, 1985," *Persuasion at Work*, Rockford Institute, Rockford, Ill., February 1985.

3. David Ellwood and Lawrence Summers, "Poverty in America: Is Welfare the Answer or the Problem," *IRP Conference Paper* (Madison, Wisconsin: Institute for Research on Poverty, 1985), pp. 26, 27, and passim. This article is a revised version of a paper prepared for presentation at the conference on "Poverty and Policy: Retrospect and Prospects," 6–8 December 1984, at Williamsburg, Virginia.

4. William Julius Wilson and Kathryn M. Neckerman, "Poverty and Family Structure: The Widening Gap Between Evidence and Public Policy Issues," *IRP Conference Paper* (Madison, Wisconsin: Institute for Research on Poverty, 1985), p. 6. This article is a revised version of a paper prepared for presentation at the conference on "Poverty and Policy: Retrospect and Prospects," 6–8 December 1984, at Williamsburg, Virginia. *See also* Mary Jo Bane and David Ellwood, "Single Mothers and their Living Arrangements," working paper, U.S. Department of Health and Human Services, 1984, and "The Dynamics of Dependence: The Routes to Self-Sufficiency," paper prepared for the Assistant Secretary for Planning and Evaluation, Department of Health and Human Services, June 1983, Table 1, p. 11.

5. Charles Murray, *Losing Ground: American Social Policy 1950–1980* (New York: Basic Books, 1984), pp. 242, 243, and passim.

6. Ellwood and Summers, "Poverty in America," p. 27.

7. The AFDC data for numbers of both children and recipients are found in Murray, *Losing Ground*, Table 4, p. 244. The data on single-parent families comes from U.S. Bureau of the Census, *Current Population Reports*, "Characteristics of the Population Below the Poverty Level, 1982" (Washington, D.C.: U.S. Government Printing Office, 1983), Table 1. In a personal correspondence, Murray speculated that the reason for the drop in fertility in AFDC families was the concentration of benefits—access to free housing, Medicaid, and other assistance—on the first illegitimate child. The marginal benefits for additional children were much lower.

8. Ibid.

9. Charles F. Westhoff, Gerard Calot, and Andrew D. Foster, "Teenage Fertility in Developed Nations: 1971–1980," *Family Planning Perspectives*, May/June 1983, pp. 105–10. Quoted in Murray, *Losing Ground*, p. 127.

10. Eugene Steuerle, "The Tax Treatment of Households of Different Size," working paper, American Enterprise Institute, Washington, D.C., 1983.

11. Ibid.

12. Scott Burns, "Irresistible Force Meets an Immovable Object," *The Boston Herald American*, 17 September 1978, p. A-26.

13. Still the most comprehensive analysis of child allowances and their implications is Eveline M. Burns, ed., *Children's Allowances and the Economic Welfare of Children* (New York: Citizens Committee for Children of New York, 1967).

14. Margaret Mead, *Male and Female: A Study of the Sexes in a Changing World* (New York: Morrow, 1949), quoted from the paperback (New York: Dell, 1968), pp. 200, 341, 343.

Chapter 10
SEXUAL POLITICS

1. Carol Felsenthal, *The Sweetheart of the Silent Majority: The Biography of Phyllis Schlafly* (Garden City, N.Y.: Doubleday, 1981). This fascinating book, by a feminist, tells of her unexpected discovery of the miracle of Phyllis Schlafly. Most of the facts on Schlafly came from this text.

2. *The Impact of the Equal Rights Amendment*, Hearings before the Subcommittee on the Constitution of the Committee on the Judiciary, United States Senate (Washington, D.C.: U.S. Government Printing Office, 1985).

3. Stanley Rothman and S. Robert Lichter are directors of a continuing study of U.S. social and political elites conducted under the auspices of Smith College, the Research Institute on International Change of Columbia University, and George Washington University. Their findings show that elites in every area of American life hold social and sexual views far more "liberal" by usual standards than the rest

of the population. The results are regularly published in issues of *Public Opinion,* American Enterprise Institute, Washington, D.C. For example, "What are Movie-makers Made of?", *Public Opinion,* December/January 1984, pp. 14–18.

4. A good compendium of public opinion polls over time is the Gallup Poll series, published by Random House until 1971 and subsequently by Scholarly Resources Inc. *See The Gallup Poll, Public Opinion 1959–1971* (New York: Random House, 1972), and *The Gallup Poll, Public Opinion, 1972–1975; The Gallup Poll, Public Opinion, 1976–1977;* and *The Gallup Poll, Public Opinion* annual through 1985 (Wilmington, Del.: Scholarly Resources Inc., in the following year). On all these issues, public opinion, even as measured by the polls, has tended to oppose elite opinion by an approximately 70 to 30 margin.

5. Victoria Sackett, ed., "Split Verdict: What Americans Think About Abortion," *Policy Review,* Heritage Foundation, Washington, D.C., pp. 18–19.

6. Quoted in Christopher Booker, *The Neophiliacs* (Boston: Gambit, 1970), p. xi.

7. Lionel Tiger, *Men in Groups,* second edition with foreword by Desmond Morris (New York: Marion Boyars, 1984), p. 44 and passim.

8. Norman Mailer, *St. George and the Godfather* (New York, NAL/World, 1972), pp. 56–61.

Chapter 11
THE PERILS OF ANDROGYNY

1. Patricia Cayo Sexton, *The Feminized Male: White Collars and the Decline of Manliness* (New York: Random House, 1969), quoted from the paperback (Vintage Books, 1970), pp. 125–32.

2. Margaret Mead, *Male and Female: A Study of the Sexes in a Changing World* (New York: Morrow, 1949), quoted from the paperback (New York: Dell, 1968), p. 273.

3. Sexton, *Feminized Male,* p. 105.

4. Ibid., pp. 104–8.

5. Ibid., pp. 108–14.

6. Ibid., p. 8.

7. Ibid., p. 105.

8. Ibid., p. 131.

9. Ibid., p. 130.

10. Ibid.

11. Ibid., p. 116.

12. Ibid.

13. Steve Fainaru, "Title IX is so effective, it's forgotten," San Jose (Calif.) *Mercury-News,* 17 April 1985, p. 2-D.

Chapter 12
WOMEN IN COMBAT

1. This chapter is a revised and updated version of George Gilder, "The Case Against Women in Combat," *The New York Times Magazine*, 28 January 1979, pp. 29 ff. Most uncredited material comes from that article.

2. Dan Cragg, "Women in the Army—I," *Washington Times*, 2 June 1983, reprinted in Part 1, *The Impact of the Equal Rights Amendment*, Hearings before the Subcommittee on the Constitution of the Committee on the Judiciary, United States Senate (Washington, D.C.: U.S. Government Printing Office, 1985), p. 378.

3. Michael Levin, "Women as Soldiers—The Record So Far," *The Public Interest* 76 (Summer 1984), pp. 31 ff. The current proportion of women in U.S. military units is highest in the world. By early 1985 there were 28,719 women officers and 172,491 female enlisted personnel, comprising some 9.5 percent of the officers and enlisted ranks, compared to less than 2 percent in 1972. *See also* Esther B. Fein, "The Choice: Women Officers Decide to Stay In or Leave," *The New York Times Magazine*, 5 May 1985, pp. 32 ff.; and Eliot A. Cohen, "Likely Effects of the E.R.A. on the Armed Forces of the United States," and interrogation, with Antonia Handler Chayes, in *The Impact of the Equal Rights Amendment*, Hearings, pp. 269–307.

4. Martin Binken, *Women and the Military* (Washington, D.C.: Brookings Institution, 1978).

5. Eleanor Emmons Maccoby and Carol Nagy Jacklin, *The Psychology of Sex Differences* (Stanford, Calif.: Stanford University Press, 1974), pp. 242–43.

6. Steven Goldberg, *The Inevitability of Patriarchy* (New York: Morrow, 1973). *See also* Robin Fox, *Kinship and Marriage* (Baltimore, Md.: Penguin Books, 1967), p. 31 and passim. Fox maintains that no marriage system can endure with a male presence unless the men exercise control.

7. D. Woal et al., "Analysis of Attrition, Retention, and Criterion Task Performance of Recruits during Training," *Technical Report T2/82* (Washington, D.C.: U.S. Army Research and Development Command, 1982). Summarized in Levin, "Women as Soldiers," pp. 34–35. *See also* W. L. Daniels et al., "The Effects of Two Years of Training in Aerobic Power and Muscle Strength," Report No. M-12/80 (Washington, D.C.: U.S. Army Institute for Environmental Medicine, 1980).

8. Lionel Tiger and Joseph Shepher, *Women in the Kibbutz* (New York: Harcourt Brace Jovanovich, 1975), pp. 183–205 and passim. *See also* Cohen, Hearings, p. 345.

9. Colin Turnbull, *The Mountain People* (New York: Simon & Schuster, 1972).

10. Margaret Mead, *Male and Female: A Study of the Sexes in a Changing World* (New York: Morrow, 1949), quoted from the paperback (New York: Dell, 1968), pp. 116–17 and passim.

Chapter 13
THE JOBS FRONT

1. U.S. Department of Labor, "Special Review: The 1995 Labor Force," *Monthly Labor Review*, November 1983.

2. Victor R. Fuchs, *How We Live: An Economic Perspective on Americans from Birth to Death* (Cambridge, Mass.: Harvard University Press, 1983), p. 127.

3. Ibid, p. 128, and Labor Department, "Special Review," November 1983.

4. Quoted in Cullen Murphy, "A Survey of the Research," *The Wilson Quarterly*, Winter 1982, p. 75.

5. For a survey of the record of women in the work force, see Andrew Hacker, *U.S.: A Statistical Portrait of the American People* (New York: Viking Press, 1983); and "Women Vs. Men in the Work Force," *The New York Times Magazine*, 8 December 1984, pp. 124-29. Statistics updated from later issues of *Monthly Labor Review*.

6. Hacker, *Statistical Portrait*.

7. Fuchs, *How We Live*, p. 165.

8. Labor Department, "Special Review," November 1983.

9. U.S. Bureau of the Census, *American Women: Three Decades of Change* (Washington, D.C.: U.S. Government Printing Office, 1983), pp. 12-15. *See also* U.S. Bureau of the Census, *Current Population Reports*, Series P-60, No. 146, "Money Income of Households, Families, and Persons in the United States, 1983" (Washington, D.C.: U.S. Government Printing Office, 1985), Table 47 ("Education and Money Income in 1983").

10. Hacker, "Women Vs. Men," pp. 124-29.

11. Thomas J. Peters and Robert H. Waterman, Jr., *In Search of Excellence: Lessons from America's Best-Run Companies* (New York: Harper & Row, 1982).

12. Unpublished data for 1983 from the U.S. Department of Labor, Bureau of Labor Statistics; and data for 1973 from U.S. Department of Labor, Special Labor Force Report, Bureau of Labor Statistics, *Marital and Family Characteristics of the Labor Force* (Washington, D.C.: U.S. Government Printing Office, 1974), Table K ("Contribution of wife's earnings to family income"). These figures show an increase from 26 percent to 28 percent in the contribution of the wife's earnings in two-earner families between 1973 and 1983 (attributable largely to declining fertility), but also indicate a significant drop in the earnings per working wife as a share of total intact family incomes. The decline in the woman's role on farms suggests a decline in total contribution to family earnings since the beginning of the century.

13. Fuchs, *How We Live*, p. 128.

14. Computed from Census Bureau, "Money Income," Table 46.

15. Ibid., Table 31, and Bureau of Labor Statistics, unpublished data (see note 12).

16. Solomon William Polachek, "Women in the Economy: Perspectives on Gender Inequality," in *Comparable Worth: Issue for the 80's* (Washington, D.C.: U.S. Commission on Civil Rights, 1984), Vol. 1, Table 7, pg. 43.

17. Irwin Garfinkel and Robert Haveman, with the assistance of David Betson, *Earnings Capacity, Poverty and Inequality*, Institute for Research on Poverty Monograph Series (New York: Academic Press, 1977), pp. 27–35, and Table 3.3, p. 32.

18. Ibid., p. 32.

19. Ibid.

20. Census Bureau, "Money Income," Table 47.

21. Louis Harris Public Opinion Poll conducted for Virginia Slims, 1981.

22. Louis Harris Public Opinion Poll conducted for Virginia Slims, 1982.

23. U.S. Small Business Administration, *The State of Small Business: A Report to the President* (Washington, D.C.: U.S. Government Printing Office, 1984), Appendix A ("Women-Owned Businesses"), p. 347.

24. Ibid., p. 357.

25. Michael Finn, "The Earnings Gap and Economic Choices," in Phyllis Schlafly, ed., *Equal Pay for Unequal Work: A Conference on Comparable Worth* (Washington, D.C.: Eagle Forum Education & Legal Defense Fund, 1984), p. 113.

26. Ibid., p. 114.

27. Census Bureau, "Money Income," Table 56; and Kim B. Clark and Lawrence H. Summers, "Labor Market Dynamics and Unemployment: A Reconsideration," Brookings Papers on Economic Activity, no. 1 (Washington D.C.: The Brookings Institution, 1979), p. 52. For a detailed analysis, see Polachek, "Women in the Economy," pp. 42–46.

28. Solomon Polachek sums up his own and other findings on the absence of effective or measurable discrimination against women: "In short, even when using the most primitive models, the human capital approach that links lifetime labor force participation to earnings in the marketplace explains almost 50 percent of the gender difference in earnings. When using statistical specifications that more accurately reflect the impact of expected intermittency on initial schooling and job choices, close to 100 percent of the wage gap can be explained. Even the skeptic of the human capital framework must note that even the crudest of the human capital models explains more of the wage gap than the most sophisticated of the occupational segregation models." (Polachek, "Women in the Economy," p. 45.)

29. Hacker, "Women Vs. Men," p. 128.

30. Jim Kaplan, "In the World of Chess, Man Thinks of Himself as King, Woman as Pawn," *Sports Illustrated*, 8 April 1985, pp. 18–19.

31. Sara Kiesler, Lee Sproull, and Jacquelynne S. Eccles, "Second Class Citizens," *Psychology Today*, March 1983. Also subsequent observations and reports from more recent computer camps and classes.

32. Camilla Persson Benbow and Julian C. Stanley, *Sex Differences in Mathematical Reasoning Ability: A Five Year Longitudinal Study* (Baltimore, Md.: The Johns

Hopkins University, 1980). Steven Goldberg has reported in an unpublished paper (1985) that "a score on the mathematics section of the Scholastic Aptitude Test (SAT) that puts a girl in the ninetieth percentile among girls places a boy in only the sixty-eighth percentile among boys; among mathematically precocious students (13 years old), a 700 score is thirteen times more likely to be scored by a boy than by a girl (with equal numbers of boys and girls with similar mathematical backgrounds taking the test)."

33. Hacker, *Statistical Portrait,* passim. *See also* Barbara R. Bergmann, "Women's Plight: Bad and Getting Worse," *Challenge,* March/April 1983, p. 24 (Table 3).

34. Fuchs, *How We Live,* pp. 164–70.

35. Ibid., p. 266. *See also* Warren T. Brookes, *The Economy in Mind* (New York: Universe Books), pp. 169–71.

36. Brookes, *Economy in Mind,* pp. 169–71 and passim.

37. Bergmann, "Women's Plight," p. 24 (Table 4).

38. Lionel Tiger and Joseph Shepher, *Women in the Kibbutz* (New York: Harcourt Brace Jovanovich, 1975).

39. Jane Gross, "Against the Odds: A Woman's Ascent on Wall Street," *The New York Times Magazine,* 6 January 1985, p. 16.

40. Michael Levin, "Comparable Worth: The Feminist Road to Socialism," *Commentary,* September 1984, pp. 13–19.

41. Allan Carlson, "Toward 'The Working Family': The Hidden Agenda Behind the Comparable Worth Debate," *Persuasion at Work,* July 1984. *See also* Paul Bernstein, "Work In Sweden: Trouble in Paradise," *The Wharton Magazine,* Summer 1982, pp. 46–52.

42. Carlson, "Hidden Agenda," p. 4.

43. Ibid.

44. United Nations, *Demographic Yearbook,* 1984.

45. Ibid.

46. Carlson, "Hidden Agenda," p. 5.

Chapter 14
SEX AND THE SOCIAL SCIENTIST

1. The summer of the absurd at *Society* was 1977, the July/August issue. But the magazine was continuing with occasional howlers as this book went to press.

2. Alan M. Klein, "Pumping Iron," *Society,* September/October 1985, pp. 68–75.

3. Charles C. Moskos, "Female G.I.s in the Field," *Society,* September/October 1985, pp. 28–33.

4. Dennis Brissett and Lionel S. Lewis, "The Big Toe, Armpits, and Natural Perfumes: Notes on the Production of Sexual Ecstasy," *Society,* January/February 1979, pp. 63 ff.

5. Frank R. Scarpitti and Ellen C. Scarpitti, "Victims of Rape," *Society,* July/August 1977, pp. 29–32. In 1983, the magazine returned to the subject with an article by

Lynda Lytle Holmstorm and Ann Wolbert Burgess on "Rape and Everyday Life" (*Society*, July/August 1983, pp. 33 ff.). In general, the authors concluded that while a program of "equal pay for comparable worth" would probably stop rapists in their tracks, until then the victims would do well to kick and scream.

6. James W. Raney, "Alternative Life-Styles," *Society*, July/August 1977, pp. 43-47.

7. Robert Francoeur, "Sex Films," *Society*, July/August 1977, pp. 33-37.

8. C. S. Lewis, *The Abolition of Man* (New York: Macmillan, 1976).

Chapter 15
THE HOME FRONT

1. Karl Marx and Frederick Engels, *The German Ideology* (London: Lawrence & Wishart, 1965), p. 44.

2. Midge Decter, *The New Chastity and Other Arguments Against Women's Liberation* (New York: Coward, McCann & Geoghegan, 1972).

3. Betty Friedan, *The Feminine Mystique* (New York: Norton, 1963).

4. Herbert J. Gans, *The Levittowners* (New York: Pantheon, 1967).

5. Helen Z. Lopata, *Occupation Housewife* (New York: Oxford University Press, 1971), p. 376.

6. Ibid., p. 373.

7. Gans, *Levittowners*, pp. 230, 231.

8. See the story of the Ik tribe in Colin Turnbull, *The Mountain People* (New York: Simon & Schuster, 1972), p. 290-95 and passim.

9. Carol Gilligan, *In a Different Voice: Psychological Theory and Women's Development* (Cambridge, Mass.: Harvard University Press, 1982). In attacking the shallow notions of male maturation and male moral superiority offered by developmental psychologists, Gilligan performs an important service. But her alternative moral view comes perilously close to a slough of situational ethics. In her interesting comparison of George Eliot's *Mill on the Floss* (1860) with Margaret Drabble's retelling of the tale in *The Waterfall* (1969), Gilligan can even condone the stealing of another woman's husband. The most telling female offense against the sexual constitution, this violation is at the root of the princess's problem in chapter 5 of this book and a source of the breakdown of monogamy that causes so many problems for women in modern society.

10. Ibid., pp. 70-71 and passim.

11. Jessie Bernard, *The Future of Marriage* (New York: World, 1972), pp. 336, 338, 339.

12. Margaret Mead, *Male and Female: A Study of the Sexes in a Changing World* (New York: Morrow, 1949), quoted from the paperback (New York: Dell, 1968), p. 110.

13. Jose Ortega y Gasset, *The Revolt of the Masses* (New York: Norton, 1932), pp. 94-95.

14. Allan Carlson, "Toward 'The Working Family': The Hidden Agenda Behind the Comparable Worth Debate," *Persuasion at Work*, Rockford Institute, Rockford, Ill., July 1984, p. 5.

15. Carlson, "The Time Bomb Within Social Security," *Persuasion at Work*, September 1985, p. 7.

16. Norman Ryder, "Two Cheers for ZPG," *Daedalus: Journal of the American Academy of Arts and Sciences*, Fall 1974, pp. 45–62.

17. Carlson, "Time Bomb," p. 7.

Chapter 16
THE SEXUAL SUICIDE TECHNOCRACY

1. Leon R. Kass, *Toward a More Natural Science: Biology and Human Affairs* (New York: Macmillan/Free Press, 1985). *See also* Kass, "Making Babies—The New Biology and the 'Old' Morality," *The Public Interest*, Winter 1972, pp. 18–56; and "'Making Babies' Revisited," *The Public Interest*, Winter 1979, pp. 32–60.

2. Edward Grossman, "The Obsolescent Mother," *Atlantic*, May 1971, pp. 39–50.

3. "The Hexaparental Mouse," *Science*, 6 October 1978, p. 5.

4. Michael Gold, "Conception in a Dish: Hopes, Technology, and Ethics in the Baby Lab," *Science85*, April 1985, pp. 26–38; and Michael Kramer, "Last Chance Babies: The Wonders of In Vitro Fertilization," *New York*, 12 August 1985, pp. 34–42.

5. Kass, "The New Biology," p. 35.

6. C. S. Lewis, *The Abolition of Man* (New York: Macmillan, 1976).

7. Lionel Tiger, *Men in Groups*, second edition with foreword by Desmond Morris (New York: Marion Boyars, 1984).

Chapter 17
WHY MEN MARRY

1. Studs Terkel, *Working* (New York: Random House, 1974), passim.

Afterword:
THE FAITH OF FATHERS

1. Allan Carlson, "Calculating the Malthusian Budget Deficit," *Persuasion at Work*, Rockford Institute, Rockford, Ill., March 1985, p. 4.

2. E. J. Mishan, "Women's Lib—Was the Movement Really Necessary," *Encounter*, January 1985.

3. Dale Vree, "Origins of the Sexual Revolution," *New Oxford Review*, April 1983, pp. 22–26.